Business Communication

Workbook

mit interaktiven Übungen

IHK/KMK

von
Chris Caridia
und
Peadar Curran

unter Mitarbeit der Verlagsredaktion

Deine **interaktiven übungen** und **Audios** findest du auf scook.de. Dort gibst den unten stehenden Zugangscode in die Box ein.

Dein Zugangscode auf
www.scook.de | kp9mm-ds47t

Cornelsen

Business Communication

Verfasser:	Chris Caridia, International Publishing Services
Verlagsredaktion:	Kari-ann Warnakulasuriya
Umschlaggestaltung:	Rosendahl Grafikdesign
Berater:	Paul Donhauser, Amberg; Frauke Fröhlich, Zeven; Matthias Wolf, Weiden
Layout:	Oxana Rödel, Berlin
Technische Umsetzung:	SPi Global, Chennai
Coverfoto:	Shutterstock.com/SFIO CRACHO

www.cornelsen.de

1. Auflage, 1. Druck 2021

Alle Drucke dieser Ausgabe sind inhaltlich unverändert und können im Unterricht nebeneinander verwendet werden.

Druck: H. Heenemann, Berlin

ISBN 978-3-06-452196-4

PEFC
PEFC/04-31-1156

PEFC zertifiziert
Dieses Produkt stammt aus nachhaltig bewirtschafteten Wäldern und kontrollierten Quellen.

www.pefc.de

CONTENTS

1 Getting started

We usually think of companies as organizations which sell products or services to us, the consumer. But businesses also buy and sell among themselves all the time. Car manufacturers, for example, buy car parts made in many different countries. There is a lot of communication in English between colleagues or customers in different countries, even though English is not their native language.

A INTRODUCING YOURSELF AND OTHER PEOPLE

1 Introduce yourself to the class. Give your name and an interesting fact about yourself. Then write about yourself for your profile.

MyProfile

Name: Hannes Schwedtke
Date of birth: 21 June 20..

I was born in Stuttgart and live in Munich, Germany. I graduated from commercial school last year, and now I'm a trainee office management assistant in a large insurance company. When I finish my training, I'm going to apply for a position in the Sales Department because I enjoy the contact with customers.

MyProfile

Name:
Date of birth:

2 Abdi Patel works in the same insurance company as Hannes. Here he is introducing a new American colleague to two of his office colleagues. Put the lines of the dialogue into the correct order.

a OK, guys. I have to take Dan to meet the boss now. See you later.
b I come from Louisiana.
c Nice to meet you, too.
d I'd be happy to do that.
e Hi, Dan. Nice to meet you.
f Where are you from, Dan?
g Hi, Amy. Hi, Sven. This is Dan. Dan, these are my colleagues, Amy and Sven.
h That's interesting. I've never been to Louisiana. You must tell us more about it sometime.
i No, it isn't. I visited Berlin last year.
j Welcome to Germany. Is this your first visit?

1	2	3	4	5	6	7	8	9	10

VOCABULARY

company – *Unternehmen*; **consumer** – *Verbraucher/in*; **manufacturer** – *Hersteller/in*; **colleague** – *Kollege/Kollegin*; **customer** – *Kunde/Kundin*; **to introduce** – *vorstellen*; **office management assistant** – *Kaufmann/-frau für Büromanagement*; **insurance** – *Versicherung*; **to apply** – *sich bewerben*; **position** – *Stelle*; **Sales Department** – *Vertrieb, Verkaufsabteilung*

B WELCOMING A VISITOR

1 Read the four text messages and complete the sentences below.

1 Zoe Kline is on her way to a __________ in __________.
2 She's late because __________.
3 Helena and Zoe __________ met before.
4 Zoe expects to be at Helena's office about __________ after she lands.

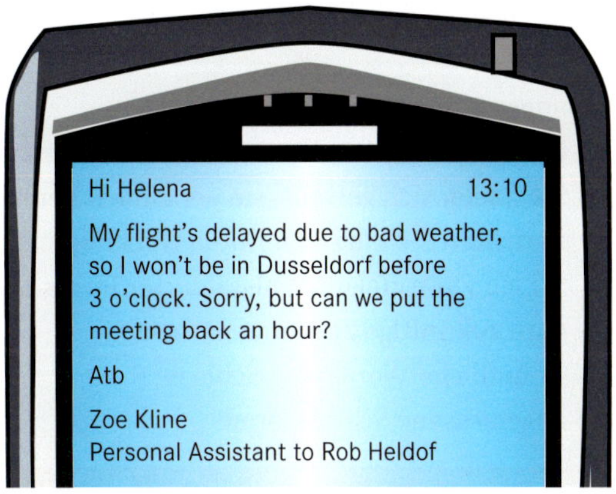

Hi Zoe 14:12
No problem! Come when you can. I'm here all day. Looking forward to meeting you personally at last.
Best wishes
Helena

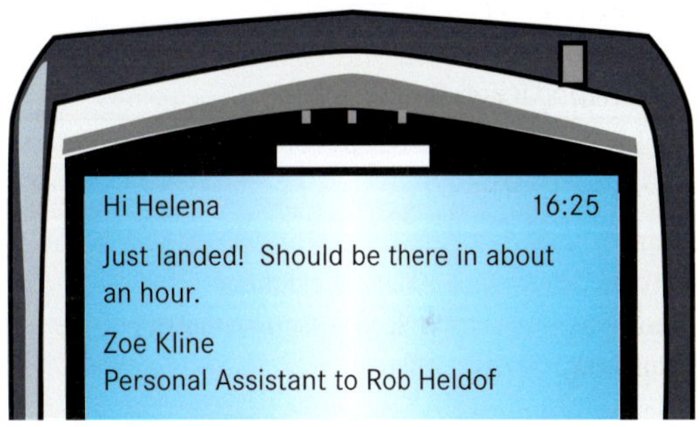

Hi Zoe 16:29
Great! See you soon.
Best
Helena

02 **2 Use the phrases in the box below to complete the dialogue and then listen to the recording to check your answers. There are more phrases than you need.**

Helena: Hello, you must be Zoe Kline! I'm Helena Sawicki. __________[1] Düsseldorf! It's so __________[2] at last!

Zoe: Hello, Helena. It's nice to meet you, too. I'm so __________[3]. I hope I haven't spoiled your plans for this afternoon!

Helena: Not at all. Did you __________[4]?

Zoe: Apart from the delay it was fine.

Helena: Good. Now, __________[5] before the meeting – tea, coffee, mineral water?

Zoe: __________[6] a cup of coffee!

Helena: Black or white? Sugar?

Zoe: Black, no sugar, please.

Helena: __________[7].

Zoe: Thanks.

Helena: Now __________[8] for the meeting. We've made a few changes, but nothing big. And here's the programme for the next two days.

Zoe: Thanks.

Helena: Now just let me __________[9], in case you need to phone me on my mobile.

Zoe: Thanks. And __________[10].

sorry I'm late ▪ give you my business card ▪ I'd love ▪ nice to be here ▪ nice to meet you ▪ have a good flight ▪ have a good journey ▪ can I get you anything ▪ here's the agenda ▪ Welcome to ▪ Here you are ▪ here's mine

VOCABULARY

text message – *SMS*; **delayed** – *verspätet*; **to put sth back** – *etw verschieben*; **to look forward to sth** – *sich auf etw freuen*; **at last** – *endlich*; **to spoil** – *verderben, durcheinander bringen*; **delay** – *Verspätung*; **business card** – *Visitenkarte*; **agenda** – *Tagesordnung*

C WRITING A THANK-YOU EMAIL

1 **Sie sind Zoe Kline und sind von Ihrem Besuch bei Helena Sawicki zurückgekehrt. Schreiben Sie ihr eine E-Mail.**

- angemessene Anrede
- Danken Sie ihr für den freundlichen Empfang und die aufschlussreiche Besprechung in Düsseldorf.
- Sie haben sich gefreut, sie persönlich kennenzulernen.
- Berichten Sie kurz von Ihrem Rückflug nach Oslo.
- Sie sind von Helenas Düsseldorfer Firma und ihren Produkten sehr beeindruckt und hoffen auf eine gute zukünftige Zusammenarbeit.
- freundliche Worte zum Schluss
- angemessene Schlussformel

Useful phrases	
Liebe Helena; Sehr geehrte Frau Sawicki	Dear Helena; Dear Ms Sawicki
Ihr/dein freundlicher Empfang	your kind welcome
nützliche/aufschlussreiche Besprechung	useful meeting
Es war sehr schön/nett …	it was very nice
Ich war von … sehr beeindruckt	I was most impressed by/with …
auf eine gute zukünftige Zusammenarbeit hoffen	hope to work together
sich auf ein baldiges Wiedersehen freuen	look forward to seeing … soon
Mit freundlichen Grüßen	Best wishes

From: z.kline@heldof.nex
To: H.Sawicki@greenmail.det
Subject: Thanks

____

____
____
____
____

____

____

2 **Match the words 1–8 with the definitions a–j. There are two more than you need.**

1 agenda
2 hobbies
3 colleagues
4 delayed
5 flight
6 rush
7 trainee
8 department

☐ **a** another word for 'hurry'
☐ **b** noun from 'fly'
☐ **c** somebody learning to do a job
☐ **d** things we do in our free time
☐ **e** friends
☐ **f** a part of a big company
☐ **g** a list of items to discuss at a meeting
☐ **h** not on time
☐ **i** people we work with
☐ **j** somewhere we work

3 Circle the correct preposition.

1 Hi! Welcome to / in / with Germany.
2 I've never been in / to / from Munich before.
3 Helena expects to arrive at / near / on 4 p.m.
4 I'm looking forward for / about / to meeting you.
5 Can we put the meeting away / back / of by about an hour?
6 The train will arrive to / at / --- the station in twenty minutes.
7 Is she coming in / with / by taxi?
8 The train wasn't in / on / about time and we were late in / to / for the meeting.
9 Hannes works by / for / to an insurance company.
10 There has been a change of / in / to plan.

4 Find a verb from the box which goes best with the words below. Use each verb only once.

ask ▪ change ▪ do ▪ have ▪ improve ▪ listen ▪ make ▪ work

1 ______________ small talk
2 ______________ your skills
3 ______________ plans
4 ______________ together
5 ______________ a good flight
6 ______________ the first question
7 ______________ a good job
8 ______________ carefully

5 Helen Brown wants to arrange a meeting with Ben Jackson. She calls his assistant Chris Jones.

03

Listen to the dialogue. Make a note of the times and places to complete the email below.

From: ChrisJones@Jackson.nex
To: Ben@Jackson.nex
Subject: Visit from Helen Brown

Hi Ben

Helen Brown called. She will be in ______________ [1] next week on ______________ [2] and would like to meet you. She is busy in the ______________ [3] and you are tied up all ______________ [4], so she suggested meeting you for ______________ [5] at ______________ [6] in a ______________ [7] in ______________ [8] – it's called the ______________ [9]. I've pencilled it in and promised to confirm first thing ______________________________ [10]. Is that OK? Can you make it?

Regards

Chris

VOCABULARY

skill – *Fähigkeit, Fertigkeit*; **to arrange** – *vereinbaren*; **to be tied up** – *beschäftigt sein*; **diary** – *Kalender*; **to pencil sb/sth in** – *jdn/etw vormerken*; **to confirm** – *bestätigen*

D MAKING AN ONLINE TRAVEL BOOKING

1 Marco Spina is booking a hotel on his company's new online business travel platform. His colleague Birgit Meyer is explaining how it works.

Fill in the gaps with the words in the box. There are more than you need.

available ▪ booked ▪ breakfast included ▪ clicked on ▪ confirmation ▪ enter ▪ facilities ▪ change ▪ filter your search ▪ live chat ▪ logged in ▪ payment method ▪ return ▪ select ▪ reserve

Birgit: OK, so you've ____________________[1], right?

Marco: Yes, and I've ____________________[2] English because my German is still not good enough.

Birgit: Now ____________________[3] your destination in this box and ____________________[4] your departure and arrival dates here.

Marco: That's … Milan … 9th to 10th April. And I press '____________________[5]'.

Birgit: Now the system shows you 416 ____________________[6] hotels! That's a lot, so you need to ____________________[7] by price and perhaps 'distance to the airport' or '____________________[8]'. All the options and hotel ____________________[9] or services are listed here on the left of the screen. Just tick the boxes. When you find what you want, it asks you to choose your ____________________[10], for example, by credit card. At the end, a message will confirm your booking. I think it says, "Hotel successfully ____________________[11]." And they also send you a separate email ____________________[12].

Marco: That's a great help Birgit. I'll get on with it now and then I have to book my flight as well.

2 **Read about booking a flight online. Match sentence halves 1-6 and a-f.**

1 To get the best price you must be …
2 A day before the flight, go to the airline's website, …
3 Before you book, check the airline's fees …
4 You may not need insurance because …
5 Many airlines allow you to select …
6 Another way to get a good price is …

☐ **a** check in online and get your boarding pass.
☐ **b** companies often have insurance which covers their employees.
☐ **c** flexible about your travel dates.
☐ **d** for cancelling or changing your ticket.
☐ **e** to book a ticket months in advance.
☐ **f** your seat online at the time of booking.

VOCABULARY

to book – *buchen*; **available** – *verfügbar*; **to include** – *beinhalten*; **confirmation** – *Bestätigung*; **facilities** – *Einrichtungen*; **to log in** – *einloggen*; **payment method** – *Zahlungsart*; **return** – *Eingabetaste*; **to select** – *auswählen*; **destination** – *(Reise-)Ziel*; **departure** – *Abreise*; **arrival** – *Anreise*; **distance** – *Entfernung*; **services** – *Leistungen*; **screen** – *Bildschirm*; **airline** – *Fluggesellschaft*; **boarding pass** – *Bordkarte*; **insurance** – *Versicherung*

E KMK EXAM PRACTICE

1 Hörverstehen

04

Situation: Benno Koch von der Firma Berghain GmbH ruft seinen Geschäftspartner Peter Michaels an.

Aufgabe: Hören Sie sich das Telefongespräch an und füllen Sie die Tabelle aus.

1 Hauptgrund für Bennos Anruf:	
2 Die Wochentage, die im Gespräch besprochen werden:	
3 Grund, weshalb Peter Bennos ersten Vorschlag nicht annehmen kann:	
4 Grund, weshalb 3 Uhr am zweiten Tag Peter nicht passt:	
5 Was die beiden schließlich vereinbaren:	

2 Produktion

Situation: Sie arbeiten für Ben Jackson. Er bittet Sie darum, eine E-Mail an Helen Brown zu schreiben, um einen Termin zu bestätigen.

Aufgabe: Schreiben Sie die E-Mail. Vergessen Sie nicht, eine Betreffzeile und eine passende Schlussformel hinzuzufügen.

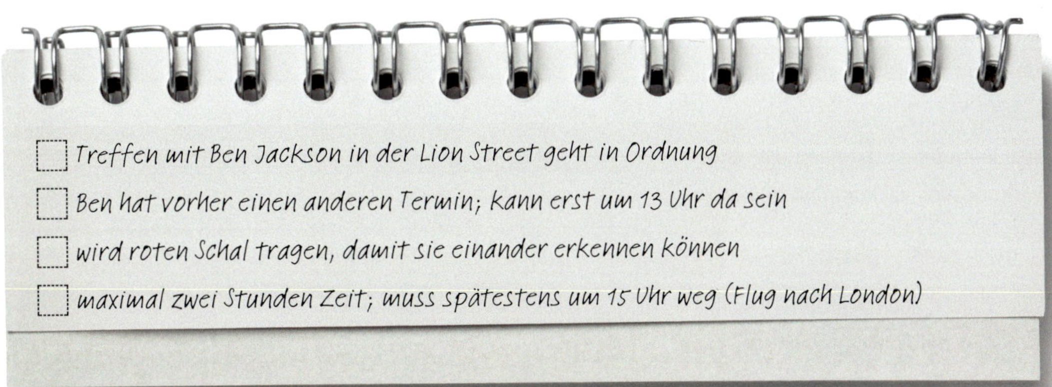

3 Leseverstehen

Situation: Ihre Firma möchte den Empfangsmitarbeitern im Haus Empfehlungen für richtiges Verhalten gegenüber Besucherinnen und Besuchern an die Hand geben. Ihr Chef bittet Sie, folgenden Text zu lesen, den er in einem Wirtschaftsmagazin entdeckt hat, und ihm den Inhalt auf Deutsch zusammenzufassen.

Aufgabe: Lesen Sie den Text genau durch und füllen Sie die Tabelle auf der folgenden Seite stichwortartig auf Deutsch aus.

Top tips when welcoming visitors

First impressions are vital, especially when future clients or business partners visit your premises for the first time. That's why it is essential that you make every visitor, whether they be workers delivering goods or important new clients, feel welcome. How can you make sure that your offices make that all-important good impression? Here are our top tips:

Remind your colleagues at reception how important they are: Reception workers are the first people visitors will see as they arrive, so they are key to making that first impression. Even if they're busy or on the phone already, they can still make friendly eye contact, use hand gestures to show they will be with the visitor immediately and offer assistance after getting off the phone.

Make your visitors feel special: Greet your customers with a board in the lobby that says, "Welcome, Joe Smith from XYZ Company" for example. This incredibly simple gesture is quick to put together and shows your visitors that you thought about them before they arrived. And if it's a potential client, this small welcome gesture shows you really care about their experience.

Train your employees: Everyone should treat every visitor as their personal customer, even if they have nothing to do with the visitor. This means making eye contact, smiling, saying hello, and offering help. Remember: it only takes one rude or inconsiderate employee to make your client's visit a negative experience.

Keep your workplace clean and welcoming: You should make sure that every area a visitor might see is kept clean and tidy, not just the reception area. Workers should of course keep their workspaces organized, but you also need to pay attention to the general appearance of your office building: Are the walls clean? Does the carpet look old? Are there old magazines in the waiting area? Make sure your workplace looks good and freshly cleaned, just as you would do with your own personal appearance when meeting clients.

Make refreshments available: It's nice to make your visitors feel comfortable. Place a nice coffee and water system somewhere where visitors can serve themselves while they wait or prepare for their meeting. Leaving fruit and other snacks at different places around your workplace can also make a good impression.

Say thank you: After an important visitor leaves, think about sending a thank you card or small gift to thank them for taking the time to visit your office. While this is yet another small thing, it can go a long way towards impressing a client and giving them a reason to choose your company instead of someone else.

1 Wie sollen sich die Empfangsmitarbeiter und -mitarbeiterinnen verhalten?	______ ______
2 Wie kann man Gäste einfach, aber wirkungsvoll willkommen heißen?	______ ______
3 Was sollten alle Mitarbeiter beim Umgang mit Gästen beachten?	______ ______
4 Welches Erscheinungsbild sollte die gesamte Arbeitsumgebung abgeben?	______ ______
5 Was kann man im Nachgang machen?	______ ______

F IHK EXAM PRACTICE

1 Vermerk in Deutsch über ein Gespräch in Englisch

05

Situation: Im folgenden Gespräch sind Sie Benno Koch von der Firma Berghain GmbH. Heute ist der 15. März. Sie erhalten einen Anruf von Ihrem irischen Geschäftspartner Peter Michaels.

Aufgabe: Verfolgen Sie das Gespräch und fertigen Sie anschließend für Ihre Chefin, Frau Marie Hufnagel, eine Gesprächsnotiz auf Deutsch an. Während des Hörens dürfen Sie Notizen machen. Diese Notizen werden nicht bewertet, sondern nur die Gesprächsnotiz.

Benno Koch:	Peter Michaels:
Guten Morgen, Berghain GmbH. Koch am Apparat.	…
Ah, morning, Peter. How are you?	…
I'm very well, thank you.	…
Yes, of course, it would be a pleasure.	…
Well, how about 11 a.m. on Monday? I'm free then.	…
No, unfortunately that won't work. I have to see another supplier.	…
Let me see. No, sorry, that's not possible either. I'm afraid I'm rather busy at the moment. Would you be able to make 3 p.m. on Tuesday?	…
Well, then. There's nothing else for it. What are you doing for lunch on Tuesday, Peter?	…
Well, why don't we meet over lunch? Say about 1 o'clock.	…
Great, Peter. See you on Tuesday.	…

2 Kurzgefasste Mitteilung in Englisch

Situation: Sie arbeiten für Ben Jackson. Er bittet Sie darum, eine E-Mail an Helen Brown zu schreiben, um einen Termin zu bestätigen.

Aufgabe: Schreiben Sie eine E-Mail an Helen Brown. Vergessen Sie nicht, eine Betreffzeile und eine passende Schlussformel hinzuzufügen.

- ☐ Treffen mit Ben Jackson in der Lion Street geht in Ordnung
- ☐ Ben hat vorher einen anderen Termin; kann erst um 13 Uhr da sein
- ☐ wird roten Schal tragen, damit sie einander erkennen können
- ☐ maximal zwei Stunden Zeit; muss spätestens um 15 Uhr weg (Flug nach London)

3 Sprachergänzungstest (Typ 1)

Aufgabe: Bitte setzen Sie 20 der 23 angegebenen Wörter oder Wendungen in die Lücken des Textes ein.

answering ▪ appreciated ▪ around ▪ attending ▪ competition ▪ desks ▪ entrance ▪ for ▪ greeting ▪ healthy ▪ impression ▪ much ▪ needs ▪ on ▪ premises ▪ staff ▪ takes ▪ their ▪ there ▪ to ▪ visiting ▪ where ▪ who

Making a good first ________________ [1] is important when meeting future business partners. The same is true when they visit your ________________ [2] for the first time. How can you make sure this happens? Make every visitor, whether they be workers delivering goods or important new clients, feel welcome. Here are some tips ________________ [3] making sure your offices make that all-important good impression.

Remind the reception ________________ [4] how important they are: Reception workers are the first people visitors will see as they arrive, so they are key to making that first impression. Even if they're busy ________________ [5] phones, they can still make friendly eye contact, use hand gestures to show they will be with the visitor immediately and offer assistance after getting off the phone.

Create an individualized ________________ [6]: Have a board in the lobby that says, "Welcome, Joe Smith from XYZ Company." This incredibly simple gesture only ________________ [7] two minutes to put together and shows your visitors that you thought about them before ________________ [8] arrival. And if it's a potential client, this small gesture shows how ________________ [9] you care about their experience.

Training: Train all employees ________________ [10] see every visitor as their personal customer, even if they do not have anything to do with the visitor. This means making eye contact, smiling, saying hello, and offering help if needed. Remember: it only takes one employee ________________ [11] acts rude or inconsiderate to ruin your efforts to make your client's visit a positive experience.

Keep your workplace clean and welcoming: Every area a visitor might see must be kept clean and tidy, especially near the ________________ [12]. This does not only mean that workers keep their ________________ [13] organized, but also the general appearance: Are the walls clean? Does the carpet look old? Are there old magazines lying ________________ [14] the waiting area? Make sure your workplace looks good and clean, just as you would do with your own appearance when ________________ [15] a meeting.

Make refreshments available: Spend a little extra money ________________ [16] a nice coffee and water system put ________________ [17] visitors can easily find it and serve themselves while they wait for their meeting. Have some fruit and ________________ [18], wrapped snacks at different places around your workplace.

After an important visitor leaves, think about sending them a thank you card or small gift to show them that you ________________ [19] them taking the time to visit. While this is yet another small thing, it can go a long way towards impressing a client and giving them a reason to choose your company over the ________________ [20].

Useful phrases

Making introductions

Greeting people you do not know	
Good morning/afternoon/evening. I'm …	*Guten Morgen/Tag/Abend. Ich heiße …*
How do you do? My name is …	*Freut mich. Mein Name ist …*
Nice/Pleased to meet you.	*Es freut mich, Sie kennenzulernen.*
Nice to meet you, too.	*Ganz meinerseits.*
Excuse me. Are you …?	*Entschuldigung. Sind Sie …?*
Yes, I am. / No, I'm not. I'm …	*Ja, das bin ich. / Nein, das bin ich nicht … Ich heiße …*
Welcome to …	*Herzlich willkommen bei/in …*
Thank you. It's nice to be here.	*Danke schön. Es ist schön, hier zu sein.*
Introducing people	
This is … . / These are my colleagues, John and Mary.	*Das ist … . / Das sind meine Kollegen, John und Mary.*
I'd like to introduce … from the … department.	*Darf ich Ihnen … aus der …-Abteilung vorstellen?*
Making small talk	
I hope you're well.	*Ich hoffe, es geht dir/Ihnen gut.*
… is such a beautiful city!	*… ist so eine schöne Stadt.*
The weather is so good today!	*Das Wetter ist heute so schön.*
Did you have a good trip/flight?	*Hattest du / Hatten Sie eine gute Reise / einen guten Flug?*

Making arrangements

Inviting sb to a meeting	
Ms Smith would like to invite you to a meeting on … (day) at … (time).	*Frau Smith möchte Sie zu einem Treffen am … (Tag) um … (Zeit) Uhr einladen.*
I would like to invite you to lunch/dinner.	*Ich würde Sie gern zum Mittagessen/Abendessen einladen.*
The meeting will take place at my office / our premises in … (place/city).	*Das Treffen findet in meinem Büro / in unseren Räumlichkeiten in … (Ort/Stadt) statt.*
Accepting/Declining the invitation	
Thank you for your invitation to meet you at … (place).	*Vielen Dank für Ihre Einladung zum Treffen in … (Ort).*
I am pleased / We are delighted to accept your invitation/offer.	*Gern nehme(n) ich/wir Ihre Einladung / Ihr Angebot an.*
I'm sorry, but I'm … (reason) on that date / at that time.	*Es tut mir leid, aber ich bin … (Grund) an diesem Tag / zu dieser Zeit.*
Making an alternative suggestion	
How about meeting on … (day) at … (time) instead?	*Wie wäre es, wenn wir uns stattdessen am … (Tag) um … (Uhrzeit) treffen?*
Conclusion	
I look forward to your reply. (*formal*)	*Ich freue mich auf Ihre Antwort.*
I hope to hear from you soon. Many thanks.	*Ich hoffe, bald von Ihnen zu hören. Vielen Dank.*

2 Basic communication

People in business usually communicate by email, phone or letter. So to be successful it is important to know how to write a business letter or talk to a business partner on the phone.

A WRITING BUSINESS LETTERS

1 **Look at the model letter and the headings in the box. Match the headings with the notes (A–J) on page 15 and add the numbers (1–12). Some notes refer to two numbers.**

Me2 MODE

Me2 Mode GmbH 1
Oststr. 44 • 40211 Dusseldorf
Germany

Tel. +49 211 59228
Fax +49 211 59227
Email info@Me2-mode.dex
www.Me2-mode.dex

•

Your ref.: SR/ah 2
Our ref.: LM/tk 3
05 July 20.. 4

•

Italian Fashions 5
Via Margarita 27
50321 FIRENZE
ITALIEN

•

Attn. Miss Ryan, Import Section 6

•

Dear Miss Ryan 7

•

Complimentary tickets 8

•

As arranged we enclose two tickets for the Body Culture Fashion Show in Dusseldorf next month and look forward to meeting you at our stand. 9

•

Yours sincerely 10

•

L. Meier 11
Linda Meier (Mrs)
Managing Director
Me2 Mode GmbH

•

•

Encs 12

•

Leave a free line for each dot (•).

Attention line ▪ Body of the letter ▪ Complimentary close ▪ Date ▪ Enclosure(s) ▪ Recipient's address ▪ Letterhead ▪ Reference 1 ▪ Reference 2 ▪ Salutation ▪ Signature ▪ Subject line

VOCABULARY

successful – *erfolgreich*; **import** – *Einfuhr*; **complimentary ticket** – *Freikarte*; **to enclose sth** – *etw beifügen*; **attention line** – *Zeile ‚zu Händen'*; **body** – *Haupttext*; **complimentary close** – *Schlussformel*; **enclosure** – *Anlage*; **recipient** – *Empfänger/in*; **letterhead** – *Briefkopf*; **salutation** – *Anrede*; **signature** – *Unterschrift*; **subject line** – *Betreffzeile*

Business letter layout

There is no standard layout for a business letter in the English-speaking world, but one of the most common layouts is the 'block' form layout shown here. After the letterhead, all the sentences are left aligned.

A ______________________________

This should include the sender's name, postal address, telephone and fax numbers, email address and website address. It often has the company's logo.

B ______________________________

References usually show the initials of the person who wrote the letter (here Linda Meyer) and of the person who typed it (here Tina Kopf). 'Your ref.' is used when someone has written to you and used that reference in their letter, 'Our ref.' is your own reference.

C ______________________________

Dates should always be given in words to avoid confusion – in the USA 05.07. would mean 7 May, whereas in Europe it is 5 July.

D ______________________________

When writing to a UK address, write the postcode on a separate line under the name of the town or city. Other countries will have rules that you may need to check.

E ______________________________

The attention line is under the recipient's address and close enough to it to be seen in a window envelope. That way, the post department in the recipient's company can see who the letter is for and deliver it to them.

F ______________________________

These are linked and depend on how formal you want to be. 'Dear Sir or Madam' is used when you do not know the name of the person you are writing to.

Salutation	Complimentary close	Formality	Notes
Dear Mrs/Ms/Mr Brown	Yours sincerely	Formal	Ms is used if you don't know if the person is married.
Dear Sir or Madam	Yours faithfully	Formal	Only used if the name is unknown
Dear Kim Dear Kim and Jim Dear Mrs/Ms/Mr Brown	Regards Best regards Best wishes	Friendly	Used in business if the writers know each other

G ______________________________

This is written in bold letters or underlined.

H ______________________________

The first word always starts with a CAPITAL LETTER. The paragraphs are separated by an empty line.

I ______________________________

Signatures are often hard to read, so the signatory's name (and position and company name), are written under the signature itself.

J ______________________________

It is sometimes enough just to write Enc or Encs but if necessary, details of the enclosure(s) can be listed like this: <u>Enc:</u> Ticket or <u>Encs:</u> Tickets

VOCABULARY

common – *gängig*; **left aligned** – *linksbündig*; **postcode** – *Postleitzahl*; **window envelope** – *Fensterbriefumschlag*; **to deliver** – *liefern*; **in bold letters** – *fett gedruckt*; **paragraph** – *Absatz*; **separated** – *getrennt*; **signatory** – *Unterzeichnete/r*

2 **The parts of the business letter below have got mixed up. Write out the letter again in the right order.**

Dear Ms Roch

Kind regards

Photo selection

Marianne Neumann

19 June 20..

I enjoyed our discussion in Cologne last week and was very pleased with the photos you took of our stand at the trade fair. Please find enclosed my choice for our new brochure. Could you let us have price details asap?

Julia Roch
Gamma Photo Agency
33 Avenue Napoléon
75019 Paris
France

Our ref.: MN/sk

Your ref.: UA/be

Marianne Neumann
Marketing Director

Encs

BIOTECH

Lehmann Biotech
Bergmannstr. 26
50667 Cologne
Germany

____
____
____

____
____
____
____
____
____

____

____

____
____
____

____

____

____
____

____

VOCABULARY

(Kind) regards – *Viele Grüße*; **selection** – *Auswahl*; **choice** – *Auswahl*; **brochure** – *Prospekt*; **details** – *Angaben, Einzelheiten*; **asap (=as soon as possible)** – *so bald wie möglich*

3 Find ten words in the box that you can use for your salutation and your complimentary close. Write them below the box.

t	r	o	p	w	m	a	d	a	m
b	e	s	t	i	q	y	l	h	a
e	g	s	o	s	u	o	r	s	i
b	a	i	t	h	f	k	i	n	d
y	r	r	d	e	a	r	u	i	l
e	d	n	k	s	y	o	u	r	s
f	s	i	n	c	e	r	e	l	y

________________ ________________

________________ ________________

4 Add words or phrases from the box to complete the letter. There are more words than you need.

23 June 20.. ▪ Encs ▪ Ms Neumann ▪ Our ref: JR/be ▪ **Photo selection** ▪ Tel. 33 (0)1 40 00 00 11 ▪ see you soon ▪ hearing from you soon ▪ Yours sincerely ▪ Lots of love

GAMMA PHOTO AGENCY

33 Avenue Napoléon | 75019 Paris | France

________________ 1

Your ref: MN/sk

________________ 2

________________ 3

Lehmann Biotech
Bergmannstr. 26
50667 Cologne
Germany

Attn. Ms Neumann

Dear ____________ 4

____________ 5

We are pleased to note that you like our photos. Please find enclosed our prices, terms and conditions as requested. I look forward to ________________ 6.

____________ 7

Julia Roch

____________ 8

VOCABULARY

Best wishes – *Mit den besten Wünschen*; **Yours sincerely** – *Mit freundlichen Grüßen*; **terms and conditions** – *(allgemeine) Geschäftsbedingungen*; **as requested** – *wie gewünscht*

B WRITING EMAILS

1 **Match the countries (1–6) with the email providers (a–f).**

1 Ireland **2** Denmark **3** Estonia **4** Turkey **5** Poland **6** Portugal

☐ **a** @mailme.dk ☐ **b** @mail.ee ☐ **c** @sapo.pt ☐ **d** @interia.pl ☐ **e** @dostmail.tr ☐ **f** @upc.ie

2 **Match the symbols (1–8) to the words (a–h) which can be used to give internet and email addresses over the phone.**

1 +	**5** .	☐ **a** at	☐ **e** number
2 _	**6** 3	☐ **b** dot	☐ **f** (forward) slash
3 @	**7** /	☐ **c** hyphen	☐ **g** underscore
4 -	**8** \	☐ **d** plus	☐ **h** backslash

06

3 **Listen and write the email addresses.**

1 ______________________ **4** ______________________

2 ______________________ **5** ______________________

3 ______________________ **6** ______________________

4 **Read the email subject lines (a–f) in Marianne Neumann's inbox. Which of them …**

1 is a request for information?
2 gives information about a meeting?
3 asks for assistance?
4 contains new information?
5 announces a change of plan?
6 is a covering letter to accompany some material?

a Need your help with English
b New location for event on Saturday
c Flyer (attached)
d Meeting 25.03. starting time?
e Update on project
f Agenda

1 ☐ 2 ☐ 3 ☐ 4 ☐ 5 ☐ 6 ☐

VOCABULARY

dot – *Punkt*; **(forward) slash** – *Schrägstrich*; **hyphen** – *Bindestrich*; **underscore** – *Unterstrich*; **backslash** – *Rückwärtsschrägstrich*; **assistance** – *Hilfe*; **covering letter** – *Begleitschreiben, Anschreiben*; **location** – *Ort, Standort*; **flyer** – *Handzettel*

5 **Write suitable subject lines for the following emails in Susan's inbox.**

1 Sorry, I have to change the date of the meeting to Friday 12 July 20..

____

2 Could you send me some information about the presentation, please?

____

3 I am on holiday from 21 March till 4 April inclusive and will answer emails when I return.

____

4 I am writing to confirm details for the Bionord Fair. Your stand number is C208.

____

5 As promised, here is the link to the website: www.tipsformails.orx.

____

6 This is just to let you know that I have booked a table for lunch in the restaurant. I suggest we meet there at 12.30.

____

6 **Add the missing words to the phrases in the box below.**

Writing emails

	Opening salutation	**Complimentary close**
Formal	Dear Ms/Mrs/Miss/Mr Smith	Regards Best ______ 1 Yours ______ 2
Less formal	Dear Paul ______ 3 morning, Paul ______ 4	Best ______ 5 ______ 6 best
Opening sentence		
Formal	With reference to … We are/I am ______ 7 to …	
Less formal	Just a quick ______ 8 to let you know …	
Closing sentence		
Formal	We/I look forward ______ 9 reply. We/I look forward to ______ 10 from you soon.	
Less formal	I hope to hear ______ 11.	

VOCABULARY

inclusive – *einschließlich*

7 You work for a Danish company in Copenhagen. Your boss, Inge Pedersen, has asked you to arrange a meeting with Gary Doyle, an important client from Dublin.
Write an email to Gary Doyle using Inge's notes and phrases from exercise 6. Don't forget the subject line.

> I'd like to have a meeting with Gary Doyle to finalize the contract.
> My suggestion: we meet at the Industrial Fair in Frankfurt next week.
> I have two free dates: Thursday, 26 at any time in the morning until 13.00
> Friday, 27 between 12.30 and 18.30
> We'll probably need about 3 hours.
> Ask him to get back to you by tomorrow as you'll need time to organize a conference room.
>
> Thanks.
> Inge

To: gdoyle@irishnation.nex
From: halltown@globalmail.orx
Subject: ____________________

____

____
____
____

____

____

8 Gary Doyle arranges to meet Inge Pedersen on Thursday. He will have to cancel a working breakfast with his business partner, Paul.
Write Paul a mail in English to cancel. Explain, apologize, and offer another appointment (say when and where). Check with Gary's calendar and use phrases from exercise 5.

Mon 23	Bank holiday		
Tue 24	Meeting: 10.00 Mr Blair	Lunch: Mr Blair 12.30–14.30 Quentins Restaurant	
Wed 25	Flight 10.50 → Frankfurt (arrive 12.20)		Dinner: Hans Treder 19.00 (Hotel restaurant)
Thur 26	~~Working breakfast: Paul 9.00–11.30~~ Ms Hall! 9.30–12.30	Presentation: 14.00–16.00	
Fri 27	Stand: 10.00–12.00		Flight 19.15 → Dublin (arrive 20.45)
Sat 28	Play golf with Harry Jones 11.00		

VOCABULARY

to finalize – *abschließen*; **contract** – *Vertrag*; **to cancel** – *absagen*; **bank holiday** – *gesetzlicher Feiertag*; **working breakfast** – *Arbeitsfrühstück*

To: paulholliday@irishnation.nex
From: gdoyle@irishnation.nex
Subject: ______________________________

____

____
____
____

____

____

C TELEPHONING

1 **Translate the useful phrases below into German.**

Identifying yourself
Good morning. My name's …

______________________ 1

Good afternoon. This is … from (company).

______________________ 2

Answering the phone
How can I help you?

______________________ 3

Speaking.

______________________ 4

Making small talk
How are you?

______________________ 5

How's the weather today?

______________________ 6

Asking for a person/department
I'd like to speak to Mr/Ms …

______________________ 7

Could you put me through to the … department, please?

______________________ 8

Explaining the reason for your call
I'm enquiring about …

______________________ 9

I'd like some information on …

____
______________________ 10

Could you tell me about … ?

____
______________________ 11

Saying what you want to do
Can I leave a message?

____
______________________ 12

I'll call again later.

______________________ 13

Ending the call
Thank you for your help.

______________________ 14

VOCABULARY

to put sb through – *jdn durchstellen, jdn verbinden*; **to enquire about sth** – *sich nach etw erkundigen*; **message** – *Nachricht*

2 Match the English sentences (1–10) to the German equivalents (a–l). There are two more than you need.

1 Could you repeat that, please?
2 I'm afraid the line is engaged.
3 I'm sorry, (person's name) is unavailable at the moment.
4 Please hold the line.
5 Who's calling, please?
6 Would you like to speak to someone else?
7 Would you like to leave a message?
8 I'm trying to connect you.
9 I'll put you through.
10 Could you spell your name, please?

☐ **a** Bleiben Sie bitte am Apparat.
☐ **b** Der Anschluss ist leider besetzt.
☐ **c** Ich stelle Sie jetzt durch.
☐ **d** Würden Sie das bitte wiederholen?
☐ **e** Würden Sie bitte Ihren Namen buchstabieren?
☐ **f** Möchten Sie mit jemand anderem sprechen?
☐ **g** Ich versuche Sie zu verbinden.
☐ **h** Möchten Sie eine Nachricht hinterlassen?
☐ **i** Herr/Frau … ist im Moment leider nicht zu sprechen.
☐ **j** Wie geht es Ihnen?
☐ **k** Mit wem spreche ich bitte?
☐ **l** Kann ich bitte eine Nachricht hinterlassen?

3 Abdi is taking a telephone call in English. Complete the dialogue using phrases from exercise 2.

L for London
not
L like London

A Can I speak to Ms Schmidt, please?

B May I ask ______________________ [1]?

A Of course. This is Liam Donnelly.

B I'm sorry, could you ______________________ [2], please?

A It's L I A M, D O double-N E double-L Y. I'm calling from Dublin, from Donnelly's Paper Mill.

B Sorry? Donnelly's Paper …? Could you ______________________ [3], please?

A Sure. Donnelly's Paper Mill, in Dublin.

B Donnelly's Paper Mill, Dublin. Thank you, Mr Donnelly. I'll try Ms Schmidt for you. Please ______________________ [4].

A Thank you.

B Sorry, this is taking a bit longer than it should. I'm still ______________________ [5].

A Thanks.

B Mr Donnelly. I'm afraid Ms Schmidt is ______________________ [6] at the moment. Would you like to speak to ______________________ [7]?

A Yes. Is Mr Müller in the office today?

B Yes, he is. I'll ______________________ [8]. I'm sorry, Mr Donnelly. His number ______________________ [9]. Would you like to ______________________ [10]?

A No, thanks. I'll try again later.

VOCABULARY

to repeat – *wiederholen*; **engaged** – *(Telefon:) besetzt*; **to be unavailable** – *nicht zu sprechen sein*; **to hold the line** – *am Apparat bleiben*; **to connect** – *verbinden*; **to spell** – *buchstabieren*

4 **Write out the telephone conversation between A and B in English.**

A	B
Nehmen Sie den Anruf an und nennen Sie Ihren Namen.	Begrüßen Sie A. (Sie kennen A.) Sagen Sie, wer Sie sind, und machen Sie ein wenig Smalltalk.
Reagieren Sie freundlich. Fragen Sie, wie Sie behilflich sein können.	Bitten Sie darum, mit einer bestimmten Person verbunden zu werden.
Die Person ist nicht erreichbar. Nennen Sie den Grund und bieten Sie an, eine Nachricht aufzunehmen/weiterzuleiten.	Hinterlassen Sie eine Nachricht.
Nehmen Sie die Nachricht auf.	Bedanken und verabschieden Sie sich.

A Hello? Steve Brown speaking.

B ______________________________

A ______________________________

B ______________________________

A ______________________________

B ______________________________

A ______________________________

B ______________________________

A Bye.

07 **5** Beatrice Kuhn works for a pharmaceutical company in Germany and often has to make phone calls in English.
Listen to a phone call and complete the following sentences with the correct ending. Tick a, b or c.

1 Ms Frey can't talk to the caller because she is …
- a talking on another line. ☐
- b writing a report. ☐
- c just leaving the office. ☐

2 Beatrice …
- a puts the caller through to someone else. ☐
- b gives the caller Ms Frey's private telephone number. ☐
- c takes a message. ☐

3 The caller would like Ms Frey to call him …
- a in the office. ☐
- b on his mobile. ☐
- c at home. ☐

4 The last three figures of the caller's number are …
- a 292. ☐
- b 922. ☐
- c 229. ☐

VOCABULARY

pharmaceutical company – *Pharmaunternehmen*; **figure** – *Ziffer*; **report** – *Bericht*; **to call sb back** – *jdn zurückrufen*; **maybe** – *vielleicht*

08

6 **Listen to the answerphone messages and complete the summaries.**

Message 1: Liam Watts is not in the office, but expects ______[1].
He asks the caller to ______[2] and promises to ______[3].

Message 2: Christine Adams apologizes because she ______[4].
She asks the caller to ______[5], and she promises to ______[6].

Message 3: Woods and Company regrets that ______[7]. They ask the caller to ______[8] and thank him/her for ______[9].

D COMMUNICATING BY EMAIL AND PHONE

1 The company Lehmann Biotech is participating in the Bionord Fair in Basel. Susann Kogel is making arrangements for her boss, Marianne Neumann.
Match Susann's emails (1–3) to the correct replies (a–c) below.

1
Lehmann Biotech is going to be at the Bionord Fair this year as usual. Ms Neumann has asked me to invite you to a working breakfast in the meeting room behind our stand (Hall 3, Stand 115) from 9.30 till 12.00 on Saturday, 3 April.

Could you let me know if the date is suitable for you? If it is, I'll book a hotel.

2
What time do you think you will arrive in Basel? Shall I arrange for someone to pick you up?

3
I'm writing to let you know that Daniel Ford from the Research Department can't be with us on Friday morning, so I'm afraid we will have to change the time of the presentation.

The presentation of the research results will now take place after lunch, at 14.00.

☐ **a** My train arrives at 8.15. I won't need anyone to pick me up as there are always a lot of taxis at the station. I expect I'll arrive just after 8.30. Please confirm that someone will be at the stand at that time.

☐ **b** Thank you for the information about the change of plans. I look forward to seeing the results on Friday afternoon.

☐ **c** This is just to let you know that the date is fine. I'm flying in from New York, and my plane lands at 23.00. Would you please inform the hotel that I'm going to arrive late?

VOCABULARY

shortly – *in Kürze*; **cooperation** – *Hilfsbereitschaft*; **to make arrangements** – *Vorbereitungen treffen*; **fair** – *Messe*; **to invite** – *einladen*; **till** – *bis*; **suitable** – *geeignet, passend*; **research** – *Forschung*; **to take place** – *stattfinden*; **to arrange for sb to do sth** – *dafür sorgen, dass jd etw tut*; **to pick sb/sth up** – *jdn/etw abholen*; **to expect** – *erwarten, annehmen*

2 **Complete these sentences using words from the emails above.**

1 Are these plans definite? Please write to ______________________ that you will be here next week.

2 Send the invitations by email so that they will ______________________ in time.

3 The date wasn't ______________________ so we changed it.

4 There are 25 participants, so I'll ______________________ the big conference room.

5 I'm sorry, but I can't come tomorrow. I hope it isn't too late to ______________________ our plans.

6 I'll ______________________ our flights so that we arrive in Madrid early.

3 **Join phrases 1–10 to phrases a–l to make sentences for making arrangements on the phone. There are two more than you need.**

1 Fine. I am looking forward to …
2 How about meeting at the …
3 I'd like to make an appointment for …
4 I'm afraid that's not possible because …
5 Shall we pick you up …
6 I'd like to …
7 Let's make …
8 Would it be possible to meet while …
9 Is Nina …
10 Is that date …

☐ a 10.30 on Monday.
☐ b at the station?
☐ c available tomorrow afternoon?
☐ d to organizing a meeting.
☐ e suitable for you?
☐ f hotel reception?
☐ g it at 11.30 instead of 10.30.
☐ h invite you to a working lunch.
☐ i she's in a meeting then.
☐ j seeing you then.
☐ k we're at the conference?
☐ l to arrive in the morning.

4 **The sentences below are from an email Susann wrote, but they are in the wrong order. Put them in the correct order.**

a She has to leave before 2 p.m. because she has another appointment.

b She asked me to tell you that she would be wearing a red coat.

c Dear Ms Andrews

d She would also like to know how long the meeting will last.

e She will arrive at your hotel at about 10 a.m. and will wait for you at reception.

f Ms Neumann asked me to email you to confirm your meeting tomorrow morning.

g Kind regards Susann Kogel

1 ☐ 2 ☐ 3 ☐ 4 ☐
5 ☐ 6 ☐ 7 ☐

VOCABULARY

in time – *rechtzeitig*; **participant** – *Teilnehmer/in*; **appointment** – *Termin*; **reception** – *Empfang, Rezeption*

5 It's normal that you have to ask people to slow down or repeat something when telephoning in English. But what is the most polite way of doing it? Answer the questions to find out how polite you are.

1 The person you are talking to is speaking unclearly. What do you say?
- a Listen! Would you speak more clearly, please? ☐
- b Sorry, could you speak a bit more clearly, please? ☐

2 The caller is speaking too fast. What do you say?
- a Could you speak a little more slowly, please? ☐
- b Slow down, please. ☐

3 You want the caller to repeat something. What do you say?
- a Sorry. I didn't get it. Say it again, please. ☐
- b Would it be possible to repeat that, please? ☐

4 You want the caller to spell something. What do you say?
- a Spell it, please. ☐
- b Could you spell it for me, please? ☐

5 The line is bad. What do you say?
- a I can't hear you. Hang up and dial again. ☐
- b I'm afraid I can't hear you. Could you hang up and dial again, please? ☐

6 Complete the grey boxes with the missing nouns or verbs, then add the German translations in the yellow boxes.

noun	verb	noun	verb
confirmation			book
Bestätigung			*reservieren, buchen*
	arrange	invitation	
meeting		enquiry	
		Anfrage	
	present	information	
	arrive		apologize

VOCABULARY

polite – *höflich*; **confirmation** – *Bestätigung*; **invitation** – *Einladung*

09

7 **Listen to the phone call and cross out the incorrect information in the dialogue. Write the correct information in the column on the right. There are thirteen mistakes. The first one has been done for you.**

Zoe: Good morning and thank you for calling Rob Heldof's press office. How can I help?

Helena: Hello, it's Helena Sawicki in Germany. Is that Zoe?

Zoe: Yes, it is. Nice to talk to you again, Helena.

Helena: Nice to talk to you too, Zoe. I'm just calling to ask you about holding a press conference with Rob Heldof when he comes here in ~~June~~. Nina Wittstock wants one either before or after his speech on Tuesday evening, and she'd also like him to go on a breakfast TV show the next day.

Zoe: Oh right. Just let me look at his diary. I have it here on my computer. OK, go ahead.

Helena: When does Rob arrive in Düsseldorf on the first?

Zoe: He arrives in the evening, but he'll have jet lag.

Helena: Oh I see. How about a press conference at six o'clock in the afternoon after his speech?

Zoe: He's going sightseeing with Katie in the afternoon. That'll take about three hours at least. What about eleven o'clock after the TV show?

Helena: I'm afraid that won't work out because he's having a meal then. How about Friday morning at about 10 a.m.?

Zoe: I'm not sure. He wants to buy some new clothes for Rio. And then his flight is at 10.30.

Helena: I see. OK. Let's look at Thursday again. What about after his show at about 9.30 p.m.?

Zoe: Yes, he's free then, but let's make it one o'clock to give him a bit more time.

Helena: Great!

Zoe: I'll check with him and get back to you.

Helena: That's marvellous. Oh, and please ask him if he wants to go on the breakfast show on Sunday morning.

Zoe: What time would that be?

Helena: It starts at 6.30 p.m., but how about eight o'clock?

Zoe: Mmm, I'm not sure. I'll ask him and get back to you as soon as possible. Talk to you soon. Bye.

Helena: Bye.

1 May ______
2 ______
3 ______
4 ______
5 ______
6 ______
7 ______
8 ______
9 ______
10 ______
11 ______
12 ______
13 ______

VOCABULARY

press conference – *Pressekonferenz*; **speech** – *Rede*; **marvellous** – *wunderbar, fantastisch*

E KMK EXAM PRACTICE

1 Hörverstehen

10

Situation: Susann Kögel hört regelmäßig die Podcasts der Webseite Your Office Matters. Im heutigen Podcast geht es um die Vor- und Nachteile von Briefen und E-Mails in der Geschäftskorrespondenz.

Aufgabe: Hören Sie sich das Podcast an und tragen Sie die Vor- und Nachteile in die Tabelle ein.

Vorteile	Nachteile

2 Produktion

Situation: Sie arbeiten für Gary Doyle und sollen auf Inge Pedersens E-Mail (Übung 7, Seite 20) antworten.

Aufgabe: Verfassen Sie eine E-Mail unter Berücksichtigung der folgenden Punkte:

- Schreiben Sie eine freundliche Einleitung.
- Sagen Sie, dass Ihnen der Terminvorschlag für Donnerstag, den 26., um 9.30 Uhr am besten passt.
- Erklären Sie, dass ein Konferenzraum nicht nötig ist, weil es am Firmenstand von Doyle eine geeignete Möglichkeit gibt.
- Geben Sie in Klammern den Standort an: Halle 3, Stand 75.
- Sagen Sie, dass Sie sich freuen, Frau Hall wiederzusehen.
- Beenden Sie das Schreiben mit einer freundlichen Schlussformel.

3 Produktion

Situation: Sie arbeiten bei Bürowelt, einer Büromöbelfirma aus München. Die Firma will vom 18. bis 20. November an der WORKPLACE-Büromöbelmesse in Earls Court, London, teilnehmen. Sie werden gebeten, eine Reservierungsanfrage an die Messeveranstalter gemäß folgender Angaben zu schreiben.

Aufgabe: Verfassen Sie die Anfrage. Berücksichtigen Sie die folgenden Punkte:

- Sagen Sie, dass Sie für Ihre Firma einen Stand in Halle 2 reservieren möchten.
- Bitten Sie darum, dass der Stand so nah wie möglich am Haupteingang ist.
- Geben Sie an, dass der Stand eine Mindestgröße von 280 m^2 haben soll.
- Schreiben Sie, dass Sie davon ausgehen, dass alle Standflächen mit Telefon-/Internetverbindung ausgestattet sind.
- Erklären Sie, dass Sie einen separaten Raum für Besprechungen benötigen.
- Bitten Sie um eine möglichst baldige Reservierungsbestätigung.
- Beenden Sie das Schreiben mit einer freundlichen Schlussformel.

4 Mediation

Situation: Your English-speaking boss, Ms Giles, wants to know more about the business travel market. You found this report on the internet which answers some of her questions.

Aufgabe: Write an email to Ms Giles summarizing the important points from the report. Include the following points:

- why you are writing
- how many companies are changing from business trips to virtual conferences
- the advantages and disadvantages of virtual conferences
- how business travellers try to keep cost and emissions low when they travel
- options that are not popular with travellers

Digitale Kommunikation: Die Zukunft des Geschäftsreisemarktes

Bis vor Kurzem galten sie in der Business-Welt noch als exotisch: Online-Konferenzen, virtuelle Meetings und digitale Workshops. Aber schon im letzten Jahr haben nachhaltige Entwicklungen und nun spätestens die Corona-Krise gezeigt, dass der Geschäftsreisemarkt vor einem Wandel steht.

Rund die Hälfte aller Unternehmen hat bereits in diesem Jahr Geschäftsreisen durch virtuelle Meetings ersetzt. Digitale Kommunikation reduziert vor allem Stress durch Verspätungen im Verkehr und ermöglicht eine bessere Weiterarbeit, da Dokumente dauerhaft verfügbar sind. Andererseits lassen sich nicht alle Dienstreisen digital durchführen, und in vielen Branchen wird der persönliche Kontakt nach wie vor als wichtig für die Geschäftsbeziehung empfunden.

Auch der Umweltschutz spielt eine große Rolle. In Studien gaben über 80 Prozent der Befragten an, dass es ihnen wichtig ist, bei Geschäftsreisen ihren ökologischen Fußabdruck möglichst gering zu halten. 59 Prozent aller Geschäftsreisenden verbinden mehrere Termine in einer Reise, um Kosten und Emissionen zu sparen. Die Hälfte nutzt die Bahn anstatt Flugzeug oder Mietwagen. Etwa genauso viele Befragte geben an, keine Papierausdrucke mehr, sondern nur noch digitale Unterlagen zu benutzen. Weniger beliebt allerdings ist die Option, Car-Sharing zu nutzen oder teurere Flugtickets zu erwerben, um CO2-Emissionen zu kompensieren.

F IHK EXAM PRACTICE

1 Geschäftsbrief in Englisch nach Stichwortangaben in Deutsch

Situation: Sie arbeiten bei Bürowelt, einer Büromöbelfirma aus München. Die Firma will vom 18. bis 20. November an der WORKPLACE-Büromöbelmesse in Earls Court, London, teilnehmen. Sie werden gebeten, eine Reservierungsanfrage an die Messeveranstalter zu schreiben.

Aufgabe: Verfassen Sie die Anfrage. Berücksichtigen Sie die folgenden Punkte:

- Sagen Sie, dass Sie für Ihre Firma einen Stand in Halle 2 reservieren möchten.
- Bitten Sie darum, dass der Stand so nah wie möglich am Haupteingang ist.
- Geben Sie an, dass der Stand eine Mindestgröße von 280 m^2 haben soll.
- Schreiben Sie, dass Sie davon ausgehen, dass alle Standflächen mit Telefon-/Internetverbindung ausgestattet sind.
- Erklären Sie, dass Sie einen separaten Raum für Besprechungen benötigen.
- Bitten Sie um eine möglichst baldige Reservierungsbestätigung.
- Beenden Sie das Schreiben mit einer freundlichen Schlussformel.

11

2 Vermerk in Deutsch über ein Gespräch in Englisch

Situation: Sie arbeiten als Assistent eines TV-Produzenten bei NRW.TV. Sie nehmen einen Anruf von June Smith entgegen. Junes Chef, Rob Heldof, soll am Sonntagmorgen an einem Fernsehinterview teilnehmen.

Aufgabe: Verfolgen Sie das Gespräch und fertigen Sie anschließend eine Gesprächsnotiz auf Deutsch für den Produzenten, Thomas Liepe an. Während des Hörens dürfen Sie Notizen machen. Diese Notizen werden nicht bewertet, sondern nur die Gesprächsnotiz.

Sie:	June Smith:
Guten Morgen, Büro von Herrn Liepe. Was kann ich für Sie tun?	…
Sure, English is no problem. How can I help you?	…
Yes, Ms Smith, I know about that interview. Please go ahead.	…
Ah, OK. I see. I will clarify that and make sure Mr Liepe knows which time suits you. And the second issue?	…
I'm sure that will not be a problem, Ms Smith. Is there anything else I can do?	…
No, not at all. We often have English-speaking guests. A translator will translate Mr Heldof's words into German and the viewers will hear that. It's normal here.	…
Yes, I will talk to Mr Liepe as soon as possible and you will hear from us shortly.	…
You're welcome, Ms Smith. Goodbye.	…

3 Sprachergänzungstest (Typ 2)

Aufgabe: In diesem Text ist jeweils nur eine der vorgeschlagenen Formen auf der nächsten Seite korrekt. Bitte setzen Sie die richtige Lösung in die entsprechende Lücke ein.

A recent study ____________________ [1] that younger people – in their 20s or 30s - tend to write ____________________ [2] informally. Is this a problem? Well, in business, it can be.

Firstly, ____________________ [3] you are one of these informal 'youngsters' in work, not everyone you write to will be your age and they may ____________________ [4] the more formal style of ____________________ [5] communication. By writing informally ____________________ [6] someone you do not know, you could unintentionally provoke a ______________ [7] reaction: "Who is this stranger calling me by my first name?!" Secondly, we live in a ______________ [8] world and English ______________ [9] the language of business, but that does not ______________ [10] the culture of English-speaking countries is the norm. Formality can show respect ______________ [11] the people ______________ [12]. English is one of the few languages that does not have a ______________ [13] form of address. In German, there is *Sie* and *du*, but in English? Only *you*. ______________ [14] this, formality – and respect – ______________ [15] by *how* you write: using Mr or Ms and ______________ [16], long forms (*I am* instead of *I'm*), and long indirect phrases ______________ [17] as *'I would appreciate it if you could send me...'*. We may think we sound friendly ______________ [18] an informal style, but the reader might think ______________ [19] shows a lack ______________ [20] respect.

But don't worry! Here's a useful tip: the sender of the first email sets the style. If you are the sender, then ______________ [21] formally. If you prefer an informal style, ______________ [22] sign your formal email with your first name, followed by your full name and work position. ______________ [23] is a signal to the ______________ [24] that you are open to a more relaxed style and it gives them ______________ [25] to write to you using your first name. Conversely, if you receive an email signed with the ______________ [26] first name, then begin your reply with ______________ [27] first name. If the communication goes on into several emails, it can be more natural to ______________ [28] less formal as you both 'get to know each other'. And ______________ [29] the rule of business: the customer is king (or queen!). If your communication partner is your customer, you ______________ [30] formally but let the customer set the tone.

1	is showing, has showed, has shown	**16**	after names, surnames, final names
2	more, much, many	**17**	such, like, that
3	if, when, that	**18**	use, used, using
4	used to be, be used to, used be to	**19**	you, it, he
5	write, wrote, written	**20**	from, in, of
6	of, to, at	**21**	write, writing, written
7	positive, negative, neutral	**22**	than, then, though
8	globalizing, globalized, globally	**23**	These, This, Those
9	may be, maybe, be may	**24**	receive, recipient, receipt
10	think, meant, mean	**25**	agreement, permission, allow
11	for, of, before	**26**	persons, person's, persons'
12	we writing to are, we are writing to, writing to are we	**27**	their, there, they're
13	formal, formally, in formal	**28**	become, becoming, getting
14	Because, Because of, That's why	**29**	not forget, do not forget, do forget not
15	expresses, is expressed, expressed	**30**	should always begin, should begin always, always begin should

Useful phrases

Telephoning	
Identifying yourself	
Good morning/afternoon. This is … from …	*Guten Morgen/Tag. Hier spricht … von …* (Firma).
Explaining the reason for your call	
I'm enquiring about …	*Ich wollte mich nach … erkundigen.*
I'd like some information on …	*Ich hätte gern nähere Informationen zu …*
Asking for a person/department	
I'd like to speak to …	*Ich würde gerne (mit) … sprechen.*
Could you put me through to …, please?	*Könnten Sie mich bitte mit … verbinden?*
Dealing with the caller	
Could you spell your name, please?	*Könnten Sie bitte Ihren Namen buchstabieren?*
Could you repeat that, please?	*Könnten Sie das bitte wiederholen?*
I'll put you through.	*Ich stelle Sie durch.*
Please hold the line.	*Bleiben Sie bitte am Apparat.*
I'm afraid the line is engaged.	*Der Anschluss ist leider besetzt.*
I'm sorry, … is unavailable at the moment.	*Es tut mir leid, aber … ist im Moment nicht zu sprechen.*
Dealing with problems	
Could you speak more slowly, please?	*Könnten Sie bitte langsamer reden?*
Could you repeat that, please?	*Könnten Sie das bitte wiederholen?*
Could you hang up and dial again, please?	*Könnten Sie bitte auflegen und nochmal wählen?*
Saying what you want to do	
Can I leave a message?	*Kann ich eine Nachricht hinterlassen?*
Could you ask … to call me back?	*Könnten Sie … bitten, mich zurückzurufen?*

Writing emails	
Salutation	
Dear Sir or Madam (*formal*)	*Sehr geehrte Damen und Herren,*
Dear Mr/Ms Smith (*formal*)	*Sehr geehrter Herr / Sehr geehrte Frau Smith,*
Dear Paul (and Paula) / Hi/Hello Paula (less formal)	*Lieber Paul (, Liebe Paula), / Hallo Paula,*
Complimentary close	
Yours faithfully (*formal*)	*Mit freundlichen Grüßen*
(Best) regards / Best wishes / Yours sincerely (*formal*)	*Freundliche/Viele Grüße*
All the best (*less formal*)	*Alles Gute / Herzliche Grüße*
Opening sentence	
I'm just writing to … (*formal*)	*Ich schreibe Ihnen, um zu / weil …*
Just a quick note/message to … (*less formal*)	*Ich wollte nur kurz …*
Conclusion	
I look forward to hearing from you. (*formal*)	*Ich freue mich auf Ihre Antwort.*
I hope to hear from you soon. (*less formal*)	*Ich freue mich, bald von Ihnen/dir zu hören.*

Applying for a job 3

Whether you apply online or offline, the key to finding a right job is good preparation. Think about what job you are interested in, research possible employers, write your application carefully and practise answering difficult interview questions.

A JOB ADVERTISEMENTS

1 Yvonne Steffens has nearly finished commercial school and would like to start an apprenticeship where she can also use and improve her English. She has found the following advertisement on the internet.

Lesen Sie die untenstehende Anzeige und notieren Sie sich:

1 für welche Stelle sich Yvonne interessiert.

____

2 welche Aufgaben die Tätigkeit umfasst.

____

3 welche Anforderungen an den Bewerber / die Bewerberin gestellt werden.

____

4 welche Zusatzleistungen angeboten werden.

____

5 wie Yvonne sich bewerben kann.

____

Date 28 May	Advert	Job ref no 20229375

ABC

We are a leading private clinic located in Munich that is looking to recruit an Office Management Assistant on a permanent basis.
The successful candidate will assist the clinic manager and work in Reception. Responsibilities include meeting and greeting international clients, providing secretarial support to the Clinic Manager, appointment management, updating the database and providing general office administration.

What we are looking for:
You will need to be a highly organized individual who is able to work under pressure.
Strong administrative skills are essential. Office experience is necessary.
You will need to be able to use standard office software, have good typing skills and an excellent telephone manner.
As we have many international clients, good English is essential. At least one other foreign language would be useful.

What's on offer:
A salary between €18,000 to €19,000 p.a.
Optional language training classes.

If you are interested in applying, please complete our application form and attach your CV and a covering letter.

Initial interviews will be conducted by telephone. Further face-to-face interviews will take place in July.

VOCABULARY

p.a. = per annum – *im Jahr*; **permanent** – *unbefristet*; **to be located in** – *in … sein/liegen*; **to recruit** – *(Personal) einstellen*; **candidate** – *Bewerber/in*; **beneficial** – *vorteilhaft*; **telephone manner** – *Telefonkompetenz*; **essential** – *unbedingt notwendig*; **salary** – *Gehalt*; **CV = curriculum vitae** (*BE*), **résumé** (*AE*) – *Lebenslauf*; **covering letter** – *Begleitschreiben*; **initial** – *erste/r/s*; **to conduct sth** – *etw durchführen*; **face-to-face** – *persönlich*

2 **Find the English equivalents of these German words in the advertisement.**

1 Bewerber/in	______________	5 Lebenslauf	______________
2 Aufgabe	______________	6 Begleitschreiben	______________
3 Verwaltung	______________	7 unbefristet	______________
4 Bewerbung	______________	8 Gehalt	______________

3 **Decide which of the jobs described in the adverts A–D would be the most suitable for the people (1–5) below. There is one person more than you need.**

☐ **A Entertainers/animators**

We are looking for young German-speakers to train as entertainers/animators at hotels in the Canary Islands.

Requirements: You speak good English and Spanish. You are a top-fit team player and a fun-loving person. Previous experience is desirable but not necessary.
Training: We'll teach you how to entertain and give classes in, for example, dancing, volleyball, aerobics, etc.
Terms of employment: Minimum age 17, board and lodging provided, €500 per month
Applications: Upload your CV to www…

☐ **B Banking customer service adviser**

Brown's Bank is looking for a German trainee banking customer service adviser to participate in an in-house training scheme in the Ingolstadt branch. If you enjoy talking to different people, speak fluent German and are interested in finance, this job could be perfect for you.

Requirements: excellent communication skills, good maths and computer skills, experience of handling cash useful but not essential.
Working hours: 9 a.m. to 6 p.m.
Starting salary: €18,000 per year
Application with CV to: Sally Clayton, HR Department, Brown's Bank, 51 Perth Street, London EC2 7HQ

☐ **C Work experience position (1 year)**

We are a major international company producing office equipment. We have a work experience vacancy in our Munich office for an office management assistant. The ideal candidate for the job will be a German native speaker with excellent English. Good telephone manner important.

Qualifications: relevant school-leaving certificate.
Salary: €15,000 p.a.
Training opportunities and possibility of a permanent position.
Please send your application together with your CV to: beate.roos@officeone.nex Tel. 089-73592

☐ **D Experienced events clerk**

This company in the city of New York organizes exhibitions, shows and events. As part of a team, you will be dealing face to face with the public, giving out information about events and distributing tickets. You should be a good communicator both orally and in writing. Standard software skills are a must. Excellent English required.

Salary: $40,000 p.a., company apartment available
Apply in writing enclosing your résumé to:
Rebecca Potter, NYNY Events, 76 Broadway, New York, NY 11580.

1 **Frank** is a native-speaker of German. His English is weak. He's a very sociable person. His best subject at school was maths.
2 **Christine** would like to live and work abroad. She is very sporty and sometimes dreams of turning her hobby into her job. She's very good at foreign languages.
3 **Annette** is bilingual. Her mother is German and her father is English. Annette doesn't want to work abroad. She wants to see what it's like to work in an office. The salary is not so important.
4 **Silvia** would like to work in an office. She is good at maths, but doesn't speak any foreign languages. She is rather shy and doesn't want a job where she has to meet a lot of people.
5 **Michael** is a good team player and gets on well with people. He would like to work abroad. He speaks German and English well, but no other languages.

VOCABULARY

terms of employment – *Einstellungsbedingungen*; **board and lodging** – *Kost und Logis*; **to upload** – *hochladen*; **customer service adviser** – *Kundenberater/in*; **to participate** – *teilnehmen*; **in-house** – *betriebsintern*; **training scheme** – *Ausbildungsprogramm*; **branch** – *Filiale*; **fluent** – *fließend*; **to handle cash** – *mit Bargeld umgehen*; **vacancy** – *offene Stelle*; **clerk** – *Sachbearbeiter/in*; **to distribute** – *verkaufen, verteilen*; **oral(ly)** – *mündlich*; **sociable** – *kontaktfreudig*; **shy** – *schüchtern*

4 **Make sentences with words from each column.**

1 The company is looking	in	good language skills.
2 The trainees can participate	to	trainees for its training programme.
3 A customer adviser talks	at	an events clerk.
4 The animator will give classes	for	dancing and aerobics.
5 A bank trainee should be good	with	brochures to the public.
6 The company has a vacancy	out	handling cash.
7 The clerk will deal	of	a better job later.
8 The team gives		different people.
9 The company says there is a possibility		the in-house training scheme.
10 The assistant needs to come		the public.

1 *The company is looking* ______________________

2 ______________________

3 ______________________

4 ______________________

5 ______________________

6 ______________________

7 ______________________

8 ______________________

9 ______________________

10 ______________________

B JOB APPLICATIONS

1 **Employers often expect job applicants to apply online. Match sentence beginnings 1–8 with the endings a–h to make sentences about online job applications.**

1 For an online job application you can apply to the employer's website or	☐ **a** and paste your complete CV into your application.
2 For an online job website you first need to	☐ **b** everything manually into different fields on the computer.
3 To add your CV to the application the simplest way is	☐ **c** if this has been successful.
4 You will receive a message	☐ **d** look for the 'help' button or link.
5 Another way is to copy	☐ **e** to an online job website.
6 But remember to check	☐ **f** register with a username and a password.
7 Some online employers ask you to write	☐ **g** the formatting afterwards.
8 If you are having trouble with the application,	☐ **h** to upload a PDF or Word file.

VOCABULARY

brochure – *Prospekt;* **applicant** – *Bewerber/in;* **manually** – *per Hand;* **field** – *Feld;* **to register** – *registrieren;* **username** – *Benutzername;* **formatting** – *Formatierung*

2 **Read the tips on writing a CV and match them with the headings.**

Education and training ▪ Hobbies and interests ▪ Personal statement ▪ *Personal details* ▪ References ▪ Skills and achievements ▪ Work experience

There is no set format for an English-language CV, but you should keep it short, using headings to guide the reader.

1 *Personal details*

Give your name and address, telephone number(s) (home/mobile) and email address.

2 ______

This should be a short message that grabs the attention of the reader and summarizes your skills and experience relevant to the job for which you are applying. Use note form and write in the third person: *Motivated office management assistant with experience in foreign trade*.

3 ______

As a general rule, CVs should be in reverse chronological order, listing the most recent position first. For each position held you should provide the dates of the start and end of employment, the employer's name and address, the job title, the main duties and responsibilities and achievements.

4 ______

Give a brief description of qualifications (school, academic and/or professional). Give the names of schools or colleges in reverse chronological order.

5 ______

Here you should write about skills gained throughout your education and work experience, such as languages, IT skills or a full, clean driving licence. These skills are of interest for any employer. You should also describe your character using words like *good organizing skills, team-orientated, flexible, reliable …*

6 ______

This feature is optional, but could help to provide something more personal to discuss at an interview. Be careful: a dangerous sport or *socializing with friends* may not be what an employer wants to hear!

7 ______

Candidates should not give referees' names and addresses on CVs, but should state that details are available on request. Always ask your referees' permission before you give someone their contact details.

3 Yvonne Steffens is applying for the job as Office Management Assistant advertised on page 33. She has written her CV in the Europass format using the tips above.
Look at Yvonne's details on page 37. What differences can you find between her CV and a German CV?

______

______

VOCABULARY

set format – *vorgeschriebenes Format;* **heading** – *Überschrift;* **to grab sb's attention** – *jds Aufmerksamkeit erregen;* **reverse** – *umgekehrt;* **duty** – *Aufgabe;* **responsibility** – *Aufgabe;* **achievement** – *Leistung, Erfolg;* **(clean) driving licence** – *Führerschein (ohne Punkte);* **reliable** – *zuverlässig;* **feature** – *Merkmal;* **to socialize with sb** – *sich (privat) mit jdm treffen;* **referee** – *Referenzgeber/in;* **available on request** – *auf Anfrage erhältlich;* **permission** - *Erlaubnis*

Yvonne Steffens
Max-Planck-Str. 236, 93047 Regensburg, Germany
Phone (+49) 941 39467
Email styvon93@gmx.nex

Personal statement
Highly-motivated office management assistant with experience in reception.
I am team-orientated but also enjoy working independently.

Previous work experience
Since March 20..: Dr Müller Rehabilitationsklinik, Bad Füssing
Dealing with administration, contact with health insurance companies, reception
September 20.. – June 20..: Training as Industriekauffrau, certified by the Chamber of Commerce, Regensburg

Education
September 20.. – July 20..: ABC Berufsschule, Regensburg
2 year, part-time vocational school: accounting, business administration, word processing
September 19.. – June 20..: Commercial School, Regensburg, including participation in the course Übungsunternehmen BAWI GmbH (simulated company designed to prepare for business transactions)
Mittlerer Abschluss, grade 2 (junior certificate exam taken at 16)

Skills
Excellent IT-Skills (MS Office)
Good at working under pressure, friendly, flexible
Fluent English (oral and written), good French, some Spanish

Hobbies and interests
Travelling, yoga, foreign languages

References
Names of referees available on request

4 **Look at Yvonne's details and find words that mean:**

1 good at working in a team	______________
2 given a certificate	______________
3 insurance in case of illness	______________
4 taking part in something	______________
5 special abilities	______________
6 can change easily in a new situation	______________
7 speak or write easily and well	______________
8 a person who gives a reference	______________

5 **Create your own Europass CV and present your skills and qualifications effectively and clearly. Go online to Europass, study an example CV and then write your own.**

VOCABULARY

health insurance – *Krankenversicherung;* **to certify** – *bescheinigen*; **business transaction** – *Geschäftsvorgang*

6 **Parts of Yvonne's covering letter are mixed up. Put the paragraphs (A–E) in the right order.**

Yvonne Steffens
Max-Planck-Str. 236
93047 Regensburg
Germany
Phone: (+49) 521 39467
Email: styvon89@gmx.nex

Dr Sanjay Patel
Best Clinic
Hauptstraße 21
80337 München

10 May 20..

Dear Dr Patel

Office Management Assistant

A As you can see from the enclosed CV, I am currently employed in a German rehabilitation clinic as an Office Management Assistant. My duties include dealing with general administration and making contact with health insurance companies. I also work at the reception desk, admitting patients and assisting visitors.

B The position of Office Management Assistant advertised on your website has caught my interest.

C Enclosed is my CV and the names of two referees. I would appreciate it if you consider my application and hope that you will grant me an interview.

D I am very interested in the job you are offering as I feel sure it will give me the opportunity to develop in my career in an interesting company. I am particularly keen to use my knowledge of English on a daily basis.

E Through the experience I have gained in my present position, I believe I can make a useful contribution to your clinic. My language abilities will also make me an asset to your team. My English is excellent as I studied it for 8 years, including business English at commercial school and during my vocational training. I also have a working knowledge of French and can speak some Spanish. My mother tongue is German.

I look forward to hearing from you soon.

Yours sincerely

Yvonne Steffens

Enc

1 ☐ 2 ☐ 3 ☐ 4 ☐ 5 ☐

VOCABULARY

to advertise (a job) – *(eine Stelle) ausschreiben*; **to admit sb** – *jdn aufnehmen*;
to be an asset to sb/sth – *für jdn/etw wertvoll sein*

7 **Choose one of the job advertisements on pages 33 and 34 and write a covering letter. Use some of the words and phrases in the box below. (You will need to refer to your letter again on page 41.)**

Writing a covering letter

Opening phrases

I was extremely interested to read In reply to With reference to	your advertisement	in … (newspaper etc.) of … (date) on your company website	for	the post of … a work experience position as …

I	see that you are looking for a/an				… (job).
	would like wish	to apply for the above-mentioned	position post	of	

Education/training

I attended … (school/college) for … (length of time).
I studied … (subjects) at vocational school in … (town/city) from … (date) to … (date).
I will complete my period of training on … (date).

As you can see from my CV, I	will take my commercial school exams in 20.. attended commercial school for … years. graduated from commercial school in 20.. took the *Abitur* (high school leaving certificate age 18) in 20.. passed my *Mittlerer Abschluss* (middle school certificate age 16) in 20..

Skills

I am a native speaker of I have a good basic knowledge of I am fluent in	German/French/English/…
My computer skills are	excellent/above-average.

Previous experience

I did my work placement/apprenticeship as a … at … (company).
I am currently working as a … for … (company)
I have been working as a … at … (company) for … years/since 20..

Further comments

I believe I am particularly suitable for the post advertised because …

Closing paragraph

I enclose Enclosed you will find	my CV/résumé. a list of my qualifications and experience.

I hope you will consider my application favourably and …
I look forward to hearing from you in the near future.
I would be pleased if you would consider me for this post.
I am available for an interview at any time/at short notice.

VOCABULARY

post – *Stelle*; **native speaker** – *Muttersprachler/in*; **to consider sth** – *etw erwägen*; **favourably** – *positiv, günstig*; **at short notice** – *kurzfristig*

C JOB INTERVIEWS

1 Yvonne wurde mitgeteilt, dass nächste Woche ein telefonisches Bewerbungsgespräch mit ihr geführt wird. Sie sucht im Internet nach Tipps und Ratschlägen.
Lesen Sie die Webseite unten und fassen sie die wichtigsten Punkte auf Deutsch für eine/n Kollegen/-in zur Vorbereitung auf sein/ihr telefonisches Vorstellungsgespräch zusammen.

Your telephone interview

One short phone call is all it takes to get you to the next level in your job application process – or not. By asking just a few questions, an interviewer can quickly decide if you are a likely candidate for the job.

Don't let your interviewer think that this phone call is not as meaningful to you as if it were a face-to-face interview:

- Don't slip into a more relaxed tone because you are on the phone. Speak clearly and stay formal.
- Listen carefully. You can't see the interviewer so it's easier to misunderstand what they say.

Be prepared!

Have these things ready beside your phone:

- a copy of the job description
- a copy of your letter of application, your CV and your references
- a notebook and a couple of pens so that you can take notes during the interview
- a list of questions you want to ask the interviewer
- a list of your strengths

Before the interview, you should also practice all your success stories. Whether they are work stories or academic achievements, a good story is much more interesting than a list of job skills.
Remember, if you don't make a good impression on the phone, you won't be invited for the face-to-face meeting.

VOCABULARY

level – *Ebene;* **meaningful** – *wichtig, bedeutsam;* **strength** – *Stärke;* **impression** – *Eindruck*

2 **Read the questions (1–5) that the telephone interviewer asked Yvonne. Decide what the interviewer wanted to find out by asking these questions. Choose from the list of suggestions (a–e).**

1 Do you have a few minutes to talk with me so that I can get a better idea of what it is you're expecting from the position?
2 What led you to apply for the position?
3 What would you like to be doing five years from now?
4 I think we've covered everything, but is there anything you'd like to ask me?
5 We'll be interviewing candidates in Dublin next week. Would you be interested in coming to talk with us?

☐ **a** If we were to hire you, would we be investing in the future of the company?
☐ **b** Have you done some research on our company?
☐ **c** Why do you think you're the right person for the job?
☐ **d** What kind of person are you? Should we go further with your application?
☐ **e** Are you still interested in the job?

3 **In exercise 7 on page 39 you applied for a job. Write down five questions the interviewer might ask you during an interview for this job.**

1 ____________________
2 ____________________
3 ____________________
4 ____________________
5 ____________________

Now write the answers to your questions.

1 ____________________
2 ____________________
3 ____________________
4 ____________________
5 ____________________

4 One of the most common questions asked in an interview is what your strengths and weaknesses are so it is important to prepare for this. You should think of examples to show your strengths and how you are working on improving your weaknesses.
Note down your strengths and weaknesses in the table below.

Strength	Example	Weakness	Improvements

VOCABULARY

to cover sth – *(Thema) behandeln;* **to hire sb** – *jdn einstellen*

12 **5** Sarah Denby has read a job advertisement for a marketing assistant. She telephones the company and is put through to Nadine Koch in the Human Resources Department.

Listen to the dialogue. Complete the notes Nadine takes in English. You need not write complete sentences.

Human Resources Department	
Name of applicant	Sarah Denby
Address	______ 1 Post code: ______ 2
Phone number	______ 3 Mobile: ______ 4
Academic qualifications	University: ______ 5 School: ______ 6
Languages	______ 7
Work experience	______ ______ 8

6 **How do you refer to your education, training and skills in English? Find the English equivalent (a–i) for each German expression (1–9).**

1 Allgemeine Hochschulreife (Abitur)
2 Berufsschule
3 Fachhochschulreife
4 Führerschein Klasse 3
5 Mittlerer Abschluss
6 Realschule
7 Hauptschule
8 Wirtschaftsschule
9 Gymnasium

☐ **a** secondary school
☐ **b** selective secondary school
☐ **c** grammar school
☐ **d** German university entrance qualifications
☐ **e** German higher education entrance qualifications
☐ **f** car driving licence
☐ **g** vocational (training) college
☐ **h** German Class 10 School Leaving Certificate
☐ **i** commercial school

13 **7** Yvonne Steffens has been invited to Munich for a second, face-to-face interview. Before she goes, she listens to a podcast in which Pat Klein, a business coach, gives tips about interviews.

Listen to the podcast and complete her notes about the 'Five stages of an interview' under the headings on the next page.

VOCABULARY

area code – *Vorwahl;* **honours degree** – *Universitätsabschluss;* **2.1** – *eine Abschlussnote;* **Highers** – *etwa: Abitur in Schottland;* **GCSE = General Certificate of Secondary Education** – *etwa: Mittlerer Schulabschluss;* **questionnaire** – *Fragebogen*

Stage 1: Greetings and introductions

Arrive ______________________[1]. Give yourself time ______________________

______________________[2].

Wear appropriate ______________________[3] because first ______________________[4].

Body ______________________[5] is important. Walk into the room as ______________________[6].

Shake hands and ______________________[7].

Don't be ______________________[8].

Stage 2: Small talk

Topics for small talk are: ______________________

______________________[9]

Get into the habit of making ______________________[10].

Stage 3: The main part of the interview

Questions will be asked ______________________[11].

Think about the questions and ______________________[12].

The interviewer may ask about your ______________________[13].

If you don't understand a question, ______________________[14].

Stage 4: Questions from the candidate

It's important to do some ______________________[15].

Find out about the company's ______________________[16].

Go to the firm's ______________________[17], read ______________________

______________________[18], or look through ______________________[19].

Make a note of ______________________[20].

Prepare some ______________________[21].

Stage 5: Further arrangements at the end of the interview

The interviewer usually says when ______________________[22].

When you leave say ______________________[23].

Give a good, ______________________[24].

VOCABULARY

appropriate – *angemessen;* **smart** – *schick, elegant;* **habit** – *Gewohnheit;* **weakness** – *Schwäche;* **to clarify** – *erklären, erläutern;* **prospects** – *Aussichten;* **to occur to sb** – *jdm einfallen;* **concerning** – *bezüglich, hinsichtlich;* **assessment** – *Beurteilung;* **evaluation** – *Bewertung;* **handshake** – *Händedruck*

8 **Read Pat Klein's list of mistakes that candidates make at interviews. Then identify which of the mistakes (1–8) candidates are making in their statements and questions (a–f).**

Common job interview mistakes

1 **Don't criticize or complain** about your current job. If you go on about the low salary or long hours, your new employer won't get a good impression. Nobody wants somebody who complains on their team.

2 **Don't appear uninterested or unprepared.** Have intelligent questions ready. Most jobs have plenty of applicants. If you aren't interested, the interviewer isn't interested in you.

3 **Don't use negative body language**, such as not smiling or not making eye contact. It will make you seem strange or shy.

4 **Don't share too much information** with interviewers. You don't want to bore them. Answer the question, then stop.

5 **Don't discuss your personal finances.** The interviewer doesn't want to know. It's a sensitive topic and not relevant for the interview.

6 **Don't ask the wrong questions.** Focus your questions on the job. Ask what a typical day is like and not when you will get the next salary increase.

7 **Don't ask a lot about holidays.** You are being interviewed to do a specific job and don't want to give the impression that you are more interested in the time you spend away from it.

8 **Don't show anger.** There could be many reasons to be angry, for example, you may have just lost your last job. But don't show anything in the interview. Angry people are not fun to work with!

☐ **a** I'm planning two nice long vacations this year. Am I free to decide when I take them?
☐ **b** I really shouted at the taxi driver because he was driving so badly!
☐ **c** My boyfriend lives near your office, so I could always go and see him after work.
☐ **d** I'm sorry, I didn't have time to think of any questions.
☐ **e** My boss at the moment gets irritated over little things, and he makes me work such long hours.
☐ **f** I have a lot of monthly expenses. My rent and car payments are the biggest items. And we eat out a lot.

14 **9** Andreas Krug is at an interview for a job in sales at an American company, Fitness Products Inc, at its European head office in Munich.

Listen to the interview and take notes to answer the questions.

1 What is the position of the people who interview Andreas?	
2 What is the position the company needs to fill?	
3 What is Andreas's current job and why does he want to leave?	
4 What are Andreas's strengths and weaknesses?	
5 Why does Andreas want the job?	

VOCABULARY

unprepared – *unvorbereitet*; **sensitive** – *sensibel, heikel*; **to bore sb** – *jdn langweilen*; **salary increase** – *Gehaltserhöhung*; **to run late** – *spät dran sein*; **to rush off** – *schnell weg sein*; **to expand** – *ausbauen*

D KMK EXAM PRACTICE

1 Leseverstehen

Situation: Sie sind fasziniert von allem Asiatischen und möchten unbedingt einmal längere Zeit in China verbringen. Die Firma, bei der Sie arbeiten, unterhält Geschäftsbeziehungen mit China - vielleicht ergibt sich hier eine Chance. Doch auch wenn das nicht klappt, wollen Sie unbedingt versuchen, einen Job in China zu finden. Doch bevor Sie Ihren Chef auf die Sache ansprechen, versuchen Sie, so viel wie möglich im Internet herauszufinden.

Aufgabe: Lesen Sie den Text und füllen Sie die Tabelle auf der nächsten Seite aus.

A Chinese adventure

Feeling bored with your job? Just stuck in a rut and looking for a new experience? Then how about getting some work experience in a different country and culture? If that sounds like fun, China is a great place to gather experience – it has a completely different culture so will provide you with lots of interesting experiences and is also one of the fastest-growing economies in the world. This is why so many people have made the move in recent years and there are a great number of fields offering jobs to foreigners including sales, marketing, IT, finance and engineering.

So how do you go about finding a job in China? Unfortunately, it's often a case of who you know not what you know which gets you the job. Many jobs are given to personal contacts of colleagues or friends but if you don't know anyone in China, don't be disheartened. There are also many websites that post different jobs and many of these are in English so can be used easily. It is not a must to be able to speak Chinese if you want a job there, but it of course helps and can give you a competitive advantage over other applicants, so trying to learn some Chinese either through a language course or online isn't a bad idea.

What else can you do to make yourself attractive to Chinese employers? Cheap labour is easy to find there so setting yourself apart with good qualifications like a college degree is a big advantage. Otherwise, the same applies as it would here. Skills like being able to speak different languages, being good at working in teams and organizational skills are all advantageous, along with a mix of other hard and soft skills.

So once you've found a job you'd like to apply for what do you need to keep in mind for your application? Firstly, be careful what you put on your CV. There are no real rules as to what needs to be included but remember that Chinese people are very modest so 'overselling' yourself may not be beneficial. Don't give too many details explaining how well you completed a certain project, just note down the facts. The same applies should you be invited for an interview – make clear that you're the right person for the job but in a quiet, modest way. Also remember how important qualifications are and send copies of your certificates along with your CV and a short covering letter. If the employer likes what they see, they'll probably invite you to an initial telephone interview and then hopefully your new adventure will soon begin. Good luck!

1 Warum China ein guter Ort für neue Erfahrungen ist:	
2 Bereiche, in denen Ausländer gesucht werden:	
3 Wie man Arbeit in China findet:	
4 Vorteilhafte Fähigkeiten und Qualifikationen:	
5 Tipps für die Bewerbung:	

2 Hörverstehen

15

Situation: Martin Spielberg hat sich für eine Stelle bei Hermes Freight Forwarding Ltd in Polen beworben. Personalleiter Brendan Mathers ruft Martin an, um ein Bewerbungsgespräch mit ihm zu vereinbaren.

Aufgabe: Hören Sie sich das Telefongespräch an und füllen Sie die Tabelle aus.

1 Grund des Anrufs:	
2 Grund für Herr Mathers Aufenthalt in Nürnberg:	
3 Grund, warum Martin nicht vor 16.00 Uhr losfahren kann:	
4 Dauer von Martins Fahrt nach Nürnberg:	
5 Datum und Zeit des vereinbarten Termins:	
6 Martins Handynummer:	

E IHK EXAM PRACTICE

1 Kurzgefasste Mitteilung in Englisch

Situation: Sie sind Trainee in der Personalabteilung der Frankfurter Niederlassung von KPMJ, einer weltweit führenden Unternehmensberatung. Ihr Vorgesetzter, Sebastian Richter, bittet Sie, eine englischsprachige E-Mail zu lesen und zu beantworten, die er von einem potenziellen Bewerber aus Irland, Patrick O'Brien, erhalten hat.

Aufgabe: Schreiben Sie unter Angabe Ihres Namens und Ihrer Position (Assistent/in in der Personalabteilung) eine kurze und freundliche Antwort an Patrick. Bedanken Sie sich bei dem Absender für die E-Mail und informieren Sie ihn über Folgendes:

- Das Umzugspaket hängt von den persönlichen Umständen des Bewerbers ab (hat er Kinder, eine Hypothek oder Mietzahlungen usw.) und kann nicht früher als in der zweiten Runde der Vorstellungsgespräche festgelegt werden. Bisherige erfolgreiche Kandidaten aus Großbritannien und Irland waren immer zufrieden.
- Die Standard-Probezeit beträgt sechs Monate.
- Zur Anerkennung Ihrer Abschlüsse in Deutschland können wir leider keine Angaben machen, empfehlen Ihnen aber, auf dem Infoportal für ausländische Bildungsabschlüsse nachzusehen und das entsprechende Bundesland (Hessen) auszuwählen.
- Wir empfehlen einen Blick auf die 'Candidate Submission Checklist' auf der KPMJ-Webseite.

From:	patobrien@outlook.ei
To:	hr@kpmj.de
Subject:	Your advertisement for a specialist in International Tax Accounting Ref. 2021915IE

Dear Mr Richter,

I read with interest your job advertisement (ref. no. 2021915IE) on the Jobs.ei website. I feel that my qualifications and experience make me an ideal candidate for the position. Moving country, however, is an important life decision and in order to decide if this is the right step for me personally and professionally, I wonder if you could clarify some questions I have. Namely:

- The advertisement says that your firm offers an attractive relocation package, could you please give me some more concrete details?
- Does the work contract contain a probationary period and, if so, how long is it?
- I possess an Advanced Diploma in International Tax Accounting. Do you know if this is recognized in Germany?

I appreciate you taking the time to answer my questions and I hope the information will confirm my decision to apply for the vacancy in your firm.

Yours sincerely,

Patrick O'Brien

2 Vermerk in Deutsch über einen Geschäftsbrief in Englisch

Situation: Sie arbeiten als Praktikant bei Sellbycom, einer deutschen Firma, die im Auftrag von deutschen und europäischen Unternehmen Callcenter-Dienstleistungen in vielen Sprachen anbietet. Die Firma benötigt mehr englische Muttersprachler und arbeitet mit einer irischen Personalvermittlung zusammen, um neue Mitarbeiter in Irland anzuwerben. Ihr Chef, Heiko Bartholomäus, erhält einen Brief von den Personalvermittlern. Er ist heute sehr beschäftigt und bittet Sie, den Brief für ihn zu lesen und zusammenzufassen.

Aufgabe: Fassen Sie die wesentlichen Punkte des Schreibens in deutscher Sprache zusammen. Verwenden Sie hierfür vollständige Sätze (keine Übersetzung).

Dear Mr Fischer,

Sellbycom Recruitment Campaign Phase 1 (Ireland)

I am writing to inform you of the results of our assessment of the first phase of our recruitment campaign on Sellbycom's behalf in Ireland. I have attached a detailed breakdown as an enclosure (it is also available in electronic form on the Client Portal on our homepage), but let me summarize our initial insights briefly here:

- Our success rate in fulfilling our goal of fifty suitable candidates in Phase 1 was less than hoped for at 60%, or thirty candidates.
- We achieved a low positive response rate to advertising and direct outreach via professional social media networks (LinkedIn, Profis.ei, etc.).
- Surveyed target professionals who declined our direct outreach gave the following reasons for their lack of interest in applying to Sellbycom:
  - Unattractive salary;
  - Insufficient financial assistance during relocation;
  - Lack of knowledge around life in Germany, especially for non-German speakers.

I understand you may feel some disappointment around these early results, but I feel with some minor changes to our strategy we can really improve the acceptance rate. As we explained in our first planning meeting, Irish professionals have salary expectations based on the high cost of living in the Republic of Ireland. Given that the cost of living is much lower generally in Germany, salaries are, compared to Ireland, understandably lower. Addressing these unrealistic expectations is key to a higher recruitment rate. Please see our proposals in the 'What next?' section of the attachment.

In conclusion, we look forward to hearing your response to our findings and our proposals especially. According to our original partnership agreement, we are due to have our planning meeting for Phase 2 in the next two weeks. I would appreciate it if your assistant could contact our office to arrange this for a mutually convenient time.

Yours sincerely

Oscar Traynor

Oscar Traynor

International Project Manager

Ahead Hunters

Useful phrases

Writing a covering letter	
Opening phrases	
With reference to your advertisement in … of …	*Bezugnehmend auf Ihre Ausschreibung in … vom …*
I would like / wish to apply for the above-mentioned position/post of …	*Hiermit möchte ich mich für die oben genannte Stelle als … bewerben.*
Education, training, past or present employment	
I studied … at vocational school in …from … to …	*An der Berufs(fach)schule in … lernte ich … von … bis …*
At present I am working for a/an … as a/an …	*Zurzeit arbeite ich bei einem/einer … als …*
I will complete my period of training on …	*Am … werde ich meine Ausbildung abschließen.*
Skills	
As you can see from my CV, I am fluent in …	*Wie Sie aus meinem Lebenslauf sehen können, spreche ich fließend …*
My computer skills are excellent / above average.	*Meine Computerkenntnisse sind ausgezeichnet/ überdurchschnittlich.*
I am particularly suitable for the post because …	*Ich bin für die Stelle besonders geeignet, weil …*
Closing paragraph	
I enclose / Enclosed is my CV (*BE*) / résumé (*AE*) / a list of my qualifications and experience.	*Anbei finden Sie meinen Lebenslauf / eine Übersicht meiner Qualifikationen und Berufserfahrungen.*
I am available for interview at your earliest convenience.	*Für ein Vorstellungsgespräch stehe ich Ihnen jederzeit gern zur Verfügung.*
I look forward to hearing from you in the near future.	*Ich freue mich darauf, bald von Ihnen zu hören.*

Job interview questions and answers	
Tell me about yourself. ▸ I would say that I'm a (sociable) person.	Erzählen Sie etwas über sich. ▸ Ich würde sagen, ich bin ein (geselliger) Mensch.
How would you describe your strengths/weaknesses? ▸ A strength that I have is that … ▸ One weakness that I have noticed is …	Wie würden Sie Ihre Stärken und Schwächen beschreiben? ▸ Eine meiner Stärken ist, dass … ▸ Eine Schwäche, die mir aufgefallen ist, ist, dass …
Why did you apply for this job? ▸ I have always been interested in the … industry/ business and this seemed a perfect opportunity.	Weshalb haben Sie sich auf diese Stelle beworben? ▸ Ich habe mich schon immer für die …-Branche interessiert, und dies schien mir eine gute Gelegenheit zu sein.
Why should we hire you? ▸ My training and experience matches well with the job advertised.	Warum sollten wir Sie einstellen? ▸ Meine Ausbildung und meine Berufserfahrung passen gut zur ausgeschriebenen Stelle.
What are your goals for the future? ▸ To find a long-term job with a company with a good management training programme.	Was sind Ihre Ziele für die Zukunft? ▸ Eine langfristige Stelle bei einer Firma mit einem guten Nachwuchsführungskräfteprogramm.
Do you have any more questions about the job? ▸ How would you describe a typical day in this position?	Haben Sie weitere Fragen zu der Stelle? ▸ Wie würden Sie einen typischen Tag auf der Position beschreiben?

4 Making and dealing with enquiries

The first step for a buyer to find goods is to find a supplier. There are several ways to do this. One is through a trade magazine, another is at a trade fair. In all cases the buyer will want more information, and this is the purpose of an 'enquiry'. Important questions to ask are about the price of the goods, the delivery time, transport (by air? sea? road?). The buyer will also want to know if there are any discounts, for example, for a large number of goods, and the terms of payment (when and how the buyer must pay).

A A FIRST ENQUIRY

Gartenmöbel Limbach GmbH
Schornstr. 5–7
79106 Freiburg im Breisgau
Germany

Tel.: +49 (0)761 77553
info@garmoeblim.dex

21 June 20..

The Greenhouse BV
Bankstraat 7
3411 AB Utrecht
NETHERLANDS

Dear Sir or Madam

Enquiry about greenhouses

We saw your advertisement in the trade magazine *Gardens and More*. We note that your company manufactures greenhouses.

Our company is a leading German importer of garden furniture. We are planning to extend our wide range of products to include greenhouses. Please send us a catalogue showing your line of products. Please let us have details of your terms of delivery and payment.

If we are satisfied with your company's products, we may place regular orders.

We would be happy to supply references on request.

We look forward to hearing from you soon.

Yours faithfully

Stefan Schwarz

1 Read Stefan Schwarz's letter of enquiry above. Which of the following statements are true and which are false? Correct the false statements using your own words.

1 Stefan Schwarz works for a company in England.

____

VOCABULARY

terms of payment – *Zahlungsbedingungen*; **discount** – *Skonto*; **greenhouse** – *Gewächshaus*; **trade magazine** – *Fachzeitschrift*; **to manufacture** – *herstellen*; **leading** – *führend*; **to extend** – *erweitern*; **wide** – *breit*; **range of products** – *Produktpalette*; **line of products** – *Produktlinie*; **delivery** – *Lieferung*; **to place an order** – *einen Auftrag erteilen*; **regular** – *regelmäßig*; **to supply** *liefern*

2 Stefan Schwarz found information about The Greenhouse BV on the internet.

____

3 Gartenmöbel Limbach makes garden furniture.

____

4 Gartenmöbel Limbach already has a lot of products in its product line.

____

5 Stefan Schwarz has downloaded The Greenhouse BV's catalogue from the internet.

____

6 Stefan Schwarz wants to know how the products will be sent and what they will cost.

____

7 Stefan is only interested in placing one order with The Greenhouse BV.

____

8 Stefan uses two polite phrases at the end of his letter.

____

2 **Find the English words for the German words 1–8 in the letter of enquiry on page 50.**

1 Anzeige	1 ___	5 Produktangebot	5 ___
2 Lieferung	2 ___	6 Importeur	6 ___
3 Bezahlung	3 ___	7 einen Auftrag erteilen	7 ___
4 Fachzeitschrift	4 ___	8 dankbar	8 ___

3 **Read the letter of enquiry on page 50 again. Find the English expressions for the German phrases and sentences below.**

1 Wir haben Ihre Anzeige … gesehen.

____

2 Unsere Firma ist ein führender deutscher Importeur …

____

3 Wir haben vor, …

____

4 … ein breites Sortiment von …

____

5 Bitte nennen Sie uns Einzelheiten …

____

6 Wenn wir mit den Produkten Ihrer Firma zufrieden sind, …

____

7 Wir können Ihnen gerne Referenzen zukommen lassen.

____

8 Wir hoffen auf baldige Antwort.

____

4 **Highlight the correct word in the text below.**

Stefan Schwarz is the managing **director/director's/direction**[1] of a company that **transports/exports/imports**[2] garden furniture. His company's product line includes a wide **list/range/offer**[3] of products. One day Stefan read this **article/advertisement/announcement**[4] of a **greenhouse/glass house/garden**[5] **importer/manufacturer/shop**[6] in a trade **magazine/catalogue/internet**.[7] Stefan decided to write an **offer/order/enquiry**[8] to the company to **request/demand/offer**[9] further **informal/information/informations**[10] about the **company/company's/companies**[11] products. He was also interested **for/with/in**[12] terms of delivery and **pay/payment/paying**.[13] As it was a(n) **business/informal/friendly**[14] letter, Stefan **opened/closed/started**[15] his letter with **Yours faithfully/Best wishes/Best regards**.[16]

THE GREENHOUSE BV

Greenhouse manufacturers since 1965!
Wide range of sizes and styles!

Contact us for more information:
The Greenhouse BV
Bankstraat 7
3411 AB Utrecht
NETHERLANDS

info@thegreenhouse.nex

B AT A TRADE FAIR

1 **Match the English sentences and phrases (1–10) with the German equivalents (a–l). There are two more than you need.**

1 Are you familiar with …?
2 I represent …
3 I'll contact you after the fair.
4 I'll explain the advantages of …
5 If you have a spare moment, …
6 … is available in …
7 It includes …
8 … give a detailed presentation of all our products.
9 … supply you with further information.
10 Would you like me to send you a quotation?

☐ **a** … unsere Produkte ausführlich vorstellen.
☐ **b** … Ihnen weitere Informationen liefern.
☐ **c** … ist erhältlich in …
☐ **d** Es enthält …
☐ **e** Ich melde mich nach der Messe.
☐ **f** Was interessiert Sie speziell?
☐ **g** Ich werde die Vorteile des/der … erklären.
☐ **h** Möchten Sie, dass ich Ihnen ein Angebot sende?
☐ **i** Lassen Sie mich wissen, wenn Sie Hilfe benötigen.
☐ **j** Wenn Sie einen Moment Zeit haben, …
☐ **k** Ich vertrete …
☐ **l** Sind Sie mit … vertraut?

VOCABULARY

offer – *Angebot*; **to demand** – *verlangern, fordern*; **spare moment** – *ein Moment Zeit*; **quotation** – *Kostenvoranschlag*; **available** – *erhältlich*

2 Jo Clarke works for Top Fit Studios in Germany. He's at a trade fair in Dusseldorf.
Complete the dialogue with a Dutch exhibitor at the fair using the phrases from exercise 1.

Evi: Hello, my name is Evi de Jong. I am the sales representative for Global Tech, Maastricht.

Jo: Hi, I'm Jo Clarke. ______________________ [1] Top Fit Studios in Dusseldorf and Cologne.

Evi: I see you're interested in our latest digital pulse counters. ______________________ [2] the instruments?

Jo: No, not really. I'm just looking for new products to sell to members in our shops.

Evi: ______________________ [3], I'll give you a demonstration and ______________________ [4] the new counter.

Jo: Thanks, that would be helpful.

Evi: Right. The Fitpulse Lite ______________________ [5] three different colours. ______________________ [6] a long-life battery …

Jo: Thank you, Evi, for a very interesting demonstration. I think it may sell well in our shops.

Evi: ______________________ [7]? Or, tell me a good time to arrange an appointment? Then I could ______________________ [8] to your staff.

Jo: Thanks. I'll discuss everything with my boss. If you give me your card, ______________________ [9].

Evi: OK. Let me know if I can ______________________ [10] about our firm. Goodbye.

16 **3** Zoe van Dijk works for Global Tech in Maastricht. She receives a phone call from Jo from Top Fit Studios in Germany, following up his enquiry.
Listen to the phone call and fill in the missing information. Before you listen, check that you know the words in the box. They will help you to understand the phone call.

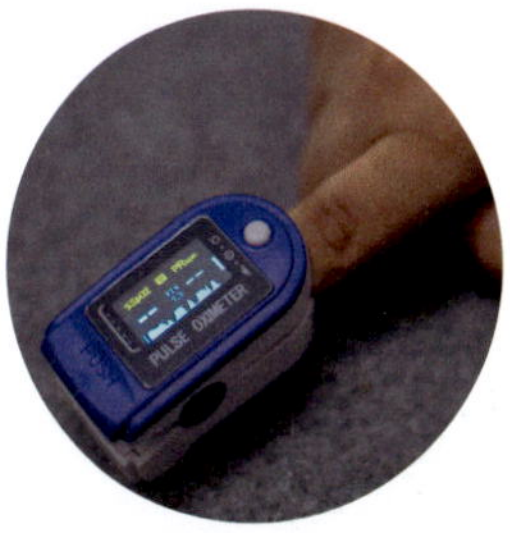

slash ▪ hyphen ▪ urgent ▪ hold on ▪ favour ▪ pressure

Enquiry for article: *digital pulse counter*	
Caller	
Company	
Date of enquiry	
Reference number	
Catalogue number	
Date of offer sent	
Email address for resend	

VOCABULARY

sales representative – *Außendienstmitarbeiter/in*; **digital pulse counter** – *digitaler Pulszähler*; **demonstration** – *Vorführung*; **urgent** – *dringend*; **to hold on** – *warten*; **favour** – *Gefallen*

C ENQUIRY ABOUT OFFICE EQUIPMENT

1 You are an office assistant at Bürowelt, a company which imports office furniture. Your boss has asked you to write a letter of enquiry to a supplier in Glasgow, Scotland.
Write the enquiry. Use phrases from the box below to help you and the following points.

- Address: Mr Duncan McTavish, Export Department, Glasgow Office Furniture plc, Tayside Industrial Estate, Glasgow G1 3GH, United Kingdom
- Write a suitable introduction.
- Describe our company.
- Say why we are writing.
- Say what we require.
- End the letter politely.

Writing an enquiry

Introduction		
We saw your With reference to your	advertisement/brochure/catalogue	in .../on...
We visited your	stand/presentation home page	at the trade fair in ... on the internet.
We have obtained	your address from	the Chamber of Commerce in Munich. one of your business partners.
About your company		
We are	a small/medium-sized/large/well-known company. distributors/importers/exporters/suppliers/producers of ...	
	a wholesaler/retailer	for ... (products). for the ... trade.
We specialize in	high-quality (products) / a wide range of ...	
Reason for writing		
We are planning to	expand our range of products. place a trial order for	
We are interested in	finding new, state-of-the-art products. including ... in our range of products.	
We are looking for	a (new) supplier.	
What you require		
Please Would you be so kind and We would be grateful if you could	send us give us let us have	a detailed description of your products. your latest catalogue/brochure/current price list. details of prices/special offers/quantity discount/trade discount. further information about ... full details of your terms of delivery and payment. a firm offer for ...
Polite ending		
If your company's products meet our requirements, we ... We are sure your product would sell well here in Germany.		
We look forward to Looking forward to	hearing from you soon. receiving your offer.	

VOCABULARY

industrial estate – *Gewerbegebiet*; **distributor** – *Vertragshändler/in,Vertriebspartner/in*; **supplier** – *Lieferant/in*; **producer** – *Hersteller/in*; **wholesaler** – *Großhändler/in*; **retailer** – *Einzelhändler/in*; **trial order** – *Probeauftrag*; **state-of-the-art** – *auf dem neuesten Stand der Technik*; **sample** – *Muster*; **current** – *aktuell*; **a firm offer** – *ein verbindliches Angebot*

2 You are the owner of *Office Props*, a retailer selling office machines (Am Winterhafen 7, 80939 Munich, Tel. +49 89 2344). You have seen a really attractive advert by an Irish company, Office Inc, in the latest issue of Fortune magazine. You decide to start a business relationship with this company.

Office Inc

149 Moulton Way, Cork City, T12 T997, Ireland
Email: office@office-inc.nex, Telephone: +35 3214 / 27947

You want a printer that can do more than just print your documents, e.g. scan them, send them on to others, save them to a hard disk, receive emails, ...? – Then the new **WLan OfficeInc 3.0** is the right product for you. But this is not all: the WLan OfficeInc 3.0 also makes it possible for you to read documents or send emails when you are not in the office. So give it a try and use our special offer: buy the WLan OfficeInc 3.0 for €298.90 instead of €349 with free delivery and 2 years' warranty.

But be quick, demand for this product is high and the offer is only valid until the end of this month.

Verfassen Sie ein Schreiben an *Office Inc*. Berücksichtigen Sie die folgenden Punkte:

- Sagen Sie, dass Sie die Annonce gesehen haben und am Produkt interessiert sind.
- Erklären Sie, dass Ihre Kunden immer an den neuesten Entwicklungen in der Computerbranche interessiert sind und Sie daher die von Office Inc angebotenen Drucker gern in Ihr Sortiment aufnehmen möchten.
- Erklären Sie, dass Ihre Einkaufsabteilung eine Sitzung für nächste Woche plant und Sie daher dringend ausführliche Produktinformationen benötigen.
- Sagen Sie, dass Sie vorhaben, größere Mengen abzunehmen, und bitten Sie um möglichst baldige Übersendung einer genauen Produktbeschreibung.
- Erkundigen Sie sich nach den Konditionen: Preise, etwaige Preisnachlässe, Mindestbestellmenge, Mengenrabatt, Liefer- und Zahlungsbedingungen.
- Beenden Sie das Schreiben mit einer passenden Schlussformel.

VOCABULARY

owner – *Inhaber/in*; **issue** – *Ausgabe*; **special offer** – *Sonderangebot*; **warranty** – *Garantie*; **demand** – *Nachfrage*; **valid** – *gültig*

D KMK EXAM PRACTICE

1 Hörverstehen

17

Situation: Ihre Chefin möchte einen Geschäftsbesuch in Schottland mit einem Kurzurlaub verbinden und bittet ihren Assistenten, sich nach einem Mietwagen zu erkundigen.

CAR RENTAL

Aufgabe: Hören Sie sich das Gespräch an und füllen Sie die Tabelle aus.

1 Ort der Wagenabholung:	______
2 Ort der Wagenrückgabe:	______
3 Fahrer des Wagens:	______
4 Tage, an den man ein Auto billiger mieten kann:	______
5 Genaue Abholzeit:	______
6 Preis für vier Tage und neun Stunden:	______
7 Folge, wenn das Auto nicht mit vollem Tank abgegeben wird:	______
8 Im Preis inbegriffen sind:	______

2 Produktion

Situation: Sie sind kaufmännische/r Assistent/in einer deutschen Druckerei. Ihr Vorgesetzter bittet Sie, eine Anfrage an eine finnische Papierfabrik zu richten, die als Lieferant infrage kommen könnte.

Aufgabe: Verfassen Sie die Anfrage. Berücksichtigen Sie die folgenden Punkte:

- Schreiben Sie die Anfrage an Finland Paper, Bulevardi 49, FI-55000 Imatra, Finnland. Verwenden Sie die korrekte Briefform und das heutige Datum.
- Nennen Sie die Quelle der Anschrift des Unternehmens, z. B. Internet, Fachzeitschrift.
- Machen Sie Angaben zum Betätigungsfeld Ihrer Firma, z. B. führende Druckerei von Fachzeitschriften.
- Geben Sie an, weshalb Sie eine Anfrage schreiben.
- Bitten Sie um Warenmuster verschiedener Papiersorten der infrage kommenden Qualitätsstufen.
- Bitten Sie um Auskunft zu Liefer- und Zahlungsbedingungen.
- Nennen Sie Referenzen für Ihre Firma.
- Bitten Sie freundlich um eine baldige Antwort.

3 Mediation

Situation: Sie arbeiten als Praktikant/in in einer Druckerei. Bisher hat das alteingesessene Familienunternehmen es nicht nötig gehabt, an Fachmessen teilzunehmen und auszustellen. Jetzt aber möchte ein neuer, jüngerer Manager die Teilnahme der Firma an Messen wieder zur Diskussion stellen und bittet Sie, Argumente für ihn zu sammeln. Sie haben im Internet den folgenden Artikel gefunden. Da Ihr Chef wenig Zeit hat und sein Englisch nicht besonders gut ist, hat er Sie gebeten, die Argumente auf Deutsch für ihn kurz zusammenzufassen.

Aufgabe: Fassen Sie die wesentlichen Punkte auf Deutsch zusammen.

Why should your company attend trade fairs?

Trade fairs bring together industry experts, enthusiasts and media under one roof for a few days. There are hardly any other occasions where this happens. Attending a trade fair is an investment which can bring great value for your company.

Whether you are a start-up or an established company, a trade fair is an ideal opportunity to become better known in your industry. There are many simple ways to do this, such as creating an eye-catching design for your stand and your company logo or placing your stand next to companies which are industry leaders, to give the impression that you are one of them.

A second benefit that trade fairs offer is the chance to make new business relationships and increase your networking opportunities. These days there is so little time for valuable face-to-face contact. A good way to do this is to check the exhibition schedule for events, such as lunch breaks or parties at the end of the day.

For the sales department, a trade fair is a perfect location: buyers who go to a fair are well informed and are looking to buy the right product for their needs. The sales staff must be well prepared with descriptions and the selling points of their products. One practical idea to support them is to organize your stand in an attractive way to highlight your latest or main products and interest customers.

A trade fair also gives you a perfect opportunity to check what the competition is doing and to follow it up with a competitor analysis which may help you to avoid some mistakes in future. Walk around the stands and take notes on those which are successful and why others don't appear to excite interest.

Finally, the educational value of a trade fair shouldn't be forgotten. It's a chance to keep up-to-date with new developments and new technologies which may have a big impact on your business in future. Look at the exhibition schedule, make a note of the sessions with topics which are most related to your business and try to find time to attend them.

E IHK EXAM PRACTICE

1 Vermerk in Deutsch über ein Gespräch in Englisch

18

Situation: Linda Paschke, die Chefin einer IT-Firma, in der Sie ein Praktikum absolvieren, möchte einen Geschäftsbesuch in Schottland mit einem Kurzurlaub verbinden. Sie bittet einen englischsprachigen Mitarbeiter, Joe Davis, die Kosten für einen Mietwagen in Schottland zu prüfen. Sie bittet auch Sie, das Gespräch mitzuhören. Heute ist der 8. April.

Aufgabe: Verfolgen Sie das Gespräch und fertigen Sie anschließend eine Gesprächsnotiz auf Deutsch für Ihre Chefin, Frau Linda Paschke an. Während des Hörens dürfen Sie Notizen machen. Diese Notizen werden nicht bewertet, sondern nur die Gesprächsnotiz.

Joe Davis:	Kim Cameron:
	Good morning...
Joe Hi. My name's Joe Davis. Look, I've got a question first. Is it possible to hire a car at Aberdeen Dyce airport but return it at Glasgow Airport?	...
Fine. In that case, what would a car cost for five days, please?	...
Well, the car's not for me, actually. It's for my boss. But I know she wants to do a lot of touring, so the car should be comfortable. She doesn't want anything luxurious, though.	...
The Peugeot sounds good. She drives a Peugeot herself. How much is the 307, then?	...
Well, she wants to pick the car up at 9 a.m. on Monday, 16 March at Dyce and return it at six p.m. on Friday, 20 at Glasgow Airport.	...
Good heavens. That's a lot, isn't it? Does that price include a full tank of petrol?	...
I see. Are there any other extras?	...
Ah, so there's no mileage surcharge?	...
OK, then. Look, can I get back to you later? I'm sure it'll be OK, but I'd better check with my boss before making a firm reservation.	...
Fine. Well, thanks for your help. Bye now.	...

2 Geschäftsbrief in Englisch nach Stichwortangaben in Deutsch

Situation: Sie sind kaufmännische/r Assistent/in einer deutschen Druckerei, Druck ohne Druck GmbH, Am Riederbruch 21, 60386 Frankfurt am Main. Ihr Vorgesetzter bittet Sie, eine Anfrage an eine finnische Papierfabrik zu richten, die als Lieferant infrage kommen könnte.

Aufgabe: Schreiben Sie die Anfrage an Finland Paper, Bulevardi 49, FI-55000 Imatra, Finnland. Verwenden Sie die korrekte Briefform und das heutige Datum. Berücksichtigen Sie die folgenden Punkte:

- Nennen Sie die Quelle der Anschrift des Unternehmens, z. B. Internet, Fachzeitschrift.
- Machen Sie Angaben zum Betätigungsfeld Ihrer Firma, z. B. führende Druckerei von Fachzeitschriften.
- Geben Sie an, weshalb Sie eine Anfrage schreiben.
- Bitten Sie um Warenmuster verschiedener Papiersorten der infrage kommenden Qualitätsstufen.
- Bitten Sie um Auskunft zu Liefer- und Zahlungsbedingungen.
- Nennen Sie Referenzen für Ihre Firma.
- Bitten Sie freundlich um eine baldige Antwort.

3 Sprachergänzungstest (Typ 2)

Aufgabe: Im Text auf der nächsten Seite ist jeweils nur eine der vorgeschlagenen Formen korrekt. Bitte setzen Sie die richtige Lösung in die entsprechende Lücke ein.

Trade fairs bring industry experts, enthusiasts and media together ______________ [1] a few days. ______________ [2] are ______________ [3] any other ______________ [4] where this happens. Attending a trade fair is an ______________ [5] which can bring great ______________ [6] for your company.

______________ [7] a start-up or an established company, a trade fair is an ideal opportunity to become ______________ [8] known in your industry. There ______________ [9] many simple ways to do this, such as creating an eye-catching design for your stand or placing your stand next to companies which are industry leaders, to give the ______________ [10] that you are one of ______________ [11].

There is also the chance to ______________ [12] new business relationships and ______________ [13] your chance to network. ______________ [14] days there is so ______________ [15] time for face-to-face contact so check the schedule for events, such as parties ______________ [16] the end of the day.

For the sales ______________ [17], a trade fair is a perfect location: buyers who go to a fair are ______________ [18] informed and are looking to buy the right product for their needs. The sales ______________ [19] must be well prepared with descriptions and the ______________ [20] of their products. Organize your stand in an attractive way to highlight your ______________ [21] products and interest customers.

You can also ______________ [22] what the ______________ [23] is doing to avoid ______________ [24] mistakes in future. Walk ______________ [25] the stands and ______________ [26] on the successful ones.

Finally, a trade fair allows you to keep ______________ [27] new developments and new ______________ [28] which may have a big impact ______________ [29] your business in future. Find sessions which deal ______________ [30] topics most relevant to your business and try to find time to attend them.

1	in, since, for	**16**	at, on, in
2	Their, There, They're	**17**	resort, divisive, department
3	hard, fast, hardly	**18**	real, good, well
4	occupations, occasionally, occasions	**19**	staff, stiff, stuff
5	investor, investment, investigation	**20**	point of sale, purchase points, selling points
6	values, value, valuables	**21**	last, late, latest
7	When are you, Whether you are, Weather are you	**22**	check, overlook, prove
8	good, better, best	**23**	compete, competition, competitors
9	is, are, be	**24**	the, much, some
10	impression, impressive, impressing	**25**	around, over, about
11	they, it, them	**26**	make notices, take notices, take notes
12	do, make, building	**27**	updating the, up to date with, with updating
13	decrease, increase, rise	**28**	technologies, technological, technique
14	Those, This, These	**29**	of, on, in
15	small, little, less	**30**	on, with, of

Useful phrases

Writing enquiries	
Source of address	
I was most impressed by the … you showed me on your stand at the …	*Ich war von den … , die Sie mir an Ihrem Stand auf der …* (Messe) *gezeigt haben, sehr beeindruckt.*
We have seen your company's advertisement in the current edition of … and are most interested in your products.	*Wir haben Ihre Anzeige in der aktuellen Ausgabe von …* (Titel des Magazins) *gesehen und interessieren uns sehr für Ihre Produkte.*
We note from your company's website that you sell a wide range of …	*Wir entnehmen der Homepage Ihres Unternehmens, dass Sie ein breites Sortiment an/von …* (Produkten) *anbieten.*
You have been recommended to us by …, who tells us that you have brought out …	*Sie wurden uns von …* (Name) *empfohlen, der/die uns mitgeteilt hat, dass Sie …* (Produkt) *auf den Markt gebracht haben.*
Description of your company	
We are a rapidly growing / leading producer/ importer/exporter/wholesaler of … with excellent business contacts all over … and beyond.	*Wir sind ein schnell wachsender / führender Produzent von … / Importeur/Exporteur/Großhändler für … mit hervorragenden Geschäftskontakten in ganz …* (Region/Land) *und darüber hinaus.*
Our company is a major/well-established (German) wholesaler of … both at home and abroad.	*Unser Unternehmen ist ein bedeutender/etablierter (deutscher) Großhändler von … im In- und Ausland.*
We have long-standing customers all over Europe.	*Wir haben langjährige Kunden in ganz Europa.*
Reason for your enquiry	
At present we are particularly interested in …	*Gegenwärtig gilt unser besonderes Interesse …*
We are looking for a supplier of …	*Wir suchen nach einem Lieferanten für …*
Your requirements	
Please send us a favourable quotation for …	*Bitte schicken Sie uns ein passendes Angebot für …*
We would be grateful if you would let us have details of your entire range.	*Wir wären Ihnen dankbar, wenn Sie uns Informationen zu Ihrer gesamten Produktpalette zukommen lassen könnten.*
Please let us have your latest catalogue …	*Bitte lassen Sie uns Ihren neuesten Katalog … zukommen.*
… including all discounts granted	*… einschließlich aller gewährten Rabatte*
… including details of your terms of delivery and payment.	*… einschließlich Einzelheiten über Ihre Liefer- und Zahlungsbedingungen.*
Please let us know if you are able to provide samples.	*Bitte teilen Sie uns mit, ob Sie uns Muster/ Proben zur Verfügung stellen können.*
We would require delivery within 6 weeks / by the end of the month at the latest.	*Die Lieferung hätten wir gerne innerhalb 6 Wochen / spätestens bis Ende des Monats.*
Polite ending	
If your products meet our requirements, we will place a substantial order.	*Wenn Ihre Produkte unseren Anforderungen entsprechen, werden wir einen größeren Auftrag erteilen.*
We look forward to hearing from you soon.	*Wir hoffen auf baldige Antwort.*

An offer is a reply to an enquiry. It will become the basis for the sale – and possibly for future sales – so it is important for the seller to make the right decisions. Will there be a discount (to encourage the buyer), and if so, how big? What will the terms of payment be? With new customers, the seller may want payment in advance. Later, when they know the buyer is trustworthy, payment can be made after delivery.

A REPLYING TO ENQUIRIES

1 Lara Smit, Sales Manager at The Greenhouse BV, sends a reply to the enquiry from Stefan Schwarz in Unit 4, page 50.
Read the reply and answer the questions.

27 June 20..

Dear Mr Schwarz

Enquiry about greenhouses

With reference to your enquiry of 21 June, we are pleased to hear that you are interested in our products and are planning to include them in your product range.

As requested, we enclose our latest catalogue. We are pleased to inform you that everything shown in the catalogue is in stock at present.

Our prices are quoted EXW. For payment within 10 days we offer a 2.5% cash discount.

Our products are carefully packed in strong cardboard boxes. We deal with orders immediately and guarantee an efficient and reliable service. We feel sure that a trial order will convince you of the quality of our products.

Please contact us if you require further details.

We look forward to hearing from you soon.

Yours sincerely

Lara Smit

Lara Smit
Sales Manager

1 If Stefan places an order soon, will The Greenhouse BV be able to deliver everything he orders? Why (not)?

______

2 How can Stefan save his company some money?

______

3 How long does it take The Greenhouse BV to make orders ready for transport?

______

4 What can Stefan do if he needs more information?

______

VOCABULARY

in advance – *im Voraus*; **trustworthy** – *zuverlässig, kreditwürdig*; **in stock** – *auf Lager*; **to quote** – *(Preis) angeben*; **EXW = Ex Works** – *ab Werk*; **discount** – *Rabatt*; **cardboard box** – *Pappkarton*; **to deal with sth** – *etw bearbeiten*; **immediately** – *unverzüglich, sofort*; **to guarantee** – *garantieren*; **reliable** – *zuverlässig*; **to convince** – *überzeugen*; **to deliver** – *liefern*; **to save** – *sparen*

2 **Find the English equivalents to sentences 1–7 in Lara Smit's letter.**

1 Unsere Preise verstehen sich ab Werk.

______

2 Bei Zahlung innerhalb von 10 Tagen gewähren wir 2,5 % Skonto.

______

3 Wir freuen uns über Ihr Interesse an unseren Produkten.

______

4 Bitte nehmen Sie Kontakt mit uns auf, wenn Sie weitere Einzelheiten benötigen.

______

5 Unsere Produkte sind sorgfältig verpackt.

______

6 Wir bearbeiten Aufträge unverzüglich und garantieren Effizienz und Zuverlässigkeit.

______

7 Wir sind sicher, dass Sie ein Probeauftrag von der Qualität unserer Ware überzeugen wird.

______

3 **Read the short text about incoterms and look at the list on the next page. Then complete the terms with the missing words.**

Incoterms

Incoterms (International Commercial Terms) are a series of groups of three letters (like EXW, CIF) that business people use when they buy and sell goods internationally. These terms are defined by the International Chamber of Commerce (ICC) and they began in 1936. The 11 terms that are used today are those that were last revised in 2020. The idea of incoterms is very simple: they tell the buyer (and the seller) exactly who pays for what. In international trade, goods have to be transported by sea, air, road or rail, and it can make a big difference whether the price of goods includes transport (or not) and if so, where to (right to the buyer or to a port in the buyer's country?). Some other things that affect the price are whether goods are loaded onto a ship (or not) and also whether the goods are insured during the journey.

VOCABULARY

to define sth – *etw definieren, etw festlegen*; **International Chamber of Commerce** – *Internationale Handelskammer*; **to revise** – *überarbeiten*; **trade** – *Handel*; **port** – *Hafen*; **to load** – *laden, verladen*; **to insure** – *versichern*

Delivery by all forms of transport			
EXW	Ex works	ab Werk	The basic cost of the goods (no transport etc.)
FCA	Free carrier	frei Frachtführer	The goods are delivered to a carrier at a lorry depot, railway station or airport. The carrier then delivers the goods.
CPT	Carriage paid to	frachtfrei bis	The goods are delivered to a (named) place in the buyer's country (e.g. a railway station or airport).
CIP	Carriage and insurance paid	frachtfrei versichert	The same as CPT but the seller also pays to insure the goods on the journey.
DAP	Delivered at place	geliefert benannter Ort	The goods are delivered to the destination. The seller bears all costs and risks until that point.
DPU	Delivered named place unloaded	geliefert benannter Ort entladen	The goods are delivered to a (named) place in the buyer's country. The seller pays all costs and risks and is also responsible for unloading them.
DDP	Delivered duty paid	verzollt geliefert	Like DPU but this time the seller also pays any duty on the goods.
Delivery by sea			
FAS	Free alongside ship	frei Längsseite Schiff	The goods are delivered to (but not loaded onto) a ship.
FOB	Free on board	frei an Bord	The goods are now also loaded onto a ship.
CFR	Cost and freight	Kosten und Fracht	The goods are delivered to a port in the buyer's country but not unloaded.
CIF	Cost, insurance and freight	Kosten, Versicherung und Fracht	The same as CFR but the seller also pays to insure the goods to the foreign port.

1 CIP: Carriage and ______________ paid

2 DPU: Delivered named place ______________

3 FOB: Free ______________ board

4 FCA: ______________ carrier

5 CFR: Cost and ______________

6 DAP: Delivered at ______________

7 DDP: Delivered duty ______________

8 CIF: Cost, ______________ and freight

VOCABULARY

carrier – *Frachtführer*; **depot** – *Lagerhalle*; **carriage** – *Beförderung, Transport*; **insurance** – *Versicherung*; **to insure** – *versichern*; **destination** – *Zielort*; **to bear** – *tragen*; **to (un)load** – *(ent)laden*; **duty** – *Zollgebühr*; **freight** – *Fracht*

4 **Match these definitions of the incoterms with the examples below.**

CPT – Carriage paid to (… named place of destination) This term is mostly used when goods are delivered by road, rail or air. It means that the goods are delivered to a named place in the buyer's country – for example, a road depot or railway station.	**DAP – Delivered at place (… named place of destination)** This is a term mostly for delivery by road or rail. It means that the goods are delivered to the destination.
EXW – Ex Works This is just the basic costs of the goods. In other words, the buyer has to pay all the costs of transport and insurance from the seller's factory to his or her own country.	**DDP – Delivered duty paid** This price is for all forms of transport. It means that the goods are delivered all the way to him/her and if there is any duty on the goods, the seller pays it.
CIF – Cost, insurance, and freight (… named port of destination) This term is used for transport by sea. The goods are delivered to a named port in the buyer's country. The seller also pays to insure the goods that far.	**FOB – Free on board (… named port of destination)** This is another maritime incoterm. The goods are delivered to a ship (in the seller's country) and loaded onto the ship.

Examples

DDP ________ 1

A company in Germany buys some goods from a company in the USA. The American seller transport the goods first by sea, then by rail all the way to the buyer's warehouse in Germany and pays the duty on the goods.

________ 2

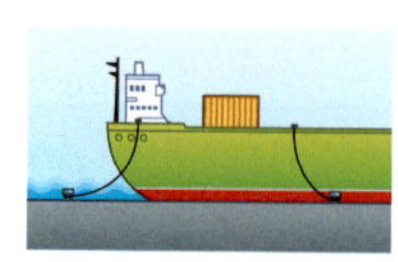

A company in Ireland buys some machines from a German company. The German company transports the machines to Bremerhaven and loads them onto a ship there. The Irish buyer pays all the costs after that.

________ 3

Dutch company A sells some goods to British company B. A pays to transport the goods by sea to Harwich in England and to insure the goods en route. B has to pay to unload the goods, however.

________ 4

German company Y sells some goods to Spanish company Z. Y delivers the goods to Z's warehouse in Spain but Z has to pay import duties and unload the goods.

________ 5

When a company in Germany buys some goods from a Polish company, it pays just the price for the goods themselves. No transport or insurance are included in the price.

________ 6

A company in Germany sells some medical equipment to a hospital in Australia. It transports the goods by air to a warehouse at Sydney airport. The hospital pays the costs of transport from there.

VOCABULARY

by rail – *per Bahn*; **warehouse** – *Lager*; **import duty** – *Einfuhrzoll*; **medical equipment** – *Medizingeräte, Medizintechnik*

5 **Look at the incoterms in exercise 4 again and decide if the following statements are true (T) or false (F).**

		T	F
1	With CPT the buyer pays all the costs of transport and insurance.		
2	With DAP the buyer has to transport the goods to their destination.		
3	With EXW the seller pays for some of the transport to the buyer.		
4	With DDP it is the seller who pays import duties on the goods.		
5	With CIF the seller pays all costs of transport and insurance all the way to the buyer.		
6	With FOB the seller has no further costs once the goods are on a ship in a port in its country.		

6 **Look at the terms of payment phrases and use them to complete the sentences below.**

Terms of payment	
(2%) cash discount	(2%) Skonto
cash in advance (CIA)	Vorkasse
cash on delivery (COD)	gegen Nachnahme
cash with order (CWO)	Kasse bei Auftragserteilung/Bestellung
(3 months') credit	(3 Monate) Ziel
payment by bill of exchange	Zahlung durch Wechsel
payment by credit transfer	Zahlung durch Überweisung
payment by irrevocable and confirmed letter of credit (L/C)	Zahlung durch unwiderrufliches und bestätigtes Akkreditiv
payment on receipt of goods	Zahlung bei Erhalt der Waren
payment on receipt of invoice	Zahlung bei Rechnungserhalt
payment within … from date of invoice	Zahlung innerhalb von … nach Rechnungsdatum

1 If a buyer places a big order, he will get 3% …
- ☐ cash discount.
- ☐ cash in advance.
- ☐ cash on delivery.

2 New customers are asked to pay at the same time as they place an order. They must pay …
- ☐ on receipt of goods.
- ☐ cash with order.
- ☐ by bill of exchange.

3 Regular customers have more time to pay their invoices. The best customers get four months' …
- ☐ payment by credit transfer.
- ☐ payment by irrevocable and confirmed letter of credit.
- ☐ credit.

4 What are your terms of payment? – Payment is within three weeks from …
- ☐ date of invoice.
- ☐ bill of exchange.
- ☐ cash discount.

5 You can't pay cash. You have to pay by …
- ☐ three months' credit.
- ☐ credit transfer.
- ☐ within three months from date of invoice.

6 Before they dispatch the goods, the company requires from new customers …
- ☐ cash in advance.
- ☐ cash on delivery.
- ☐ cash with order.

B OFFERS

1 **Read the model offer and summarize the main points in German.**

TIERBERG Stromtechnik GmbH & Co. KG
Eichenstr. 10 | 82256 Fürstenfeldbruck | Germany
+49 (0) 8141 9

5 May 20..

Silverberg Industries India Ltd.
Pensfield Business Centre
Andheri-Kula Rd.
Mumbai
400 093
Indien

Dear Mr Khurana

Offer for SCC-D-48 electrical switches

Many thanks for your enquiry dated 2 May 20... Our company manufactures a wide range of electrical switches for the home and has many satisfied customers both inside and outside the EU. You will find further information on our company and the SCC-D-48 electrical switch in the enclosed brochure.

As regards the goods requested, we are pleased to make the following offer:
For orders over 1,000 switches we can offer the SCC-D-48 switch at €6.00 each.

Our price is quoted FOB Hamburg. Our usual terms of payment for an initial order are cash with order. Delivery is made within approximately 1 month after receipt of order. This offer is valid until 30 June 20..

We hope our offer is to your liking and look forward to doing business with you.

Yours sincerely

Ralf Nordstern

Ralf Nordstern
Export Sales Department

Enc

Herr Nordstern aus der Exportabteilung bedankt sich für die Anfrage. Er ______

______

______

______

______

______

VOCABULARY

switch – *Schalter*; **as regards ...** – *was ... betrifft*; **initial order** – *Erstbestellung*; **approximately** – *circa*

2 You work in the Sales Department of Glasgow Office Furniture plc and need to reply to the enquiry from Bürowelt, an importer of office furniture in Munich. The addresses you need are in the letter on page 54.

Write a reply. Use phrases from the box below to help you. Include the following points.

- Bedanken Sie sich für die Anfrage vom (Datum).
- Bedanken Sie sich für das Interesse an den Produkten Ihrer Firma.
- Sagen Sie, dass Sie wie gewünscht einen Prospekt und eine Preisliste beifügen.
- Sagen Sie, dass alle Produkte verfügbar sind, so dass Sie sofort liefern können.
- Nennen Sie Ihre Liefer- und Zahlungsbedingungen und sagen Sie, dass sich alle Preise DDP verstehen. Sie hoffen, bald von Bürowelt zu hören.

Writing an offer

Reference to the enquiry

Many thanks for We refer to	your letter of ... (date) your enquiry of ... (date)	about ...
We are pleased to note that	you are interested in our product(s).	

Reference to information, etc.

Enclosed please find We are sending you	our brochure/catalogue/price list.	
To download our latest	catalogue/brochure/price list	please visit our website.

Price

As regards the goods requested, we are pleased to	submit the following quotation. make the following offer.

Terms

Our prices are quoted EXW/DDP/CIF/FOB ... (place).

We are able to grant a trade/quantity discount of ...

We offer a cash discount for payment within ... days.

For orders over ... we offer a discount of ...%.

Our usual terms of payment for an initial order are ...

Delivery

Delivery time is about/approximately Delivery is made within Dispatch (is) within	... hours/days/weeks/months	after receipt of order.

We can guarantee immediate delivery.

Further information

Our offer is valid	until ... (date) as long as stocks last.

Polite ending

We hope our offer is to your liking and look forward to doing business with you.
We look forward to receiving your order.

Please contact us Please do not hesitate to contact us	if you need any further details. if you require further information.

VOCABULARY

to submit a quotation – *ein Angebot unterbreiten*; **to grant sth** – *etw gewähren, etw einräumen*; **quantity discount** – *Mengenrabatt*; **receipt of order** – *Auftragseingang*; **dispatch** – *Versand*; **as long as stocks last** – *solange der Vorrat reicht*; **to hesitate** – *zögern*

3 **Match the sentence beginnings 1–8 with the endings a–j. There are two more than you need.**

1 An offer is normally
2 An offer gives the customer information
3 Companies often offer a discount
4 EXW means that the customer
5 The goods are in stock, so
6 If you need further details,
7 Please find enclosed
8 Many thanks

☐ **a** for payment within a short time.
☐ **b** we can deliver them immediately.
☐ **c** please contact us.
☐ **d** interested in our products.
☐ **e** our catalogue and price list.
☐ **f** for your enquiry of 5 May 20…
☐ **g** a reply to an enquiry.
☐ **h** has to pay the delivery costs.
☐ **i** about terms of payment and delivery.
☐ **j** a quantity discount of 2%.

4 You work for Office Inc in Ireland.
Look at the advert for Office Inc and the enquiry in Unit 4 on pages 54–55 again. Write the following letter to Office Props including all details given.

- Bedanken Sie sich für die Anfrage vom (Datum).
- Sagen Sie, dass Sie sich sehr über das Interesse des Kunden an Ihren Produkten freuen.
- Sagen Sie, dass Sie wie gewünscht detaillierte Informationen über den Drucker WLan OfficeInc 3.0 beifügen.
- Weisen Sie darauf hin, dass der Preis von 298,90 € sehr günstig (*favourable*) ist und der Drucker zu einem solch niedrigen Preis nirgendwo anders zu bekommen ist.
- Sagen Sie, dass Sie bei Abnahme von mind. 50 Stück einen Mengenrabatt von 15 % gewähren.
- Erklären Sie, dass dieses Angebot gültig ist, solange der Vorrat reicht.
- Empfehlen Sie dem Kunden, so bald wie möglich zu bestellen, da die Nachfrage nach diesem Sonderangebot sehr hoch ist.
- Sagen Sie, dass Sie sich auf die Bestellung des Kunden freuen.
- Sagen Sie, dass der Kunde, sofern er weitere Informationen benötigt, bitte nicht zögern soll, sich in dieser Sache noch einmal an Sie zu wenden.

5 DUTCH BIKES in the Netherlands is ordering dynamos for their new e-bikes.
Read the two offers they receive, then complete the table below comparing the offers and answer the questions.

Dear Mr De Vries

Your enquiry about dynamo model no. SP-11-AB

We refer to your enquiry of 2 February 20.. for our dynamo model SP-11-AB. We are pleased to note your interest in our product. Konrad Dynamos is a new, innovative company with a series of lights for e-bikes.

Regarding the model requested, we are pleased to make the following offer: on orders of over 100 dynamos we can offer a price of €140 each. In addition, we offer a cash discount of 3% on payment within 10 days.

Our prices are quoted DAP your factory in Den Haag. We can guarantee immediate delivery.

Our usual terms of payment for EU customers are payment within two weeks of date of invoice.

This offer is valid as long as stocks last.

We look forward to receiving your order. We can guarantee an efficient and reliable service.

Yours sincerely
Bernd Amberger
Sales assistant
Konrad Dynamos GmbH

Subject: Offer for AC-L. ED-600 (bike dynamo)

Dear Mr De Vries

Many thanks for your enquiry of 2 February 20.. . Our company is a leading global bicycle component producer and our new light-weight dynamo is attracting a lot of customers. I attach our brochure with the full technical details.

As regards your enquiry, we are pleased to submit the following quotation: the wholesale price is €137 per unit, but for orders of over 50 dynamos we grant a quantity discount of 7%.

Our prices are quoted FCA Taoyuan International Airport. We have good relations with local freight forwarders and will be happy to put you in touch.

Our usual terms of payment for an initial order are CWO. On later orders we will grant 60 days' credit.

Dispatch is within two weeks after receipt of order.

This offer is valid for ten days from the date of this email.

We look forward to receiving your order. Please do not hesitate to contact us if you require further information.

Yours sincerely
Ms Li Siying

Sales Manager
Chen Bike Co. Ltd.

	Chen Bike Co. Ltd. Taipei, Taiwan	**Konrad Dynamos GmbH, Munich**
Price		
Discounts		
Terms of delivery		
Terms of payment		
Delivery time		
Valid for …		

1 What would be the unit price for 200 dynamos from each supplier if DUTCH BIKES pay on time?

2 What extra costs would DUTCH BIKES have to pay in each case?

3 Which supplier grants better terms of payment?

VOCABULARY

light-weight – *leichtgewichtig, leicht*; **freight forwarder** – *Spediteur*; **to put sb in touch with sb** – *jdm den Kontakt zu jdm herstellen*

C KMK EXAM PRACTICE

19

1 Hörverstehen

Situation: Anjali Sen von Apex Leisure in Nottingham, England, ruft bei FreiLuft GmbH in Linz, Österreich, an, um zwei Anfragen zu besprechen.

Aufgabe: Hören Sie sich das Telefongespräch an und füllen Sie das Notizformular aus.

Notiz 1

Anbieter: Fa. Apex Leisure, Nottingham, England			
Menge	______	**Artikel**	Champion Solarlampen
Farbe	grün/gelb ☐ grau/silber ☐ grün/silber ☐		
Modellnummer	______		
Nachlässe/Rabatte	• ______ • ______		
Transport- und Lieferbedingungen	______		
Versand	______ nach Eingang der Bestellung		

Notiz 2

Anbieter: Fa. Apex Leisure, Nottingham, England			
Menge	______	**Artikel**	Kühltaschen
Artikelbeschreibung	Arctic Star (12 Volt) Farbe: ______ Fassungsvermögen: ______		
Modellnummer	______		
Nachlässe/Rabatte	• ______ • ______		
Transport- und Lieferbedingungen	______		
Versand	______ nach Eingang der Bestellung		

2 Mediation

Situation: Sie machen eine Ausbildung in der Verkaufsabteilung einer amerikanischen Firma in Erlangen. Sie sind auf die folgende Anzeige für eine englischsprachige Verkaufsschulung gestoßen und möchten Ihre deutsche Chefin, Frau Thiel, davon überzeugen, Sie zu dieser Schulung zu schicken.

Aufgabe: Verfassen Sie auf Deutsch eine E-Mail an Frau Thiel, in der Sie die wichtigsten Angaben zu der Schulung zusammenfassen und Ihre Argumente vorbringen.

CSC IN-COMPANY TRAINING

Basic Sales Course

This one-day sales training course offers a full introduction to successful selling. It is ideal for anyone new to sales or who has some experience but no formal training in the sales process. Before the course, participants complete a questionnaire and receive a coursebook with background information, selling tips and extra tasks.

Course objectives
The course will develop the participants' skills and self-confidence to sell over the phone and face-to-face. The training will also introduce them to key sales principles and the basic selling skills needed to make a sale.

By the end of the course, participants will understand what makes a successful sales person. They will learn how they can make a great first impression and open a sales conversation well. They will also understand the importance of effective listening and will practise presenting products by highlighting their features and benefits. They will look at ways of closing a conversation with a sale.

Course topics
- **A good sales person:** attitude, behaviour and skills
- **Opening a sales conversation:** first impressions, face-to-face meetings, non-verbal behaviour
- **The importance of relationships:** building and developing a relationship with your customers
- **Practising sales skills:** active listening (face-to-face and on the telephone), asking the right questions, summarizing
- **Presenting your product:** the features, advantages and benefits
- **Closing a sales conversation:** what 'closing' is, checking interest, asking for next steps

What participants say

"Excellent! A really useful course. It has given me the confidence to be able to go out and sell."	"Lots of helpful, practical suggestions. The trainer was also very flexible and adapted to our needs."	"A good mix of theory and practice. The role plays were great fun. The day went by really fast!"

3 Produktion

Situation: Sie sind Sachbearbeiter/-in in der Verkaufsabteilung der Firma World Navigator GmbH (Querstraße 20, 90762 Fürth). Ihre Firma ist ein bedeutender Großhändler für GPS-Geräte mit einem ausgezeichneten Ruf in ganz Europa. Aus Irland erhalten Sie eine Anfrage von Whitefriar Trekking Ltd (31 Wicklow Street, Dublin 8, Irland).

Aufgabe: Verfassen Sie ein Angebot an die irische Firma unter Berücksichtigung folgender Punkte:

- Bedanken Sie sich für die Anfrage vom (Datum).
- Weisen Sie für weitere Informationen auf Ihre Homepage mit Katalog zum Download und Exportpreisliste hin.
- Machen Sie folgendes Angebot:
  - GPS-Gerät vom Typ ‚eTreck' mit Touchscreen, Artikel-Nr. eT49, zum Preis von 250 € pro Stück
  - GPS-Handgerät vom Typ ‚Xpedition', Artikel Nr. XP1, zum Preis von 100 € pro Stück
- Bieten Sie einen Mengenrabatt von 10 % bei Abnahme von 10 oder mehr Geräten an.
- Erklären Sie, dass die Lieferung DDP Geschäftsräume des irischen Kunden innerhalb 14 Tagen nach Auftragseingang erfolgt.
- Beenden Sie das Schreiben mit einer passenden Schlussformel.

D IHK EXAM PRACTICE

1 Vermerk in Deutsch über ein Gespräch in Englisch

20

Situation: Sie sind Beate Quint und arbeiten bei FreiLuft GmbH in Linz, Österreich. Sie erhalten einen Rückruf von Anjali Sen von Apex Leisure in Nottingham, England, wegen zweier Anfragen, die Sie gestellt haben.

Aufgabe: Verfolgen Sie das Gespräch und fertigen Sie anschließend eine Gesprächsnotiz auf Deutsch für Ihren Chef an. Während des Hörens dürfen Sie Notizen machen. Diese Notizen werden nicht bewertet, sondern nur die Gesprächsnotiz.

Beate:	**Anjali Sen:**
FreiLuft Austria. Beate Quint, Einkauf. Kann ich …	…
Oh, hello, Anjali. How're you?	…
Oh, I'm fine, too, thanks. Anyway, what can I do for you?	…
Of course – the sooner the better, in fact.	…
So that'd be a trade discount of 15 % below list, plus a 2.5 % cash discount for payment within 15 days of delivery.	…
And delivery?	…
That sounds fine, Anjali. Well, thanks for your …	…
Oh, of course. The cool boxes.	…
OK. Everything's the same as in our enquiry.	…
Well, I'll just check with my boss, but I'm pretty sure I'll be able to fax you an order early tomorrow, 16 February.	…
Bye now, Anjali.	…

Notiz 1

Anbieter: Fa. Apex Leisure, Nottingham, England	
Menge	______
Artikel	Champion Solarlampen
Farbe	grün/gelb ☐ grau/silber ☐ grün/silber ☐
Modellnummer	______
Nachlässe/ Rabatte	• ______ • ______
Transport- und Lieferbedingungen	______ ______
Versand	______ nach Eingang der Bestellung

Notiz 2

Anbieter: Fa. Apex Leisure, Nottingham, England	
Menge	______
Artikel	Kühltaschen
Artikelbeschreibung	Arctic Star (12 Volt) Farbe: ______ Fassungsvermögen: ______
Modellnummer	______
Nachlässe/ Rabatte	• ______ • ______
Transport- und Lieferbedingungen	______ ______
Versand	______ nach Eingang der Bestellung

2 Geschäftsbrief in Englisch nach Stichwortangaben in Deutsch

Situation: Sie sind Sachbearbeiter/in in der Verkaufsabteilung der Firma World Navigator GmbH (Querstraße 20, 90762 Fürth). Ihre Firma ist ein bedeutender Großhändler für GPS-Geräte mit einem ausgezeichneten Ruf in ganz Europa. Aus Irland erhalten Sie eine Anfrage von Whitefriar Trekking Ltd (31 Wicklow Street, Dublin 8, Irland).

Aufgabe: Verfassen Sie ein Angebot an die irische Firma unter Berücksichtigung folgender Punkte:

- Bedanken Sie sich für die Anfrage vom (Datum).
- Weisen Sie für weitere Informationen auf Ihre Homepage mit Katalog zum Download und Exportpreisliste hin.
- Machen Sie folgendes Angebot:
  – GPS-Gerät vom Typ ‚eTreck' mit Touchscreen, Artikel-Nr. eT49, zum Preis von 250 € pro Stück
  – GPS-Handgerät vom Typ ‚Xpedition', Artikel Nr. XP1, zum Preis von 100 € pro Stück
- Bieten Sie einen Mengenrabatt von 10 % bei Abnahme von 10 oder mehr Geräten an.
- Erklären Sie, dass die Lieferung DDP Geschäftsräume des irischen Kunden innerhalb 14 Tagen nach Auftragseingang erfolgt.
- Beenden Sie das Schreiben mit einer passenden Schlussformel.

3 Kurzgefasste Mitteilung in Englisch

Situation: Sie sind Sachbearbeiter/in in der Verkaufsabteilung der Firma Schmidt Sportbekleidung GmbH, Regensburg, einem der führenden Hersteller in Deutschland. Ein Kollege aus der Marketingabteilung, dessen Englisch nicht so gut wie Ihres ist, hat Sie um Hilfe gebeten: Sie möchten bitte eine E-Mail, die gestern eingegangen ist, lesen und dringend eine kurze, aber freundliche Antwort schreiben.

Aufgabe: Verfassen Sie die E-Mail an Frau Al Kubaidi unter Berücksichtigung folgender Punkte:

- Entschuldigen Sie sich für die Verzögerung bei der Zusendung der versprochenen Informationen an Frau Al Kubaidi. Erklären Sie, dass Herr Dietrich kurz nach der Messe erkrankt ist und nicht arbeiten konnte.
- Sagen Sie, dass Sie dieser Mail den aktuellen Katalog und die Preisliste Ihrer Firma beifügen.
- Erwähnen Sie, dass Herr Dietrich in der nächsten Woche wieder zur Arbeit kommt und dann direkt mit Frau Al Kubaidi in Kontakt treten wird.
- Beenden Sie das Schreiben mit einer passenden Schlussformel.

From: m_alkubaidi@sunsand.dux
To: info@schmidtsport.nex
Subject: Enquiry for Mr Dietrich

Dear Sir/Madam,

I represent Sand and Sun Sports, a leading chain of sports equipment and clothing stores in Dubai and the United Arab Emirates. In fact, I attended a trade fair in Berlin some weeks ago and spoke with a representative from your firm, Mr Dietrich. He showed me some very nice samples of your products and proposed sending us your firm's latest catalogue, along with details of your terms and payment. Unfortunately, we've heard nothing since.

We're particularly interested in your company's line of football clothing and, with the World Championship around the corner, we'd appreciate a swift reply.

Best regards,

Miriam Al Kubaidi
Head of Purchasing

Useful phrases

Writing offers	
Reference to enquiry	
As agreed in our telephone conversation (today) …	*Wie (heute) telefonisch vereinbart …*
We were delighted to receive your enquiry dated … about our products.	*Wir freuen uns über Ihre Anfrage vom … bezüglich unserer Produkte.*
I am pleased to let you have details of our offer in writing.	*Gerne lasse ich Ihnen ein schriftliches Angebot zukommen.*
Many thanks for the above-mentioned enquiry / your enquiry dated …	*Wir danken für die oben genannte Anfrage / Ihre Anfrage vom …*
Description of your company/goods/services	
We are a major distributor of …	*Wir sind ein bedeutender Großhändler für …*
… with an excellent reputation throughout Europe.	*… mit einem hervorragenden Ruf in ganz Europa.*
Our company manufactures a wide range of high-quality (engineering) products …	*Unser Unternehmen stellt eine breite Palette von hochwertigen (Maschinenbau-) Produkten her …*
… and already has many satisfied customers throughout Western Europe and North America.	*… und hat bereits viele zufriedene Kunden überall in Westeuropa und Nordamerika.*
Sales material	
A brochure on … / Our current catalogue and price list is/are attached/enclosed for your information.	*Zu Ihrer Information ist ein Prospekt über … / sind unser aktueller Katalog und eine aktuelle Preisliste angehängt/beigefügt.*
To download our export price list, please visit our website at …	*Um unsere Exportpreisliste herunterzuladen, besuchen Sie bitte unsere Homepage unter …*
Price	
We are pleased to submit the following quotation: …	*Wir freuen uns, Ihnen folgendes Angebot zu unterbreiten: …*
… and can supply you with … at … each.	*… und liefern Ihnen gerne … zu je …* (Preis).
Terms and discounts	
Our prices are quoted FOB Hamburg.	*Unsere Preise verstehen sich FOB Hamburg.*
Delivery will be made CIP Frankfurt Airport.	*Die Lieferung erfolgt CIP Flughafen Frankfurt.*
A quantity discount of …% is granted on orders for 10 or more …	*Bei Abnahme von 10 oder mehr …* (z. B. Geräten, Artikeln) *wird ein Mengenrabatt von … % gewährt.*
Our terms of payment for an initial order are CWO.	*Bei Erstauftrag kann lediglich bar bei Auftragserteilung gezahlt werden.*
Our usual terms of payment are …	*Unsere üblichen Zahlungsbedingungen sind …*
… 10 days 3%, 30 days net.	*… 3 % Skonto bei Zahlung innerhalb von 10 Tagen, netto bei Zahlung innerhalb von 30 Tagen.*
Delivery	
Delivery is made within approximately … days after receipt of order.	*Die Lieferung erfolgt innerhalb von ca. … Tagen nach Auftragseingang.*
… while stocks last	*… solange der Vorrat reicht*
Polite ending	
We look forward to receiving your order.	*Wir freuen uns über Ihren Auftrag.*
Please do not hesitate to contact us if you require further details.	*Sofern Sie weitere Angaben benötigen, zögern Sie bitte nicht, sich an uns zu wenden.*

When the buyer receives the offer from the supplier, he/she will decide whether to go on to the next step: placing an order. When an order is placed, it is normal to repeat all the details that have been agreed (price, discounts, terms of payment, etc.). Most importantly, the order must state exactly what is being ordered. Catalogue numbers or other descriptions are used so that there are no misunderstandings.

A PLACING ORDERS

1 Sanyang GmbH imports rolls of material for advertising banners.
Read the order they have sent to the China Canvas Company Ltd and decide if the statements on the next page are true (T), false (F) or not in the text (N).

Sanyang GmbH
Am Stern 18 • 85049 Ingolstadt
Tel. +49 (0) 841 51277

04 July 20..

China Canvas Company Limited
110 Linqing Rd.
200245 Shanghai
China

Attn. Mr Andy Gao, Export Sales Director

Dear Mr Gao

Order no. BK42 for banner material

Many thanks for your offer dated 28 June 20.. .

We would like to place an order for the following goods:

Quantity	Description	Article No.	Unit Price ($)	Total ($)
50 rolls	banner material	BL 246	50	2,500.00

Delivery: FOB Shanghai within 30 days after receipt of order
Packing: Container
Payment: 30% in advance, 70% after completion by transfer to your a/c at the Bank of China

Transport and insurance of the goods from Shanghai to Ingolstadt via the Port of Rotterdam will be arranged by us.

We look forward to receiving your confirmation of order and advice of dispatch in the near future.

Yours sincerely

J. Dahlmann

Julia Dahlmann
Import Department

VOCABULARY

to acknowledge – *bestätigen*; **banner** – *Fahne, Transparent*; **order completion** – *Auftragserfüllung, Auftragsabschluss*; **a/c = account** – *Konto*; **confirmation of order** – *Auftragsbestätigung*; **advice of dispatch** – *Versandanzeige*

Decide if the following statements are true (T), false (F) or not in the text (N).

		T	F	N
1	The China Canvas Company has a branch office in Germany.			
2	Julia Dahlmann works in the purchasing department of Sanyang GmbH.			
3	Andy Gao sent Julia Dahlmann an offer on 28 June.			
4	Sanyang has placed orders with the China Canvas Company before.			
5	The seller will bear all costs and risks until the goods reach the buyer's country.			
6	The goods will be sent to Europe by ship to Rotterdam.			
7	The China Canvas Company has an account at the Bank of China.			
8	Full payment will be made in advance.			

21 **2** Katrin Troll is doing her work placement at A–Z Logistics in London. She calls Good Business Equipment and places an urgent order.
Listen to the telephone conversation and complete the table below.

Good Business Equipment		**Order form**	
Address	A–Z Logistics, North Park Industrial Estate, London ________		
Phone	020 71594	Email	Katrin@A2Z.co.nex

Order	
Item number	________
Description	________
Quantity	________
Price	________
Item number	________
Description	________
Quantity	________
Price	________
	TOTAL: ________

Method of payment		
Bank transfer	Cheque	COD
Credit card	Amex ☐ Mastercard ☐ Visa ☐	

VOCABULARY

branch office – *Zweigstelle*; **stainless steel** – *Edelstahl*; **to interrupt** – *unterbrechen*; **urgently** – *dringend*; **basic** – *einfach*; **to call sth up** – *etw aufrufen*; **moveable** – *beweglich*

3 **Match the German words and phrases (1–10) from the letter on page 75 with their English equivalents (a–l). There are two more than you need.**

1 Wir möchten einen Auftrag erteilen.
2 Versandanzeige
3 zu Händen von
4 Transport und Versicherung
5 Ihr Angebot vom
6 Auftragsbestätigung
7 nach Auftragserfüllung
8 Bestellnr.
9 Stückpreis
10 Verpackung

☐ **a** confirmation of order
☐ **b** your offer dated
☐ **c** advice of dispatch
☐ **d** will be arranged
☐ **e** unit price
☐ **f** Attn.
☐ **g** order no.
☐ **h** near future
☐ **i** We would like to place an order.
☐ **j** transport and insurance
☐ **k** after completion
☐ **l** packing

4 **Study the following order. Some of the statements below are correct, some of them are false. Correct the false statements.**

Quantity	Description	Article No.	List price	Total
100	HQ printer	HQ3000	€60.00	€6,000.00
250	Quickchip laptop	QC99	€100.00	€25,000.00
			– 30% trade discount	–€9,300.00
			Subtotal	€21,700.00
			+ 19% VAT*	€4,123.00
			Total price	€25,823.00
Delivery	CIF Rotterdam, Netherlands by 30 June 20..			
Packing	cardboard boxes			
Payment	2% 10 days, 30 days net after receipt of invoice			
* Value Added Tax = *Mehrwertsteuer*				

1 One printer costs €60.
2 There is a discount of 19%.
3 The final price of the goods is €21,700.
4 The goods will be delivered to the Netherlands.
5 The seller will pay for transport of the goods from Rotterdam to the buyer's offices.
6 The buyer wants the goods on or after 30 June 20.. .
7 The buyer will get a further discount if he pays within ten days.
8 The buyer has a maximum of 30 days to pay after he has received the invoice.

Statements ____________________ are correct.

Statements ____________________ are incorrect.

Corrections: ____

____

____

____

5 Last week Stefan Schwarz from Gartenmöbel Limbach GmbH in Freiburg received a catalogue from The Greenhouse BV in Utrecht, the Netherlands (pages 50 and 52). Stefan decides to place a trial order.

Complete Stefan's order using words and phrases from the box on the next page.

Gartenmöbel Limbach GmbH
Schornstr. 5–7
79106 Freiburg i. Breisgau
Germany

Tel.: +49 (0)761 77553
info@garmoeblim.dex

Our ref.: Order no. AB 54321

1 July 20..

The Greenhouse BV
Bankstraat 7
3411 AB Utrecht
NETHERLANDS

Attn. Ms Lara Smit

Dear Ms Smit

Trial order for greenhouses

Thank you ______________________________[1] 27 June 20..

We ______________________[2] terms and are pleased to ____________________[3] for greenhouses as follows:

Catalogue number	Item	Quantity	Unit price	Total price
S324	Solargro standard	3	€509	€1,527
E564	Solargro Elite	2	€561	€1,122
D965	Solargro Deluxe	1	€627	€627
			Total	€3,276

We ______________________________[4] are EXW.

______________________________[5] by bank transfer within 30 days of

______________________________[6].

Please ______________________[7] this order.

We look forward to ______________________[8].

Yours sincerely

Stefan Schwarz

Stefan Schwarz
Managing Director

Placing orders

- Thank you for your quotation of …
- Many thanks for your quotation.
- With reference to …, we would like to place an order for the following goods: …
- We agree to your terms and are pleased to place an order for …
- We enclose order no. …
- We note that your prices are EXW/FOB/CIF and include VAT.
- Payment will be made by (*method of payment*) on delivery of the goods.
- Payment will be made within … days of receipt of the goods.
- Please acknowledge this order.
- We look forward to receiving the goods as soon as possible.
- We trust the goods will arrive punctually and in good condition.

6 Combine a word from Box A with a word from Box B to make a compound noun. Use each word only once. Write the compound nouns in Box C and add translations into German in Box D.

Box A	Box B
bank ▪ business ▪ credit ▪ clothing ▪ market ▪ order ▪ photo ▪ sales ▪ trade ▪ transport ▪ trial ▪ unit	agency ▪ card ▪ company ▪ costs ▪ fair ▪ form ▪ letter ▪ order ▪ price ▪ representative ▪ research ▪ *transfer*

Box C	Box D
1 *bank transfer*	1 *Banküberweisung*
2 ______	2 ______
3 ______	3 ______
4 ______	4 ______
5 ______	5 ______
6 ______	6 ______
7 ______	7 ______
8 ______	8 ______
9 ______	9 ______
10 ______	10 ______
11 ______	11 ______
12 ______	12 ______

7 **Below is an order to a sports clothing company. Fill in the gaps with words from the box. There is one word more than you need.**

delivery ▪ discount ▪ enclosed ▪ following ▪ invoice ▪ item no. ▪ list prices ▪ of ▪ offer ▪ order ▪ payment ▪ pleased ▪ satisfaction ▪ sincerely ▪ within

Dear Mr Bains

We are ______[1] to note that you are prepared to give us a 10 per cent ______[2] on your ______[3]. This makes it possible for us to order the ______[4] items:

20 pairs ______[5] Road Runner jogging shoes ______[6] 1203.

For exact details on sizes please see the ______[7] order form.

Punctual ______[8] is very important.

______[9] will be made 30 days after date of ______[10] or less 2% discount ______[11] 10 days.

We trust that you will process this ______[12] to our full ______[13].

Yours ______[14]

8 **Match a sentence beginning (1–7) with the correct ending (a–g). There is one beginning and ending which don't match.**

1 We note with pleasure
2 This enables us
3 Please find enclosed
4 Please make sure
5 We understand that
6 Payment will be made
7 We trust the goods

☐ **a** your quotation of 16 September.
☐ **b** our order for 3,000 T-shirts of various sizes.
☐ **c** 30 days after date of invoice.
☐ **d** we'll be granted a 5% discount for this first order.
☐ **e** that you now offer cotton shirts.
☐ **f** to increase our business with you.
☐ **g** that our packing instructions are strictly observed.

9 **Complete the sentences with the correct prepositions from the box. You can use some prepositions more than once.**

at ▪ by
for ▪ of
on ▪ to

1 We wish to place an order ______ the following goods.
2 We sent you an offer ______ 28 June.
3 The goods will be sent to Rotterdam ______ ship.
4 We will soon send advice ______ dispatch.
5 Please transfer the deposit to our account ______ the Bank of China.
6 We agree ______ your terms.
7 Payment will be made ______ bank transfer.
8 Full payment will be made ______ delivery of the goods.

VOCABULARY

satisfaction – *Zufriedenheit*; **to trust** – *hoffen*

B ACKNOWLEDGING ORDERS

1 **Look at the polite phrases in the box (a–h). Choose the right phrase. Sometimes there is more than one.**

		Phrases	
1	den Eingang einer Bestellung bestätigen		
2	sich für eine Bestellung bedanken		
3	die Hoffnung auf eine zukünftige Zusammenarbeit ausdrücken		
4	Zuversicht hinsichtlich einer ordnungsgemäßen Lieferung ausdrücken		
5	eine unverzügliche Bearbeitung der Bestellung versprechen		
6	dem Kunden versichern, dass die Bestellung zufriedenstellend durchgeführt wird		
7	den Kunden wissen lassen, dass man ihm ggf. zur Verfügung steht		

Polite phrases

a Please do not hesitate to contact us.
b We were very glad/happy/pleased to receive your order.
c We are pleased/happy to confirm your order.
d We are sure that the items/goods will arrive in good condition.
e We will execute your order to your complete/full satisfaction.
f We look forward to doing business with you again / to further orders in the future.
g We can assure you that your order will be dealt with immediately.
h Thank you for your order of … (date) for … (goods).

2 **Find the phrases in the email to Julia Dahlmann at Sanyang GmbH to complete the chart 'Structure of an acknowledgement' on the next page.**

To: julia.dahlmann@sanyang.dex
Subject: Your order No. BK 42 dated 4 July 20.. for banner material

Dear Ms Dahlmann

Many thanks for the above-mentioned order. We are pleased to confirm the details as follows:

Quantity	Description	Article No.	Unit Price ($)	Total ($)
50 rolls	banner material	BL 246	50	2,500.00

As agreed, the goods will be packed in a container and delivered FOB Shanghai by 15 August 20.. We note that you will arrange for transport and insurance of the goods from the Port of Shanghai to the Port of Rotterdam and then to your premises in Ingolstadt, Germany.

Payment of 30% of the total amount is now due. Please therefore transfer $750 to our account at the Bank of China. We expect to complete your order in approx. 20 days and will inform you as soon as the goods are ready. Payment of the remaining 70% will then be due. When the total amount has been received, the goods will be transported to the Port of Shanghai for shipment, and we will send you our advice of dispatch.

If you have any queries about your order, please do not hesitate to contact us.

Thank you for placing your order with the China Canvas Company.

Yours sincerely
Andy Gao

Structure of an acknowledgement

1 Reference to the order

Your order No. BK 42 dated ____________________

2 Confirmation of receipt of the order

Many thanks for ____________________

3 Confirmation of prices and discounts

____

4 Terms of payment

____

____

5 Date and mode of delivery

____

____

6 Suitable ending

____

3 **You are Lara Smit, Sales Manager of The Greenhouse BV in Utrecht, the Netherlands. Write to Stefan Schwarz and acknowledge his order of 1 July (exercise 5 on page 78). Use some of the phrases from exercise 1 on page 81.**

____

____

____

____

____

____

____

____

____

____

____

VOCABULARY

acknowledgement – *Bestätigung*; **above-mentioned** – *oben genannt*; **remaining** – *restlich*; **due** – *fällig*; **query** – *Frage*; **mode of delivery** – *Art der Zustellung*

C KMK EXAM PRACTICE

1 Leseverstehen

Situation: Die Firma, für die Sie arbeiten, möchte ihre Exporte über Europa hinaus ausdehnen, hat aber bislang nur innerhalb Europas Erfahrungen. Ihr Abteilungsleiter bittet Sie, im Internet zu spezialisierten Fachfirmen zu recherchieren. Sie stoßen auf die folgende Webseite.

Aufgabe: Lesen Sie den Text und füllen Sie die Tabelle aus.

1	Art von Firmen, die Schwierigkeiten haben, ins Ausland zu expandieren:	
2	Wie diese Firmen vorhaben vorzugehen:	
3	Drei Dienstleistungen, die Ashdown Exporting Services anbietet:	
4	Angebotene Hilfe in Sachen Werbung:	
5	Nötige Details der Marketing-Pläne:	
6	Informationen, die in der Preisliste enthalten sein sollte:	
7	Angebotene Hilfe beim Produktkatalog:	
8	Entlohnung von Ashdown Exporting Services:	

Do you want to expand the countries you export to but don't know where to start? Things are complicated for your company because you only have a small marketing budget and no office in the country you want to expand in? Your plan is to advertise your services on different business websites and wait for foreign companies to contact you to find out about distributing your products in their home markets? There is a better way.

Ashdown Exporting Services can help you!

We can help you with almost any problem but specialize in exports to Central and South America. Before you start with your business plans, it is essential that you are aware of the various rules and regulations that are associated with customs, duties and taxes in the region you are targeting as well as the market conditions you will be confronted with. That's where we come into the equation. We can help you by providing:

- Detailed reports covering import duties and regulations for specific products.
- Access to extensive marketing research of the different markets.
- Analysis of the marketing of various goods and services in a region. This includes names of competitors who currently export the goods to the market, names of domestic buyers of the products and statistics showing how many similar products are currently imported.
- Access to our advertising experts to help plan campaigns and decide which media suit your marketing needs.
- Help finding business partners to purchase your goods.

In return all we need from you to help build a successful export business in your chosen region is:

- Your marketing ideas for which type of company could be interested in your products.
- Your current price list with comprehensive details of terms of payment and delivery, minimum order amount, quantity discounts and details of packaging and insurance.
- A brochure or website showing your goods and services. We can help you to translate this into the appropriate language using our large pool of translators if required.
- Details of the commission we would receive on successful business transactions.

It's that simple! Just click here to contact us. We look forward to hearing from you!

2 Produktion

Situation: Sie sind Einkaufsleiter/in bei der Firma TT Autobeschriftung GmbH (Tempelstr. 99, 47918 Tönisvorst). Ihre Firma vertreibt selbstklebende Autobeschriftungsfolien und Zierstreifen und bezieht das Material dafür aus China. Sie haben ein Angebot der chinesischen Firma Guangzhou Materials im Internet gesehen (Guangzhou Materials Ltd, Unit 2099, Panyu District, 511450 Guangzhou, China) und die Firma anschließend angerufen.

Aufgabe: Erteilen Sie der chinesischen Firma einen Probeauftrag unter Berücksichtigung folgender Punkte:

- Ihr Ansprechpartner ist Ms Susan Wang, Verkaufsabteilung.
- Beziehen Sie sich auf das Angebot im Internet und auf das Telefongespräch.
- Bestellen Sie mit Auftrags-Nr. VF247 je 100 Rollen Go faster tape, 0,08 mm × 1,07 m zu 7,50 $ pro Rolle, Katalog-Nr. VF8107, und Self-adhesive film, 0,10 mm × 1,27 m zu $9,00 pro Rolle, Katalog-Nr. SAF10127, Gesamtpreis 1.650 $.
- Bestätigen Sie, dass die Lieferung im Container CIF Rotterdam innerhalb von 30 Tagen nach Auftragserhalt erfolgt.
- Nennen Sie folgende Zahlungsbedingungen: 30 % im Voraus, 70 % nach Auftragserfüllung per Banküberweisung.
- Bitten Sie um eine Auftragsbestätigung und eine Versandanzeige.
- Drücken Sie Ihre Hoffnung auf eine pünktliche Lieferung der Ware in gutem Zustand aus.
- Beenden Sie das Schreiben mit einer passenden Schlussformel.

3 Mediation

Situation: You are doing a placement in an English-speaking company looking to expand into the import-export business. Your boss found this article about the subject in German and asks you to inform her about the details.

Aufgabe: Write a short summary of the article for your boss. Include:

- the theme of the article
- importance of a business plan
- things an importer must check
- things an exporter must check

Wenn Sie eine Firma im Import oder Export gründen, gibt es verschiedene Regeln, die Sie beachten müssen. Gerade für kleine Exportfirmen sind die Herausforderungen groß. Außerdem sind fundierte Kenntnisse der Branche unerlässlich. Besonders wenn man auf Fremdkapital angewiesen ist, benötigt man einen Businessplan. Dieser ist erforderlich, um mögliche Geldgeber von Ihrer Idee überzeugen zu können. Er beinhaltet auch einen Finanzplan, der die Kosten auflistet und im Gespräch mit dem Bankberater hilft.

Mit folgenden Fragen sollten Sie sich auseinandersetzen:

Importunternehmen – der Bezug von Gütern aus dem Ausland:

- Aus welchen Ländern möchten Sie Waren in angemessener Qualität oder zum geeigneten Preis einführen?
- Besitzen Sie genügend Kenntnisse über die Märkte und finden sich mögliche Geschäftspartner?
- Gibt es Beschränkungen, was den Import oder Export anbelangt?
- Wie hoch sind die Transportkosten und ggf. Zollgebühren?

Export – die Ausfuhr von Waren über Staatsgrenzen hinweg:

- Welche ausländischen Märkte sind für Sie interessant?
- Besitzen Sie die notwendigen Kenntnisse für den ausländischen Markt (Sprache, Kultur, Gesetze etc.)?
- Gibt es bereits Geschäftspartner vor Ort?
- Gibt es für Ihr Produkt Beschränkungen beim Export? Kennen Sie sich mit Einfuhrbestimmungen und Zoll aus?
- Was müssen Sie beim Marketing beachten?

D IHK EXAM PRACTICE

1 Vermerk in Deutsch über einen Geschäftsbrief in Englisch

Situation: Sie arbeiten als Auszubildender bei Gartenmöbel Limbach GmbH, Schornstr. 5-7, 79106 Freiburg im Breisgau. Ihr Vorgesetzter, Stefan Schwarz, ist heute (4. September 202..) nicht im Büro. Es kommt ein Brief von einem neuen niederländischen Lieferanten, The Greenhouse BV, Bankstraat 7, 3411 AB Utrecht, Niederlande.

Aufgabe: Lesen Sie den Brief des Lieferanten und fassen Sie den Inhalt für Herrn Schwarz in deutscher Sprache zusammen. Schreiben Sie vollständige Sätze (keine Übersetzung).

Dear Mr Schwarz

Trial order for greenhouses, order no. AB54321

We were very pleased to hear that you were satisfied with the quality of our *Solargro* greenhouses and that you are interested in placing regular orders.

To this end, we enclose our latest product catalogue featuring our brand new *Solargro Next* range. We are very excited to expand our range and are confident our valued clients will share our excitement.

Indeed, we feel so confident in our *Solargro Next* range that we are delighted to offer you a launch discount of 5% for orders of 5-10 items, rising to 7.5% for orders higher than 10.

Finally, in the spirit of furthering our new business relationship, it is our pleasure to offer you open account terms. This means your firm may avail of the possibility of quarterly settlement by bank transfer within 30 days of your statement of account.

We hope you enjoy exploring our new catalogue and look forward to serving you again in the near future.

Yours sincerely

Lara Smit

Lara Smit
Sales Manager

2 Kurzgefasste Mitteilung in Englisch

Situation: Sie sind Auszubildende/r im Vertrieb der Trixie Mode GmbH in Passau. Ein Kollege hat vor einer Woche eine Auftragsbestätigung an einen irischen Kunden (Sky High Fashion) geschickt. Aus einer E-Mail, die heute eingetroffen ist, geht allerdings hervor, dass der Brief dort nie angekommen ist.

Aufgabe: Verfassen Sie eine kurze, aber freundliche E-Mail in englischer Sprache an den Kunden. Beachten Sie alle formalen Einzelheiten (E-Mail-Adresse, Datum, Betreff usw.). Bedanken Sie sich beim Kunden für die E-Mail und informieren Sie ihn über Folgendes:

- Die Auftragsbestätigung wurde vor einer Woche an den Kunden verschickt und sollte theoretisch angekommen sein.
- Danken Sie dem Kunden für die Zahlung, die ohne Verzögerung eingetroffen ist.
- Drücken Sie die Hoffnung aus, dass dem Kunden dadurch keine Unannehmlichkeiten entstanden sind.
- Eine Kopie der Auftragsbestätigung und eine Kopie der Versandanzeige sind der E-Mail beigefügt.
- Bedanken Sie sich beim Kunden und teilen Sie ihm mit, dass er sich bei weiteren Fragen gerne melden soll.

From: j_ryan@skyhigh.ei
To: sales@trixiemode.nex
Subject: Order no.42BK

Dear Trixie Mode team,

I'm writing you a quick email to check whether you received our order (see below). We sent the order eight days ago and we paid by bank transfer on the same day as stipulated in your offer. But we haven't heard anything since.

Quantity	Item	Article No.	Unit Price (€)	Total (€)
20	ladies' silk scarves	HB49	€40	€800
			Quantity discount 5 %	€40
			Total price	€760

We've experienced some issues with our post not arriving so maybe it has nothing to do with you. If you did post an acknowledgment, maybe you could email us a soft copy as an attachment.

Thanks in advance,

Jill Ryan

3 Sprachergänzungstest (Typ 1)

Aufgabe: Bitte setzen Sie 20 der 23 angegebenen Wörter in die Lücken des Textes ein.

accept ▪ account ▪ advance ▪ after ▪ before ▪ agreed ▪ confirmation ▪ discount ▪ doing ▪ due ▪ follows ▪ fulfil ▪ in ▪ making ▪ provide ▪ receipt ▪ requirements ▪ ship ▪ that ▪ trust ▪ unable ▪ understanding ▪ within

Many thanks for your order. Unfortunately, ________ 1 to unforeseen circumstances, we are ________ 2 to ________ 3 item VF8001 MaxStrength tape. As ________ 4 with your colleague, Mr Ritter, on the phone on 21 June, we are pleased to ________ 5 you with a ________ 6 of order for the other items. The details are as ________ 7:

Quantity	Description	Catalogue	Unit price ($)	Total ($)
150 rolls	Go faster tape, 0.08 mm × 1.07 m	VF8107	$7.50	$1,125.00
50 rolls	Double-sided adhesive film, 0.10 mm × 1 m	DSAF0100	$8.50	$425
Total price				$1,550.00

Delivery: CIF Rotterdam ________ 8 30 days after ________ 9 of order

Payment: 30% in ________ 10, 70% ________ 11 completion by transfer to our ________ 12 at the Bank of China

We are ________ 13 our best efforts to ________ 14 the outstanding element of your original ________ 15 and ask you to ________ 16 a 2% ________ 17 on the total cost of ________ 18 part of your order. We thank you for your ________ 19.

We ________ 20 you will be satisfied with the goods.

Useful phrases

Writing orders	
Reference to offer	
Many thanks for your offer dated …	*Vielen Dank für Ihr Angebot vom …*
Having seen your offer on the internet and spoken to you on the telephone …	*Nachdem wir Ihr Angebot im Internet gesehen und mit Ihnen gesprochen haben …*
Details of goods/services ordered	
We now wish to place an order / a trial order for the following goods: ...	*Wir möchten einen Auftrag/Probeauftrag über folgende Waren erteilen: ...*
Quantity / Description / Size / Article no.	*Menge / Beschreibung / Größe / Artikel-Nr.*
Price(s) and discount(s)	
Unit price / List price / Catalogue price / Total	*Stückpreis / Listenpreis / Katalogpreis / Gesamt*
Subtotal / Total price	*Zwischensumme / Gesamtpreis*
19 % VAT (value added tax)	*19 % USt / MwSt (Umsatzsteuer/Mehrwertsteuer)*
Delivery	
delivery date/period	*Liefertermin/-zeit*
within 10 days after receipt of order	*innerhalb 10 Tagen nach Auftragserhalt*
by 30 June 20..	*bis zum 30. Juni 20..*
Transport / Insurance	
Transport and insurance of the goods from … to … via …	*Versand und Versicherung der Ware von … nach … über …*
… will be arranged by us/you.	*… wird von uns/Ihnen übernommen.*
Payment	
30 % in advance, 70 % after completion	*30 % im Voraus, 70 % nach Auftragserfüllung*
by transfer to our a/c at …	*per Überweisung auf unser Konto bei …* (Geldinstitut)
Acknowledgement / Advice of dispatch	
We look forward to receiving your advice of dispatch.	*Wir freuen uns auf den Erhalt Ihrer Versandanzeige.*
Please send us your confirmation of order and advice of dispatch in the next few days.	*Bitte schicken Sie uns Ihre Auftragsbestätigung und Versandanzeige in den nächsten Tagen zu.*
Polite ending	
We trust the goods will arrive punctually and in good condition …	*Wir hoffen, dass die Ware pünktlich und in gutem Zustand ankommt ….*
… and will place further/regular orders if they sell well.	*… und werden weitere/regelmäßige Aufträge erteilen, wenn sie sich gut verkauft.*

7 Making and adjusting complaints

Even in the best companies, there can be mistakes. In fact, mistakes are just part of business life and they are not always one person's fault. It is important, therefore, to be firm when you write a letter of complaint but never to be personal or angry. Typical problems are that the wrong goods are sent or arrive damaged, that a delivery is delayed for various reasons, or that the goods are not of the quality that buyer expected.

A MAKING COMPLAINTS

1 Global Medical GmbH, based in Passau, sells reconditioned medical equipment to companies all over the world. The company has good business relationships with its customers, but today a new customer sends a complaint.

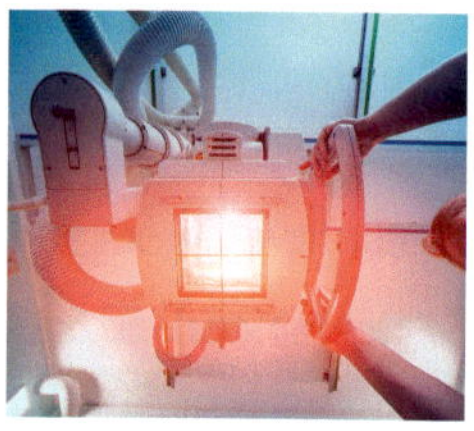

Read the email below and answer the questions.

1 What has gone wrong?

___

2 What does the writer want the addressee to do?

___

___

3 Why does the writer want the addressee to do this?

___

4 How does the writer close his email?

___

___

Dear Ms Wolf

Regarding our order number 942761 of 11 April for two reconditioned x-ray machines, the agreed date of delivery was 7 May. To date, the machines have not been delivered.

Please look into the matter immediately, and let us know when we can expect delivery. We need the equipment urgently, so if you cannot deliver within the next week, we will have to look for another supplier.

As you know, this is a trial order. We feel sure you will understand that your handling of this matter will determine whether we will be able to place future orders with you.

Yours sincerely

Jerzy Adamczyk
Clinic Manager

VOCABULARY

complaint – *Beschwerde, Reklamation*; **to adjust a complaint** – *eine Reklamation bearbeiten*; **fault** – *Schuld*; **firm** – *bestimmt, entschlossen*; **addressee** – *Empfänger/in*; **regarding** – *mit Bezug auf*; **to recondition** – *generalüberholen*; **x-ray** – *Röntgen*; **to date** – *bis jetzt, bislang*; **to look into sth** – *einer Sache nachgehen*; **handling (of sth)** – *Umgang (mit etw)*; **to determine** – *bestimmen, entscheiden*

2 Global Medical ships their orders in special containers made by Swedish Metals AB in Stockholm. Global Medical is waiting for delivery of some containers, so Melissa Wolf calls her colleague, Elisabeth Felix, in the Purchasing Department to find out what has happened. The latest consignment of containers has not arrived, so Elisabeth Felix writes to Peter Johansson at Swedish Metals' Sales Department to complain about the delay in delivery. Elisabeth has dealt with Peter for several years.

Dear Peter

I'm sorry to inform you that order no. 923/EF/04 for containers hasn't arrived yet. The order was sent almost one month ago on 18 April, and delivery was promised by 3 May.

Could you please explain what has happened to the goods, and let me know as soon as possible when we can expect the consignment?

As you realize, we can't fulfil our orders until we have your containers. I have heard from the Sales Department that we have, in fact, just received a complaint from a new customer who has been waiting for a delivery from us since 7 May.

We've been doing business with Swedish Metals for over five years, and we've had no cause for complaint up to now. You'll understand, however, that this delay is causing us some problems.

Could you look into this and get back to me as soon as possible? Thanks for your help.

Best wishes

Elisabeth

Your colleague, whose English is not as good as yours, has written a summary of the email. Cross out the mistakes and write the corrections in the column on the right.

1 Elisabeth Felix ordered containers from Swedish Metals ~~at the beginning of April~~.	on 18 April
2 The containers should have been delivered by the end of April.	
3 Global Medical does not need the containers to fulfil their orders.	
4 A new customer ordered some goods on 7 May.	
5 Global Medical and Swedish Metals have just started to do business with each other.	
6 Elisabeth has often sent complaints to Swedish Metals.	
7 She would like an explanation by the end of the week.	

VOCABULARY

container – *Behälter*; **consignment** – *Sendung*; **delay** – *Verzögerung*; **to fulfil** – *erfüllen, abwickeln*; **cause for complaint** – *Anlass zur Klage/Beschwerde*; **to cause problems** – *Probleme bereiten*

3 Find words or phrases in the email on page 88 that mean:

1 Mit Bezug auf unsere Bestellung …

____

2 der vereinbarte Liefertermin war …

____

3 bislang …

____

4 Bitte gehen Sie der Sache nach …

____

5 Wir benötigen die Geräte dringend.

____

6 Sie werden sicherlich verstehen, dass …

____

22

4 Listen to the dialogue about a delayed consignment and complete the sentences.

1 Jenna thinks it's a good thing that _______________

2 The consignment should have arrived on (date) _______________

3 The dialogue between Jenna and Anton takes place on (date) _______________

4 Anton asks Jenna to treat the matter as urgent because _______________

____

5 Some of Anton's customers _______________

6 Jenna promises to get on with it immediately and _______________

5 These sentences are from letters of complaint. Fill in the reasons for the complaints using the words from the box. Then translate the sentences.

poor quality ▪ wrong goods ▪ delay ▪ part of delivery is missing ▪ damaged goods

1 We had stressed that punctual delivery was very important. REASON: delay

____

2 The trousers are not of the quality we had expected. REASON: _______________

____

3 We hope you can send us the correct goods without delay. REASON: _______________

____

4 As we need the complete quantity urgently, please forward the missing 100 units immediately.

REASON: _______________

____

5 We are prepared to keep the scratched machines if you grant us a 20% price reduction.

REASON: _______________

____

VOCABULARY

delivery schedule – *Lieferplan*; **delivery date** – *Liefertermin*; **restless** – *unruhig*; **to forward sth** – *etw senden, etw verschicken*; **scratched** – *zerkratzt*

6 **Complete the text using the correct form of the words in brackets.**

1 We have received a complaint ______ about the goods we sent last week. (complain)
2 The consignment ______ four days after the deadline. (arrival)
3 We are still ______ for our order XY31 to arrive. (wait)
4 We insist on a price ______ for the damaged articles. (reduce)
5 We are ______ to keep the goods if you grant us a 30% discount. (prepare)
6 Please confirm ______ of this email. (receive)
7 We expect a ______ for damaged articles. (replace)
8 Our ______ have let us down. (supply)
9 We invite you to inspect the ______ goods in our warehouse. (damage)
10 We ask you to inform us by email when the ______ will be made. (deliver)
11 While ______ the equipment, it became clear that it was not working. (test)
12 Please find a ______ to this problem. (solve)

7 **The parts of this letter of complaint are mixed up. Put them in the correct order.**

1 about the late delivery
17 and that you will be able to avoid mistakes like this in future.
2 We did not receive them
7 until this morning
3 ordered on 3 March.
15 We hope you will understand that we are not satisfied
8 delivery within a week.
4 We have to complain
9 Unfortunately,
11 although you had guaranteed
10 that we placed the order.
12 business between us
6 of the tennis shoes
5 It was on this understanding
13 there have been similar delays before.
14 under conditions such as these.
16 We cannot continue

Correct order:

4																

VOCABULARY

replacement – *Ersatz*; **to inspect** – *prüfen, kontrollieren*; **on this understanding** – *unter dieser Voraussetzung*; **similar** – *ähnlich*

B ADJUSTING COMPLAINTS

1 As soon as he received her email, Peter Johansson phoned Elisabeth Felix to apologize for the delay. Later, Peter sent Elisabeth an email.

Read the email, then do the following tasks.

1 Describe the problem which led to the delay.

____

2 Say what the current state of the order is.

____

3 Explain what Swedish Metals has done to make sure that the goods arrive as soon as possible.

____

Subject: Order No. 923/EF/04 for containers

Dear Elisabeth

I refer to your complaint of 15 May regarding order no. 923/EF/04.

We are sorry for the delay in delivery of the goods. As I explained in our phone call this morning, this was caused by late delivery of materials from one of our business partners.

I have checked and am pleased to be able to tell you that your order was dispatched two days ago. Logistics will send you an advice of dispatch by email today.

We have sent the consignment by rail this time so that transport is not interrupted by the weekend. The containers should arrive in Passau on Monday, 23 May.

We hope that the goods arrive safely and apologize once again for the delay.

Regards
Peter

2 **Read the email again and find the English equivalents of these German words and phrases.**

1 Wir bedauern die Verzögerung.	______________
2 Die Ursache dafür war …	______________
3 Ihre Ware wurde vor zwei Tagen verschickt.	______________
4 Sendung	______________
5 Wir hoffen, dass die Ware wohlbehalten ankommt.	______________
6 Wir entschuldigen uns nochmals für …	______________

VOCABULARY

to cause – *verursachen*; **to refer to sth** – *sich auf etw beziehen*; **to dispatch** – *versenden*

3 Once she knows the containers are on their way, Elisabeth gets in touch with Jerzy Adamczyk at Denta Dental Clinic.

Complete her email using words and phrases from Peter Johansson's email (exercise 1 on page 92).

Subject: Order no. 942761 for x-ray machines
From: efelix@globalmedical.dex

Dear Mr Adamczyk

Your ____________ [1] about your order number 942761 of 11 April has been passed on to me.

We are sorry that you have not yet received this order. This was caused by a ____________ [2] of containers from one of our ____________ [3].

I am pleased to tell you that your order will be ____________ [4] within the next few days.

Our Logistics Centre will send you an ____________ [5] by email as soon as the ____________ [6] is on its way.

I am sure that the ____________ [7] will arrive safely and will be to your satisfaction.

Once again, I ____________ [8] for the delay.

Yours sincerely

Elisabeth Felix

23

4 **Eleven pieces of information in the part of a dialogue below are wrong. Listen and cross out the wrong information. Write the correct information in the column on the right. The first one has been done for you.**

Jenna Well, the consignment left our stores last ~~Tuesday morning~~ as planned. I've been in touch with our forwarding agents, and they told me that the truck was on schedule until it was involved in a bad pile-up in snow on the main road near Nuremberg in Bavaria on Wednesday.
Anton Oh, that's bad. Was our consignment damaged in the accident?
Jenna Well, the forwarding agents say yes, it was. It's being transferred to another train today, and it should arrive in Vienna at about nine o'clock tomorrow morning, 13 October.
Anton Good heavens. What took so long? Nuremberg's not all that far away. It's only about 300 kilometres or so.
Jenna Sure, but I'm afraid it's the old story, Anton. As far as I can see, in Bavaria the weekend starts about Friday at four o'clock. Anyhow, I'll confirm all this by letter, OK?
Anton Fine, Jenna. I'd appreciate that.

1 Monday afternoon
2 ____________
3 ____________
4 ____________
5 ____________
6 ____________
7 ____________
8 ____________
9 ____________
10 ____________
11 ____________

VOCABULARY

forwarding agent – *Spediteur*; **on schedule** – *im Zeitplan*; **pile-up** – *Massenkollision*; **fog** – *Nebel*

5 Here are reactions to three different complaints. Mark the sentences which are not suitable for the situation.

1 a We apologize for the inconvenience we caused you. ☐
b Of course we are prepared to replace the damaged items. ☐
c But things like this can happen to anyone. ☐

2 a It's annoying to get letters like yours when it isn't really our fault. ☐
b We will do our best to send the missing goods as soon as possible. ☐
c We will make sure that similar errors will not happen again. ☐

3 a We very much regret the delayed delivery of your consignment. ☐
b You got the goods in the end, so what's the problem? ☐
c We apologize for the errors which happened in connection with your order. ☐

6 Match four of the reasons for a complaint (a–f) with the replies (1–4).

a The wrong goods were sent.
b The invoice was not sent with the goods.
c Some of the goods were damaged.
d None of the goods has been delivered.
e Some of the goods were missing.
f The goods were not of the expected quality.

1 We are prepared to replace the broken goods as soon as you have returned them. ______
2 We apologize for the oversight and are sending you a further 50 colour monitors by express freight. ______
3 The mistake was caused by an error in our new computer software, which mixed up some catalogue numbers. ______
4 If you refer to our main catalogue, you will see that the sample we sent you was 301A-1 (100% cotton), while you ordered 301A-2 (80% cotton). ______

7 Fill in the gaps in the letter of apology with suitable words from the box. Use each word or phrase only once. There are more words than you need.

accept ▪ address ▪ care ▪ connection ▪ consignment ▪ executed ▪ expense ▪ giving ▪ good ▪ inconvenience ▪ packing ▪ placing ▪ regret ▪ return ▪ staff ▪ well

We very much __________[1] the errors which happened in __________[2] with your order. Normally our __________[3] department works very __________[4], but at this time of year we always have a lot of extra work, and obviously some of our temporary __________[5] didn't manage to pack your __________[6] properly.

We would be happy for you to __________[7] the wrong items at our __________[8] and have already arranged for the correct ones to be sent to your __________[9].

Please accept our apologies for this __________[10]. We hope it will not prevent you from __________[11] further orders with us, which will be __________[12] with more __________[13] than this one.

VOCABULARY

inconvenience – *Unannehmlichkeiten*; **by express freight** – *per Eilsendung*; **in connection with** – *im Zusammenhang mit*; **temporary staff** – *Aushilfspersonal*; **at our expense** – *auf unsere Kosten*

C KMK EXAM PRACTICE

1 Hörverstehen

24

Situation: Bei Denta Dental Clinic in Warschau ist eine Sendung mit Röntgengeräten von Global Medical eingetroffen. Die Geräte sind allerdings beschädigt, so dass Jerzy Adamczyk bei Global Medical anruft, um sich zu beschweren.

Aufgabe: Hören Sie sich das Telefongespräch an und füllen Sie die Tabelle aus.

1 Abteilung, die den Anruf entgegennimmt:	______
2 Art der Beschädigung:	Gerät 1: ______ Gerät 2: ______
3 Bestellnummer:	______
4 Art des Auftrags:	______
5 Letzte Beschwerde (wann?):	______
6 Grund der ersten Beschwerde:	______
7 Herr Adamczyks Telefonnummer:	______
8 Name von Frau Wolfs Vorgesetzter:	______

2 Leseverstehen

Situation: Kollegen in Ihrer Firma beklagen sich öfters über verärgerte Kunden und wissen nicht, wie sie mit ihnen umgehen sollen. Sie bilden mit zwei Ihrer Mitarbeiter eine Arbeitsgruppe, um den betroffenen Kollegen Tipps im Umgang mit verärgerten Kunden zu geben. Bei einer Betriebsversammlung berichten Sie von Ihren Ergebnissen.

Aufgabe: Lesen Sie sich den Text auf der nächsten Seite genau durch. Beantworten Sie die nachfolgenden Verständnisfragen stichpunktartig auf Deutsch.

1 Was „kosten" verärgerte Kunden die Firma?

______

2 Warum sind Probleme eigentlich gut fürs Geschäft?

______

3 Nennen Sie drei im Text erwähnten Gründe, warum ein Kunde verärgert sein kann.

______

4 Wie sollte man sich einem aufgebrachten Kunden gegenüber verhalten?

5 Was sollte man niemals tun?

6 Warum hilft es, leise zu sprechen?

7 Wie reagiert man, nachdem man die Situation verstanden hat?

8 Welcher Schritt sollte der Problemlösung immer folgen, und warum?

From angry complaints to five-star reviews: dealing with unhappy clients

Anyone working in a client-facing role knows that dealing with complaints is part of the job. But just because it's inevitable doesn't mean it's easy. In fact, many wholesale and retail workers list angry customers as their biggest source of work-related stress. And unresolved issues eat up a lot of time and resources that companies rarely have to spare. But there is an alternative. We've put together some tips to bring angry clients back from the brink – or even turn them into trusting regulars. After all, satisfactory problem-solving is a great way of nurturing customer loyalty – and you can't do that if there aren't any problems in the first place!

Tip 1: Put yourself in the customer's shoes. Though you're the professional on this occasion, you still know how it feels to receive wrong or damaged goods, be overcharged for an order or have issues with insurance. So listen carefully to what's happened and let the customer know that you understand why they are frustrated.

Tip 2: Stay calm. Even if the customer is very angry, remember that they are not attacking you personally but presenting an interesting challenge for you to solve. Wait for the customer to finish speaking – never interrupt! – and then respond in a soft and even tone. This encourages the customer to calm down and shows that you want to work with them, not against them.

Tip 3: Repeat the problem back to the customer. This will help ensure you've understood the problem correctly and also reassure the customer that they are being heard. But stick to the facts – blaming another person or department will only further diminish the customer's trust in your business.

Tip 4: Know your limits. If the issue falls outside your expertise, put the customer in touch with someone who can help – for example, by getting management involved. The customer will appreciate your self-awareness in knowing when it is time to escalate.

Tip 5: Take action. Listening and nodding is all very well, but what the customer really wants is for their problem to be solved. A quick fix isn't always possible, and that's OK. But you should still outline to the customer what steps you're going to take to resolve the issue, and then follow through.

Tip 6: Check in. Once the problem is resolved at your end, send a follow-up email or give the customer a call, to check that they are satisfied with the results. This demonstrates to the customer that you sincerely care about how they experience your company's service.

D IHK EXAM PRACTICE

1 Vermerk in Deutsch über ein Gespräch in Englisch

25

Situation: In dem folgenden Gespräch sind Sie Melissa Wolf von der Firma *Global Medical* in München. Heute ist der 15. September. Sie erhalten einen Anruf von einem Kunden in Polen.

Aufgabe: Verfolgen Sie das Gespräch und fertigen Sie anschließend eine Gesprächsnotiz auf Deutsch für Ihre Chefin, die Vertriebsleiterin Mia Richter, an. Während des Hörens dürfen Sie Notizen machen. Diese Notizen werden nicht bewertet, sondern nur die Gesprächsnotiz.

Melissa Wolf:	Jerzy Adamczyk:
Guten Morgen. Verkaufsabteilung. Melissa Wolf am Apparat.	...
Yes, of course. How can I help you?	...
Yes, this is the Sales Department. My name's Melissa Wolf.	...
It depends on what it's about. Could you give me some details?	...
Oh, I'm sorry to hear that. Could you give me the order number, please?	...
Just a moment, please. Right. I have it here.	...
Oh, dear. I'm extremely sorry to hear that you've had so much trouble. I'm sure my superior would like to discuss this with you. Can I ask her to phone you when she comes in to work tomorrow?	...
Yes. You'll get a call from my superior tomorrow, Mr Adamczyk.	...
It's Mia Richter.	...
You're welcome, Mr Adamczyk. Thank you for calling.	...

2 Vermerk in Deutsch über einen Geschäftsbrief in Englisch

Situation: Sie arbeiten als Auszubildender in der Qualitätsabteilung eines Glasunternehmens in Bodenmais, Bayern. Heute, am 22. Februar, erhalten Sie einen Brief von einem langjährigen französischen Kunden, Événements Merveilleux SARL, 33 Avenue du Sergent Maginot, 67082 Strasbourg Cédex, Frankreich.

Aufgabe: Verfassen Sie für Ihren Vorgesetzten, Herrn Fischer, eine Zusammenfassung des Inhalts des Briefes in deutscher Sprache (vollständige Sätze, keine wörtliche Übersetzung).

Dear Mr Fischer

I am writing with regard to our order no. CG25005 of 17 December 20.. for 300 champagne glasses.

The consignment of glasses arrived even later than you had promised. As you explained in your email of 21 December, a delay of 1-2 weeks was to be expected due to difficulties with your suppliers over the holiday period and we accepted that. The fact that our order eventually arrived 4 weeks behind schedule, however, is unacceptable.

Furthermore, on examining the consignment we found that in one box of 50 glasses, nearly every single glass was broken and those that were not had cracks. I have enclosed photos of the damaged goods in question and you will see that your logistics provider's delivery vehicle is also in the photos. This confirms the goods arrived damaged.

Regrettably, these two issues mean that our previously positive business relationship is now in question and any future relationship will depend on how these matters are dealt with. We expect you at the very least to supply us with replacements for the damaged and broken items free of charge and without delay.

Yours sincerely
Cécile Nexer

3 Sprachergänzungstest (Typ 2)

Aufgabe: In diesem Beschwerdebrief ist jeweils nur eine der unten vorgeschlagenen Formen korrekt. Bitte setzen Sie die richtige Lösung in die entsprechende Lücke ein.

_______________ [1] our order no. SB 7174

I am writing _______________ [2] our order no. SB 7174 of 28 March 20.. .

The _______________ [3] finally arrived _______________ [4] morning, one week later _______________ [5] agreed. _______________ [6], _______________ [7] we _______________ [8] the packing cases, we _______________ [9] that _______________ [10] contained 200 boxes of welding goggles _______________ [11] of the 250 boxes of safety goggles _______________ [12] we had ordered.

We are now _______________ [13] and have a large number of orders from customers _______________ [14] have to meet new safety regulations. Could you please look _______________ [15] this matter _______________ [16], as we need the safety goggles _______________ [17] and we are in danger of _______________ [18] important customers.

Whatever the _______________ [19] for the mistake, we must _______________ [20] you to _______________ [21] the replacement _______________ [22] an absolute _______________ [23] and to send it as _______________ [24] express shipment _______________ [25] your expense.

Please _______________ [26] today when we can expect _______________ [27] the correct goods and also what we should _______________ [28] with the _______________ [29] goods.

Yours _______________ [30]

1	Re, Asap, Attn	**16**	so forth, straight ahead, immediately
2	reference, regard, regarding	**17**	urging, urgently, urgent
3	containing, consigning, consignment	**18**	losing, to lose, lose
4	this, that, today	**19**	ground, reasons, fault
5	as, than, then	**20**	asking, ask, to ask
6	However, Nevertheless, Fortunately	**21**	do, make, take
7	if, when, then	**22**	deliver, delivering, delivery
8	are opening, open, opened	**23**	emergency, urgency, priority
9	find, are finding, found	**24**	the, a, an
10	she, it, they	**25**	at, of, to
11	except, place, instead	**26**	say something, let me inform, let me know
12	which, what, them	**27**	to receive, receipt, receiving
13	not in store, not available, out of stock	**28**	make, do, doing
14	where, they, who	**29**	false, mistaken, wrong
15	in, inside, into	**30**	faithful, sincere, sincerely

Useful phrases

Making complaints	
Description of the problem	
We regret to inform you that we are dissatisfied with the goods delivered.	*Leider müssen wir Ihnen mitteilen, dass wir mit der Lieferung nicht zufrieden sind.*
On examining the goods, we discovered that some articles were (badly) damaged.	*Bei Prüfung der Ware mussten wir feststellen, dass einige Artikel (stark) beschädigt sind.*
Request for explanation and consequences	
We would welcome your explanation of the damage.	*Wir würden eine Erklärung für den Schaden begrüßen.*
We are returning the damaged goods to you.	*Wir schicken die beschädigte Ware an Sie zurück.*
Request for action	
We must therefore insist that you …	*Wir müssen daher darauf bestehen, dass Sie …*
... as the goods are urgently needed.	*… da die Waren dringend benötigt werden.*
We must therefore ask you to supply us with replacements free of charge by return.	*Wir müssen Sie deshalb bitten, uns umgehend kostenlosen Ersatz zu liefern.*
Polite ending	
Our future business relationship will depend on how this matter is dealt with.	*Die Fortsetzung unserer Geschäftsbeziehung ist von der Regelung dieser Angelegenheit abhängig.*
We trust you will deal with this matter without delay.	*Wir vertrauen darauf, dass Sie sich unverzüglich mit dieser Angelegenheit befassen werden.*

Responding to complaints	
Acknowledgement and expression of regret	
We have (just) received your email regarding …	*Wir haben (soeben) Ihre E-Mail bezüglich … erhalten.*
We are sorry to hear the consignment was delayed and that some of the goods are below standard.	*Es tut uns leid zu hören, dass die Sendung verspätet eingetroffen ist und einige Waren nicht den Qualitätsanforderungen entsprechen.*
Action taken	
Since receiving your email, we have investigated the matter and found out / discovered that ...	*Nach Erhalt Ihrer E-Mail haben wir die Angelegenheit untersucht und herausgefunden, dass ...*
… the wrong component was used.	*... das falsche Bauteil benutzt wurde.*
… there was an error in the dispatch department.	*… es einen Fehler in unserer Versandabteilung gab.*
Solution	
We are sending you replacements at no extra charge.	*Wir schicken Ihnen umgehend kostenlosen Ersatz.*
If you are prepared to keep the …, we will grant you a reduction in price of …%.	*Wenn Sie sich bereiterklären, die … (Waren) zu behalten, gewähren wir Ihnen einen Rabatt von … %.*
Second apology and polite ending	
Please accept our apologies for the delay.	*Bitte entschuldigen Sie vielmals die Verzögerung.*
We assure you it will not happen again.	*Wir versichern Ihnen, dass dies nicht wieder vorkommen wird.*
We look forward to doing further business with you.	*Wir freuen uns darauf, weiterhin Geschäfte mit Ihnen zu tätigen.*

8 Dealing with payments and reminders

Every successful business needs a smooth cashflow to survive. In order to be able to pay its running costs, it needs reliable sources of money coming in. As customers, we need to be sure we receive the correct goods or services we ordered and that invoices are correct. As suppliers, we need our customers to pay us on time. Pointing out mistakes on invoices or asking for payment in a polite but firm manner is a delicate issue, but balance can be achieved.

A CHECKING A COMMERCIAL INVOICE

1 Julia Dahlmann receives an invoice for the rolls she ordered from China Canvas Company. She checks the invoice carefully and discovers some errors.

Compare the invoice to Sanyang GmbH's order on page 75 and find the mistakes.

China Canvas Company Limited
110 Linqing Rd. | 200245 Shanghai | China

Sanyang GmbH
Am Stern 18
85049 Ingolstadt
GERMANY

Shanghai, 18.07.20..

COMMERCIAL INVOICE NO.: 210915421

Purchase Order: BK 42		**Date:** 04.07.20..	**Client no.** 0365	
Item	**Quantity**	**Description**	**Unit Price ($)**	**Total Price ($)**
BL 246	55	Banner material	50.00	2,750.00
			Total	2,750.00

Two thousand, seven hundred and fifty United States dollars only

Terms of payment: 50 % in advance, 50 % after completion
Terms of delivery: FAS Port of Shanghai
Packing: Container
Name of bank: Bank of China, 600-618 Yan'an East Road, 200244 Shanghai, China
Account number: 0918-0-311076

Notes: We have received your advance payment. Thank you. Please note that the outstanding balance is due once the goods have been delivered to Port of Shanghai.

Title to the aforementioned goods shall remain vested in China Canvas Company Ltd. until the purchase price for said goods has been paid in full and received by China Canvas Company Ltd.

Best regards,

Michael Wong
Export Dept.

This is an electronically generated invoice, hence does not require signature.

VOCABULARY

running costs – *Betriebskosten*; **reliable** – *zuverlässig*; **outstanding balance** – *ausstehender Betrag, Restforderung*; **the title to sth is vested in sb** – *etw ist Eigentum von jdm*; **aforementioned** – *(vorstehend) genannt*; **electronically generated** – *elektronisch erzeugt*; **hence** – *daher, deshalb*

2 English does not have a formal style of address like languages such as German, French and Spanish do. That means when English speakers need to say something negative, they use a more indirect style so the other person does not lose face.
Read the statements below and decide if they are direct (D) or indirect (I).

1 I am afraid you made some mistakes.		6 The delivery and payment terms are obviously wrong, too.	
2 It seems the quantity in the invoice is not correct.		7 We want a corrected invoice as soon as possible.	
3 I am afraid some mistakes have been made.		8 We would appreciate it if you could send us a corrected invoice without delay.	
4 The quantity in the invoice is wrong.		9 Inaccurate billing such as this is not acceptable.	
5 An error also appears to have been made with the payment and delivery terms.		10 It would be unfortunate if such mistakes were to happen again.	

3 **Use your answers to exercise 2 to complete Julia's email to her supplier, China Canvas Company Limited.**

From: julia.dahlmann@sanyang.dex
To: sales@ccc_shanghai.ci
Subject: Order BK42, Invoice no. 210915421

Dear Sir or Madam,

We received your invoice no. 210915421 for order BK42. However, after checking it against our records, ______________________[1]. Namely:

- ______________________[2]. We ordered 50 items, not 55.
- ______________________[3]. As per our communication with Mr Andy Gao, payment was 30 % in advance, 70 % after completion. Delivery terms were also FOB Port of Shanghai, not FAS.

______________________[4]. Until now, we have had a positive business relationship with China Canvas Company Limited and ______________________[5].

Yours sincerely,

Julia Dahlmann

Import Department

VOCABULARY

to lose face – *das Gesicht verlieren*; **to appreciate sth** – *etw schätzen*; **without delay** – *unverzüglich*; **inaccurate** – *fehlerhaft*; **billing** – *Abrechnung, Rechnungserstellung*

B DEALING WITH LATE PAYMENTS

1 **Complete the grey boxes with the missing translations. You have been given some letters of the missing words.**

German	English	German	English
Mahnung	r________	*fällig sein*	book
ü ________	(to) remit	*überfällig*	o________
u______ ______	(to) escape notice	*offenstehend*	o________
Saldo	b________	o________	above-mentioned

2 Joe Li works in the Accounting Department of Guangzhou Materials Ltd. in China. A German client, TT Autobeschriftung GmbH, should have paid the remaining 70% of the price for an order it placed in January. Joe understands that everyone can make mistakes, so he writes a short but friendly email to the client.

Complete his email with words from exercise 1. Pay attention to the form of the verbs.

Subject: Invoice no. VF251-01 for $2,450.00 dated 30 January, 20.. .

Dear Ms Winster

It has most likely __________[1] your __________[2] that payment of the __________[3] __________[4] of the __________[5] invoice __________[6] __________[7] on 7 March, 20.. .

We look forward to receiving the __________[8] sum in the next few days. If it has already been __________[9], please kindly ignore this __________[10].

Yours sincerely

Joe Li

Accounting Department

Guangzhou Materials Ltd

3 In exercise 2, a friendly reminder was all the customer needed. In other cases, a second reminder and even a third and final warning may be needed. Each step is stronger in tone and the final reminder often says what consequences will follow if payment is not made.
Complete these sentences which are taken from second and third (or final) reminder letters with the correct words from the box.

refer to ▪ regret to note ▪ to charge ▪ set a final deadline ▪ will be remitting ▪ will result in ▪ would welcome

1 As we have received neither an explanation nor a remittance, we must ______ for payment of seven days.

2 We ______ that the above-mentioned invoice remains unpaid despite our email/letter dated ... .

3 We ______ an explanation as to why the payment has not been made but, whatever the case may be, we request that you pay without any further delay.

4 We ______ our two previous letters/emails, dated ... and ..., and the invoice which is still overdue.

5 Failure to settle the outstanding payment ______ our taking the necessary steps, up to and including legal action, to recover the amount owed.

6 We trust you ______ the amount in question in the next few days.

7 We are left with no choice but ______ you a late fee and interest due to the unacceptable delay.

4 **Now decide whether the sentences in exercise 3 belong to a second reminder letter or a final reminder.**

5 Sie arbeiten als Auszubildender in der Buchhaltung der Wir Fahren Gut GmbH, einem deutschen Logistikdienstleister in Hamburg mit Sitz in der Elbchaussee 498, 22588 Hamburg. Frau Ines Steven, Leiterin der Buchhaltung, bittet Sie, unter ihrem Namen ein zweites Mahnschreiben in englischer Sprache an einen irischen Kunden, Foyle Foods, Donore Road Industrial Estate, Donore Road, Drogheda, Irland, zu schreiben.

Schreiben Sie die zweite Mahnung. Heute ist die 4 Oktober. Verwenden Sie ein Standard-Layout für Geschäftsbriefe. Schreiben Sie höflich, aber bestimmt. Erwähnen Sie in Ihrem Brief die folgenden Punkte:

- Der Kunde hätte die Rechnung Nr. 21-1549 in Höhe von 10.454,00 € am 21. September bezahlen sollen.
- Am 25. September wurde eine Erinnerungs-Mail an den Kunden gesandt; leider gab es darauf keine Reaktion.
- Der Kunde möchte bitte darlegen, weshalb die Zahlung nicht fristgerecht erfolgt ist; auf jeden Fall muss die Zahlung ohne weitere Verzögerung erfolgen.
- Sie vertrauen darauf, dass die ausstehende Summe in den nächsten Tagen gezahlt wird.

VOCABULARY

to regret sth – *etw bedauern*; **to set a final deadline** – *eine endgültige Frist setzen*; **to remit** - *(Geld) überweisen*; **to result in sth** – *zu etw führen*; **remittance** – *Überweisung*; **despite** – *trotz*; **failure to settle a payment** – *Nichtzahlung, Ausbleiben einer Zahlung*; **legal action** – *rechtliche Schritte*; **to recover sth** – *(Schulden) einbringen, zurückerlangen*; **interest** – *Zinsen*

C KMK EXAM PRACTICE

1 Mediation

Situation: During your term at business school in the UK, your teacher asks the class to look for interesting articles about the business/client relationship which you should summarize for a lesson next week. You have found an article about encouraging clients to pay invoices promptly.

Aufgabe: Write a short summary of the article in English to read to the class. Include:

- the theme of the article
- summarize the article into five recommendations and the reasons behind them

Ein gutes Verhältnis zu Ihren Kunden ist der Schlüssel für jede erfolgreiche und langanhaltende Geschäftsbeziehung. Wie bei jeder Beziehung geht es um Respekt und gegenseitiges Vertrauen - beides muss aufgebaut werden, und das passiert nicht von alleine. Wenn Sie sich dem Kunden gegenüber Mühe geben, werden diese die Geschäftsbeziehung zu Ihnen wertschätzen und folglich nichts tun, was diese beschädigen könnte - etwa durch verspätete Zahlungen.

Auch wenn Ihre Kunden längere Zahlungsfristen lieber sähen, sollten Sie im Interesse Ihres Unternehmens versuchen, den Zeitrahmen kurz zu halten. Ein einfaches Mittel ist es, den Kunden um eine Anzahlung im Voraus bitten. Sehr wirkungsvoll ist auch, die Bezahlung an konkrete Phasen der Auftragsabwicklung zu binden: 25 % bei Bestellung, 25 % bei Versand und 50 % bei Lieferung. So ist besonders bei längerfristigen Projekten und Geschäftsvorgängen ein konstanter Geldzufluss gewährleistet.

Die Einräumung eines Rabatts für frühe oder pünktliche Zahlungen ist eine lohnende Investition. Pünktliche und frühzeitige Zahlungen seitens Ihrer Kunden helfen Ihnen, Ihre Buchhaltung korrekt zu führen, und der Rabatt ermutigt die Kunden, ihre ausstehenden Rechnungen nicht länger aufzuschieben. Bieten Sie einen Rabatt an, der großzügig, aber geschäftlich sinnvoll ist, z. B. 2 oder 3 %. Stellen Sie sicher, dass dieser Anreiz auf der Rechnung deutlich ins Auge fällt (etwa durch Fettdruck). Es wird Sie überraschen, wie bereitwillig Kunden zahlen, wenn für sie damit eine Ersparnis verbunden ist!

Die Erweiterung der Liste der Zahlungsarten ist eine weitere Möglichkeit, Ihre Kunden zu schneller Zahlung zu animieren. Neben dem traditionellen Weg der Banküberweisung sind Kreditkarten für jedes Unternehmen längst ein Muss. Zusätzlich dazu sollten Sie darüber nachdenken, PayPal-Zahlungen und vielleicht sogar Kryptowährungen wie Bitcoin zu akzeptieren. Hierzu sollten Sie zuvor allerdings sorgfältig recherchieren.

Nun ist es gerade bei Inhabern kleiner und mittlerer Unternehmen, die sich meist persönlich auch um kleinere Vorgänge in ihrer Firma kümmern, keine Seltenheit, dass eine Rechnung auf ihrer To-Do-Liste ganz nach unten rutscht. In diesen und ähnlichen Fällen - ganz besonders natürlich bei chronischen Spätzahlern - ist für Ihr Unternehmen ein CRM-System (Customer Relationship Management) praktisch und sinnvoll. Dieses kann in Ihr geschäftliches E-Mail-System integriert werden und versendet automatisch Zahlungserinnerungen an säumige Kunden.

2 Produktion

Situation: Sie arbeiten in der Abteilung Buchhaltung bei MegaKauf Großhandel GmbH, Oberkasseler Str. 200, 40545 Düsseldorf. Sie haben einige Fehler in einer vierteljährlichen Abrechnung gefunden, die von einem Lieferanten, Winter Gear Ltd, 222 Grampian Road, Aviemore PH22 1RH, Großbritannien, gesendet wurde.

Aufgabe: Schreiben Sie im Namen von Hannah Schmidt, der Einkaufsleiterin bei Megakauf, einen Brief, in dem Sie auf die Unstimmigkeiten hinweisen und um eine geänderte Quartalsabrechnung bitten. Folgende Angaben sind wichtig:

- Datum: 5. April 20..
- Ansprechpartnerin: Ms Sheena Murray (E-Mail: s.murray@wintergear.org), Accounts Director
- Bezug auf Abrechnung Nr. GBST/375 vom 2. April 20.. über 31.550,00 €
- falscher Nachlass bei Positionen 1 und 2 für Skischuhe, nur 15 % statt der vereinbarten 50 %
- Gutschrift Nr. RBM/6 vom ... (15. des vergangenen Monats) über 185,00 € nicht berücksichtigt
- falsch berechnete Abrechnung liegt bei
- Bitte um berichtigte Abrechnung über 25.065,00 €
- Überweisung des entsprechenden Betrags nach Erhalt der korrigierten Abrechnung
- höfliche Schlussformel

3 Produktion

Situation: Sie arbeiten als Auszubildender in der Buchhaltung der Wir Fahren Gut GmbH, einem deutschen Logistikdienstleister in Hamburg. Frau Ines Steven, Leiterin der Buchhaltung, bittet Sie, eine Antwort auf eine E-Mail zu schreiben, die ein irischer Kunde, Foyle Foods, gestern, am 9. Oktober, geschickt hat. Sie war die Antwort auf ein zweites Mahnschreiben, das am 4. Oktober verschickt wurde.

Aufgabe: Schreiben Sie eine dritte und letzte Zahlungsaufforderung. Achten Sie in Ihrer Antwort auf die folgenden Punkte:

- Betreff: Rechnung Nr. 21-1549, fällig am 21. September
- Danken Sie dem Kunden für die E-Mail und die Darlegung der Gründe für den Zahlungsverzug, aber stellen Sie fest, dass der ausstehende Betrag von 10.454,00€ nunmehr seit drei Wochen überfällig ist.
- Ihre Firma kann keine weitere Verzögerung akzeptieren und muss eine endgültige Zahlungsfrist von sieben Tagen setzen.
- Außerdem muss aufgrund der unzumutbaren Verzögerung ein Säumniszuschlag in Höhe von 200 € auf den Betrag aufgeschlagen werden.
- Weisen Sie darauf hin, dass Ihre Firma bei Nichtbegleichung des überfälligen Betrags und des Säumniszuschlags die notwendigen Maßnahmen zur Eintreibung des Betrags ergreifen wird, bis hin zu rechtlichen Schritten.

D IHK EXAM PRACTICE

1 Vermerk in Deutsch über einen Geschäftsbrief in Englisch

Situation: Sie machen ein Praktikum bei der Garden Gekko GmbH, einem deutschen Händler für Gartengeräte und -möbel. Diese Woche sind Sie in der Buchhaltung tätig. Da Peter Konrad, der sich normalerweise um die Lieferanten im englischsprachigen Raum kümmert, seit Januar krank ist, bittet Ihr Vorgesetzter Sie, sich um die liegengebliebene Korrespondenz zu kümmern. Sie entdecken einen wichtigen Brief eines irischen Lieferanten.

Aufgabe: Fassen Sie die wesentlichen Inhaltes des Schreibens in deutscher Sprache zusammen. Verwenden Sie hierfür vollständige Sätze (keine Übersetzung). Achten Sie darauf, dass Sie alle die angegebenen relevanten Details (Firmenname, Datum usw.) korrekt wiedergeben.

Green Isle Gardens Limited
17 Station Road | Newbridge | County Kildare | Ireland

27 February 20..

Peter Konrad
Garten Gekko GmbH
Richthofener Str. 400
40699 Erkrath
GERMANY

Dear Mr Konrad

Invoice no. GIG-45129 for €9,995.00 dated 15 Jan 20..

It is most unfortunate that we must write to you again on the subject of the above-mentioned invoice, which has now been overdue for four weeks, given that a reminder was sent on 2 February by email and an additional reminder was issued by us on the tenth of this month.

As we have received neither an explanation nor a remittance, we have no choice but to set a final deadline for payment of 10 working days. We must also apply a late payment penalty of €526, which was the 5% discount on your original order offered by us for payment within 7 days.

If we have not received payment of the outstanding sum of €10,521 by 9 March 20.., we will suspend your firm's account with us and take the necessary steps to recover the sum owing, including possible legal action.

Please attend to this matter with urgency.

Yours sincerely

Emily O'Connor

Head of Accounts

2 Geschäftsbrief in Englisch nach Stichwortangaben in Deutsch

Situation: Sie arbeiten in der Abteilung Buchhaltung bei MegaKauf Großhandel GmbH, Oberkasseler Str. 200, 40545 Düsseldorf. Sie haben einige Fehler in einer vierteljährlichen Abrechnung gefunden, die von einem Lieferanten, Winter Gear Ltd, 222 Grampian Road, Aviemore PH22 1RH, Großbritannien, gesendet wurde. Das Datum ist 5. April 20..

Aufgabe: Schreiben Sie im Namen von Hannah Schmidt, der Einkaufsleiterin bei Megakauf, einen Brief, in dem Sie auf die Unstimmigkeiten hinweisen und um eine geänderte Quartalsabrechnung bitten. Beachten Sie alle für das Verfassen von Geschäftsbriefen wichtigen Details (korrektes Brieflayout, korrekte Absender- und Empfängeradresse usw.). Folgende Punkte sollen Sie berücksichtigen:

- Ansprechpartnerin: Ms Sheena Murray (E-Mail: s.murray@wintergear.nex), Accounts Director
- Bezug auf Abrechnung Nr. GBST/375 vom 2. April 20.. über 31.550,00 €
- falscher Nachlass bei Positionen 1 und 2 für Skischuhe, nur 15 % statt der versprochenen 50 %
- Gutschrift Nr. RBM/6 vom … (15. des vergangenen Monats) über 185,00 € nicht berücksichtigt
- falsch berechnete Abrechnung liegt bei
- Bitte um berichtigte Abrechnung über 25.065,00 €
- Überweisung des entsprechenden Betrags nach Erhalt der korrigierten Abrechnung
- höfliche Schlussformel

3 Kurzgefasste Mitteilung in Englisch

Situation: Sie arbeiten als Auszubildender in der Buchhaltung der Wir Fahren Gut GmbH, einem deutschen Logistikdienstleister in Hamburg. Frau Ines Steven, Leiterin der Buchhaltung, bittet Sie, eine E-Mail zu lesen, die ein irischer Kunde, Foyle Foods, gestern, am 9. Oktober, geschickt hat. Sie war die Antwort auf ein zweites Mahnschreiben, das am 4. Oktober verschickt wurde.

Aufgabe: Lesen Sie die E-Mail des Kunden und schreiben Sie eine Antwort in Form einer E-Mail. In Form und Tonfall soll es eine dritte und letzte Zahlungsaufforderung sein. Achten Sie darauf, alle wichtigen Details (E-Mail-Adresse, Datum, Betreff usw.) korrekt anzugeben.
Achten Sie in Ihrer Antwort auf die folgenden Punkte:

- Betreff: Rechnung Nr. 21-1549 fällig am 21. September
- Danken Sie dem Kunden für die E-Mail und die Darlegung der Gründe für den Zahlungsverzug, aber stellen Sie fest, dass der ausstehende Betrag von 10.454,00€ nunmehr seit drei Wochen überfällig ist.
- Ihre Firma kann keine weitere Verzögerung akzeptieren und muss eine endgültige Zahlungsfrist von sieben Tagen setzen.
- Außerdem muss aufgrund der unzumutbaren Verzögerung ein Säumniszuschlag in Höhe von 200 € auf den Betrag aufgeschlagen werden.
- Weisen Sie darauf hin, dass Ihre Firma bei Nichtbegleichung des überfälligen Betrags und des Säumniszuschlags die notwendigen Maßnahmen zur Eintreibung des Betrags ergreifen wird, bis hin zu rechtlichen Schritten.

From: seanduignan@foyle.ei
To: accounts@wfg.dex
Subject: Your letter recvd 8 October re: Invoice No.21-1549

Dear Ms Steven

Thank you for your letter which we received yesterday. Unfortunately, due to IT problems in the last week of September, your reminder email was neither received or read. Please accept our sincere apologies for that.

With reference to your invoice no. 21-1549, we fully accept that we are late in settling. Due to circumstances beyond our control, namely the insolvency of one of our largest customers, we are currently experiencing serious cashflow issues. Please rest assured that we are doing our best to address these issues and fully expect to be in a position to remit the overdue balance soon.

We appreciate and thank you for your patience in this matter and assure you that we value our longstanding business relationship.

Yours sincerely
Sean Duignan

Useful phrases

Querying invoices	
We refer to your/our statement / invoice no. … dated … for … (amount).	*Wir beziehen uns auf Ihre/unsere (Ab)Rechnung Nr. … vom … über … (Betrag).*
Having checked your statement/invoice against our (own) records, we must point out that it is incorrect in the following points:	*Nachdem wir Ihre (Ab)Rechnung mit unseren (eigenen) Aufzeichnungen verglichen haben, müssen wir darauf hinweisen, dass sie in folgenden Punkten nicht korrekt ist:*
… you have not included our credit note no. XYZ123 for €200 dated 10 August.	*… Sie unsere Gutschrift Nr. XYZ123 über € 200 vom 10. August … nicht berücksichtigt haben.*
… items 1 and 2 of your statement have been incorrectly charged.	*… die Posten 1 und 2 Ihres Kontoauszugs nicht richtig belastet worden sind.*
… you have omitted to include the quantity/special discount of …% granted on orders for 100 units or more.	*… Sie haben versäumt, den Mengen-/Sonderrabatt von … %, der für Aufträge über 100 Stück oder mehr gewährt wird, einzubeziehen.*
… the (special) discount granted on items 1 and 2 for … (e.g. skiing boots) is only 15% instead of 50%, as promised.	*… der auf den Posten … / die Posten … und … gewährte (Sonder)Rabatt für … (z. B. Skischuhe) nur 15 % beträgt statt wie versprochen 50 %.*
… you have overcharged/undercharged us by (a total of) €200.	*… Sie uns (insgesamt) € 200 zu viel / zu wenig berechnet haben.*
We are returning your statement/invoice and would request you to send us an amended statement/ invoice.	*Wir schicken Ihnen Ihre (Ab)Rechnung zurück und bitten Sie, uns eine berichtigte (Ab)Rechnung zu schicken.*
As soon as we have received your amended statement/invoice we will remit the sum owing.	*Sobald wir Ihre berichtigte (Ab)Rechnung erhalten haben, werden wir Ihnen den geschuldeten Betrag überweisen.*

Writing reminders	
I am writing in connection with the attached unpaid invoice for …	*Ich schreibe in Zusammenhang mit der angefügten unbezahlten Rechnung für …*
I would like to draw your attention to invoice no. …	*Bitte sehen Sie sich Rechnung Nr. … noch einmal an.*
We are sure this must be an oversight and have included a copy of the invoice for your convenience.	*Wir sind uns sicher, dass es sich hierbei um einen Irrtum handelt, und fügen zu Ihrer Information eine Kopie der Rechnung bei.*
Would you please settle your account by the end of the month at the latest.	*Bitte begleichen Sie die Rechnung bis spätestens zu Ende des Monats.*
If your payment of our invoice has crossed with this letter, we kindly ask you to ignore this reminder.	*Falls Sie die Rechnung schon beglichen haben sollten, betrachten Sie dieses Schreiben bitte als gegenstandslos.*
Payment is now … (length of time) overdue.	*Ihre Zahlung is nun … (Zeitspanne) überfällig.*
If we have not received your payment within the next seven days, we will have to instruct our solicitors to take legal action.	*Wenn wir Ihre Zahlung nicht innerhalb der nächsten sieben Tage erhalten, werden wir unseren Anwalt hinzuziehen, um rechtliche Schritte einzuleiten.*

1 Hörverstehen

Teil 1
26

Situation: Das Betriebsklima in Ihrer Firma hat sich in letzter Zeit spürbar verschlechtert. Sie wollen das heikle Thema im Betriebsrat ansprechen und mit Ihren Kollegen erörtern, wie man das Betriebsklima verbessern könnte. Zuvor möchten Sie sich darüber informieren, wie mit dem Thema in anderen Ländern umgegangen wird. Bei Ihrer Recherche im Internet stoßen Sie auf einen interessanten Podcast, über den Sie in der nächsten Betriebsratssitzung referieren möchten.

Aufgabe: Hören Sie sich den Podcast zweimal an und beantworten Sie dann die Verständnisfragen in Stichworten auf Deutsch.

1 Welche Erfahrungen hat Lewis bei seinem ersten Job gemacht? Nennen Sie drei Aspekte.

____

2 Welche zwei Möglichkeiten gibt es, wenn man sich in seinem Job langweilt?

____

3 Welche Eigenschaften machen einen Chef zu einem schrecklichen Chef?

____

4 Welchen Rat gibt Lewis, wenn man einen solchen Chef hat?

____

5 Wie kann man die Monotonie durchbrechen? Nennen Sie drei Beispiele.

____

Teil 2
27

Situation: Sie sind von der Mittagspause zurück und hören Ihren Anrufbeantworter ab: Ein Anrufer aus Argentinien hat Ihnen eine Nachricht hinterlassen.

Aufgabe: Hören Sie sich die Nachricht zweimal an und tragen Sie die Angaben in das Formular ein.

Anrufer	
Grund des Anrufs	
Inhalt des Anrufs	
E-Mail-Adresse	

2 Leseverstehen

Situation: Einer Ihrer Schwesterfirmen in Amerika geht es schlecht. Sie kennen dort ein paar junge Kolleginnen und Kollegen und machen sich große Sorgen, was aus Ihnen wird. Sie haben viel von Rettungspaketen seitens der Regierung gehört. Sie wollen mehr wissen und stoßen bei einer Internetrecherche auf einen interessanten Artikel.

Aufgabe: Lesen Sie den Text genau durch. Beantworten Sie die nachfolgenden Verständnisfragen in Stichworten auf Deutsch.

1 In welchen beiden Bereichen ist Nkechi Ikande Expertin?

___

2 Nennen Sie die wichtigste Funktion, die die Regierung in einer freien Marktwirtschaft hat.

___

3 Wann muss die Regierung eingreifen?

___

4 Zählen Sie auf, wer alles bei einer Firmenpleite betroffen ist.

___

5 Wie kann ein großer finanzieller Verlust vermieden werden?

___

6 In welchen Bereichen sind Firmenpleiten besonders schlimm? Nennen Sie ein Beispiel.

___

7 Wer ist bei solchen Pleiten besonders betroffen?

___

8 Welche Bedingungen müssen erfüllt sein, bevor die Regierung einschreiten kann? Nennen Sie zwei.

___

Time to intervene?

Nkechi Ikande is a team lead for marketing and strategy at a New York consultancy firm that specializes in financial relations between government and private business.

On first thoughts, many people believe it is not the government's place to intervene in a private business, even one that is close to bankruptcy. But, in a free-market society, any government's biggest responsibility is to protect the interests of its citizens. If a company's financial struggles pose a threat to the general public, the government has to step in.

When a company fails, many people are affected: most obviously, its customers and employees. That might already be over 100,000 people. But while disastrous for those individuals, and even the city or region where the company is based, these numbers will not be felt on the national level. So why intervene? Well, remember that investors will also be affected, who put not only their own assets, but also those of others, on the line. Suddenly, corporate collapse could affect over a million people around the world. In such situations, the government must carefully weigh up the costs and benefits of intervening. Handled well, a local investment of one to five billion dollars may prevent the global loss of 100 times as much.

And what about companies that provide important services, like electricity, water supply, or healthcare? If they go bankrupt, everyone is affected, with the most powerless members of society being hit the hardest. For a government to allow these companies to fail would be morally unacceptable: it would mean disregarding the welfare of the very people it is supposed to protect.

But there are some checks and balances in place to ensure that government intervention does not happen prematurely. Governments will only get involved if the company has already taken steps to improve its financial situation and those steps have not worked. This ensures that private companies remain private for as long as possible before the state intervenes to prevent a financial catastrophe.

3 Produktion

Situation: In Ihren Aufgabenbereich in der Firma fällt die Materialverwaltung. Sie haben den Lieferschein Ihrer letzten Bestellung in der Hand und stellen fest, dass da einiges schiefgelaufen ist:

Bestellt	Geliefert
10.000 Blatt Kopierpapier	1000 Blatt Kopierpapier
50 Klebestifte	100 Klebestifte
20 Rollen Klebeband	kein Klebeband
20 Sets Whiteboard-Stifte	20 Sets Folienstifte
10 DIN-A4-Ordner groß	10 DIN-A4-Ordner klein

Aufgabe: Schreiben Sie eine E-Mail auf Englisch mit folgendem Inhalt und achten Sie auf die korrekte Form (Anrede, Betreff, Schlussformel). Schreiben Sie vollständige Sätze.

- Beschreiben Sie die Situation.
- Führen Sie sämtliche Mängel auf (siehe Tabelle).
- Zeigen Sie sich verärgert. Sie sind immerhin ein guter Kunde.
- Bitten Sie, das fehlende Material schnellstmöglich zuzusenden.
- Bitten Sie um einen kostenfreien Retourenaufkleber, damit Sie die überzählige oder falsch gelieferte Ware zurückschicken können.
- Fragen Sie nach einem Rabatt wegen der Unannehmlichkeiten.
- Machen Sie ein wenig Druck, indem Sie durchklingen lassen, dass Sie sich anderweitig orientieren werden, wenn diese Probleme öfters auftreten.

4 Mediation

Situation: Sie wollen Ihre organisatorischen Fähigkeiten in puncto Konferenzen verbessern. Im Internet haben Sie dazu einen Artikel gefunden. Sie möchten sich das Wichtigste auf einen kleinen Zettel schreiben und an Ihren Computerbildschirm kleben. Ihre Kollegin sieht Sie beim Lesen und findet, dass Ihre Erkenntnisse eine große Hilfe für das ganze Planungsteam sein könnten. Sie bittet Sie, doch eine etwas genauere Zusammenfassung des Artikels zu erstellen.

Aufgabe: Lesen Sie den Text genau durch und erstellen Sie auf Deutsch ein Infoblatt in Listenform mit Tipps zum perfekten Organisieren eines Meetings.

How to organize the perfect business conference

You've heard it a million times before: the secret to organizing a successful business conference lies in good planning and logistics. But what does that actually look like? We've put together our own top tips for organizing a productive business meeting.

1. **Location, location, location.** You need to factor in travel time for your attendees and ensure you are not making unreasonable demands. People don't want to spend hours travelling to and from a conference that only lasts an afternoon.
2. **Pick the perfect venue.** The number of people you are inviting determines the space and facilities you will need – but the themes or form of the conference may also play a role.
3. **Time it right.** Sending out your invitations at the correct time is essential, but what is 'correct' can vary. Your own colleagues will be grateful to receive informal notice well in advance, so they can 'save the date' until you follow up with a formal invitation. But people from other companies or organizations are unlikely to commit to attending until shortly before the event – they might even forget about it! So wait a while before inviting them.
4. **Make use of online platforms.** There are many online systems that can save you time and effort. For example, you can direct your invitees to a web-based registration system, where they can register for the event simply by entering their details. Some services even tie in accommodation and travel arrangements at this stage, which can make your life and your guests' lives much easier.
5. **Money matters.** Be transparent about what is included in the conference fee. For example, will complementary food and drink be available, or will guests have to pay their own way? Even if these questions are awkward, make sure you answer them, or you might end up in an even stickier situation.
6. **Plan out your time.** After dealing with the pre-conference logistics, it's time to plan the conference itself. Organize a strict but realistic time plan, with enough time built in for unexpected happenings or extra questions from your guests.
7. **Smarten up!** Appropriate attire is a must for making a good impression in the corporate world – it can even be important in advancing your career – so make sure you are well-presented.
8. **Send round the minutes.** That's it, your conference was a success! Congratulations. But before you put your feet up, collate all the findings from the conference in either a printed or electronic format and forward them on to your attendees for future reference.

A Geschäftsbrief in Englisch nach Stichwortangaben in Deutsch

Bearbeitungszeit: 45 Minuten

Situation: Sie machen ein Praktikum bei einer internationalen Spedition: Speedy GmbH, Karolingerstraße 56, 85059 Ingolstadt. Das Auftragsvolumen der Firma wächst und in Kürze müssen mehrere Mitarbeiter im Home-Office am Firmen-Laptops arbeiten. Der Leiter der Einkaufsabteilung bittet Sie, ein Angebot von einem irischen Anbieter von Computerhardware, Pete's PCs, Ballycoolin Industrial Estate, Dublin 15, Irland, einzuholen.

Aufgabe: Erstellen Sie für den Leiter der Einkaufsabteilung, Herrn Peter Schmeichel, ein unterschriftsfertiges Schreiben an den irischen Anbieter. Achten Sie auf die korrekte Form (Brieflayout, heutiges Datum, Absender- und Empfängeradresse usw.). Berücksichtigen Sie die folgenden Punkte:

- angemessene Anrede
- eigene Firma kurz vorstellen
- im Internet auf die interessante Preise der irische Firma aufmerksam geworden
- Vorhaben, zehn Laptops für Mitarbeiter/innen im Home-Office anzuschaffen
- Anforderungen an das Produkt:
  - 13 Zoll-Bildschirm (13-inch screen)
  - Gewicht nicht mehr als 1,5 kg
- dringender Bedarf: Lieferzeit maximal zwei Wochen nach Auftragserteilung
- um die Zusendung von Produktinformation bitten
- Preisliste zusammen mit eventuellen Mengenrabatten/Sonderangebote anfordern
- Lieferungs- und Zahlungsbedingungen
- zweite Bestellung möglich
- freundlicher Schluss
- Schlussformel

B Kurzgefasste Mitteilung in Englisch

Bearbeitungszeit: 30 Minuten

Situation: Sie arbeiten in der internationalen Vertriebsabteilung der Gesund und Munter GmbH, einem deutschen Vertrieb für Medizingeräte mit Sitz in Frankfurt am Main. Ihre Vorgesetzte, Frau Anna Pollack, erhält eine E-Mail-Anfrage von einem irischen Krankenhaus.

Aufgabe: Verfassen Sie unter dem Namen von Frau Pollack eine kurze, aber höfliche E-Mail-Antwort auf die Anfrage. Achten Sie darauf, dass die untenstehenden Informationen, die sie Ihnen gegeben hat, enthalten sind, und achten Sie auf die korrekte Form (E-Mail-Addresse, Datum, Betreff usw.).

- dem Kunden für die Anfrage danken
- bedanken Sie sich für das Interesse an Ihren Produkten: der E-Chair BP075 ist eine gute Wahl, da es sich um ein hochmodernes Produkt handelt, das sich durch Zuverlässigkeit, Komfort und Sicherheit auszeichnet
- bestätigen, dass Produkt- und Preisangaben aktuell sind
- nennen Sie Liefer- und Zahlungsbedingungen:
  - Lieferung - DAP Dublin
  - Zahlung - 33 % bei Bestellung, 67 % bei Lieferung
- Lieferzeit: drei Wochen nach Auftragseingang
- aktuelle Preisliste und Katalog wie gewünscht beifügen
- hoffen, dass Sie bald von Frau O'Meara hören werden

From: helenom@dubhs.nex
To: int_sales@gesundum.dex
Subject: Enquiry about battery-powered wheelchairs (item no. BP075)

Dear Sir/Madam,

I work in the purchasing department of Dundrum Hospital, situated in Dublin, Ireland.

We currently require ten electric wheelchairs and are interested in the E-Chair BP075 (battery-powered wheelchair) as advertised on your website. As we are considering models from a range of suppliers, some additional information would be very helpful to us in making our decision, namely:

- Is the unit price (€2,320 per unit) as featured on your website up to date?
- What are your terms payment and delivery?
- How long will delivery take?
- Do you offer any quantity discount?

We would also appreciate a copy of your latest catalogue and price list.

Best regards,

Helen O'Meara
Purchasing Officer

Dundrum Hospital
Eastern Health Service
Donegal Road
Dublin 16
DN65 7EC
Ireland

C Vermerk in Deutsch über ein Gespräch in Englisch

28 **Bearbeitungszeit:** 20 Minuten (ausschließlich Aufgabendarbietung)

Situation: Im Rahmen Ihrer Ausbildung verbringen Sie einen Tag in der Münchner Niederlassung von *Hermes Freight Forwarding*, einem großen europäischen Logistikdienstleister. Sie sitzen mit Brendan Mathers, Recruitment Manager in der Personalabteilung, zusammen. Herr Mathers arbeitet normalerweise in England, aber diese Woche ist er in der Münchner Niederlassung. Er versucht gerade, eine freie Stelle als Export Clerk zu besetzen. Im Rahmen der Bewerberauswahl ruft er einen Bewerber aus Nürnberg, Martin Spielberg, an.

Aufgabe: Verfolgen Sie das Gespräch und fertigen Sie anschließend die untenstehende Gesprächsnotiz auf Deutsch für Herrn Mathers' deutschen Kollegen im Münchner Büro aus. Sie werden das Gespräch zweimal hören und dürfen sich währenddessen Notizen machen. Diese Notizen werden nicht bewertet, sondern nur die Gesprächsnotiz. Achten Sie darauf, dass Sie alle angegebenen Details (Firmenname, Datum usw.) berücksichtigen.

Brendan Mathers:	**Martin Spielberg:**
	Spielberg. Guten Morgen.
Good morning, Mr Spielberg. It's Brendan Mathers here from Hermes Freight Forwarding. I'm phoning about the position you applied for as Export Clerk. Do you mind if we speak English?	…
Mr Spielberg, I read through your CV and covering letter and would be very interested to meet you to find out a bit more about you. You wrote in your covering letter that you'd be available for an interview at short notice. Is that still the case?	…
Well, I'm actually in Nuremberg on business from Wednesday, 29 July until Monday, 3 August. What about Thursday, 30 July?	…
What about the next day? Would Friday be convenient for you, at about 5 p.m.?	…
Yes, that's OK with me. Now, I was thinking we could meet at Restaurant Backstein. Do you know it?	…
That's right. There's just one more thing. Would you mind giving me your mobile number, just in case there are any changes to the plan?	…
Thank you. Right, well, I'll see you on Friday, 31 July at 6 p.m.	…
Goodbye.	…

D Vermerk in Deutsch über einen Geschäftsbrief in Englisch

Bearbeitungszeit: 30 Minuten

Situation: Sie arbeiten als Auszubildender in der Exportabteilung der Generalgroßhändler MegaKauf Gmbh, Oberkassler Str. 200, 40545 Düsseldorf. Heute, am 25. Juni, haben Sie einen Brief von einem irischen Kunden, Safety First Ltd., Drumcondra Road, Stoneybatter, Dublin 3, D3 FA7, erhalten.

Aufgabe: Lesen Sie den Brief des Kunden und fassen Sie alle wesentlichen Informationen für die Leiterin der Exportabteilung, Frau Tamara Beck, in deutscher Sprache zusammen. Schreiben Sie vollständige Sätze und übersetzen Sie nicht wörtlich. Achten Sie darauf, dass Sie alle angegebenen Details (Firmenname, Datum usw.) berücksichtigen.

Safety First Ltd.,
Drumcondra Road,
Stoneybatter,
Dublin 3,
D3 FA7
IRELAND

MegaKauf GmbH,
Oberkassler Str. 200,
40545 Düsseldorf,
GERMANY

21 June, 20..

Attn. Ms Beck, Head of Exports

Dear Ms Beck

Order No.VBF900 for 5,000 EW1 smoke alarms dated 12 May 20..

The above-mentioned smoke alarms were delivered on 12 June 20.. and forwarded to various customers all over the British Isles. When they opened the boxes, they discovered that many were without batteries and mounting screws while others did not work at all when tested. Furthermore, all of the alarms in two boxes (200 units) were not white but discoloured and slightly yellow.

We enclose photographs of these items for your information.

This standard of quality falls far below what we have come to expect of MegaKauf and we would appreciate an explanation.

Whatever the case may be, you will understand that we cannot sell these articles and must therefore ask you to urgently replace the entire consignment free of charge by return.

We feel sure you will appreciate that our future business relationship will depend on how this matter is dealt with.

We expect to hear from you in the very near future.

Yours sincerely
Fiona Murphy
Fiona Murphy
Purchasing Department
Enc: 5 photos

E Nachweis der Fremdsprachenbeherrschung durch einen Sprachergänzungstest

Text 1

Bearbeitungszeit für beide Texte zusammen: 25 Minuten

Aufgabe: Bitte setzen Sie 20 der 23 angegebenen Wörter in die Lücken des Textes ein.

about ▪ agreed ▪ approximately ▪ brochure ▪ circa ▪ CWO ▪ enclosed ▪ FCA ▪ hesitate ▪ initial ▪ major ▪ Many ▪ mayor ▪ range ▪ receipt ▪ receiving ▪ references ▪ reputation ▪ require ▪ supply ▪ Very ▪ visit ▪ with

Schmidt Großhandel GmbH
Binzstrasse 20
40124 Düsseldorf
GERMANY

Mr Paul O'Connor
The Great Outdoors Ltd
3 Shop Street
Galway
GA1 4GR
IRELAND

Dear Mr O'Connor

Your enquiry dated 20 October 20.. ____________[1] charcoal barbecues

____________[2] thanks for the above-mentioned enquiry.

We are a ____________[3] distributor of high-quality products and have an excellent ____________[4] throughout Europe and North America. A ____________[5] with our Greber charcoal barbecues is ____________[6] for your information and to download details of our entire ____________[7] together with our export price list, please ____________[8] our website at www.SchmidtGh.de.

As ____________[9] in our telephone conversation this morning, we will be pleased to ____________[10] you ____________[11] 200 Greber Smoker charcoal barbecues. Our price of €15,000 is quoted ____________[12] Dusseldorf. Our terms of payment for an ____________[13] order are ____________[14] or, with favourable ____________[15], 10 days 3 %, 30 days net. Delivery will be made ____________[16] 6 weeks after ____________[17] of order.

Please do not ____________[18] to contact us if you ____________[19] further details.

We look forward to ____________[20] your order.

Best regards

Leonie Hartmann

Text 2

Aufgabe: In diesem Text ist jeweils nur eine der auf der folgenden Seite vorgeschlagenen Formen korrekt. Bitte setzen Sie die richtige Lösung in die entsprechende Lücke ein.

Companies now ______________ [1] all the tools of the digital age to find ______________ [2] for new positions and they are also very ______________ [3] to how the online behaviour of ______________ [4] current employees can reflect on ______________ [5]. If you're looking for a job, social media can ______________ [6] you find the job of your dreams, and if you ______________ [7] have a good position, be careful not to blow it with a tweet that others could find offensive.

Experts agree all of your social media should reflect you as a ______________ [8]. Keep ______________ [9] eye on your privacy settings and when you post something public (and profile pictures are always public!) – ______________ [10] it clean and professional. ______________ [11] departments are not ______________ [12] to judge you on your social media, but ______________ [13] recruiters can't resist checking candidates' internet ______________ [14]. Unfortunately, you ______________ [15] know if the profile picture of you pouring beer into your mouth was the reason you ______________ [16] called for an interview, but it very well could be.

If celebrities can lose their jobs over tweets, ______________ [17] can you. One woman lost her job in ______________ [18] for tweeting angry remarks ______________ [19] rude customers. Have a ______________ [20] through your public social media posts, tweets, etc. for anything that your boss ______________ [21] think reflects badly on their company and delete it. ______________ [22] includes any negative comments about ______________ [23] employers you may have had. If you can complain about a past boss, you might complain about your present or future ______________ [24], too.

But it's not just a one-way street – if you ______________ [25] invited for an ______________ [26], you can look up the interviewer's professional social media. You might find an interesting topic you could bring up in the interview. But don't be too ______________ [27], and don't let pro-active, acceptable research become stalking! Whether you are employed or still searching, educate yourself on the company's social media ______________ [28] and read your ______________ [29] carefully for any rules they might have on it – ignorance of the rules won't be any defence if you unintentionally break them by tweeting something Friday night that you might ______________ [30] Saturday morning.

1	using, use, uses	**16**	didn't get, didn't got, not got
2	vacancies, recruitment, candidates	**17**	too, also, so
3	sensitive, sensible, sensing	**18**	retale, retail, retailer
4	their, they're, there	**19**	in, about, around
5	them, they, her	**20**	good looks, good looking, good look
6	helps, helping, help	**21**	might, must, maybe
7	yet, already, had	**22**	These, This, Those
8	profession, occupational, professional	**23**	passed, before, previous
9	the, an, a	**24**	employer, employee, employ
10	hold, keep, stay	**25**	will be, had been, have been
11	Personal, Personnel, Resource	**26**	job, talk, interview
12	supposing, supposed, suppose	**27**	directly, direct, directing
13	much, several, many	**28**	politic, police, policy
14	presence, presents, present	**29**	employee profile, work contract, job offer
15	wont, wo'nt, won't	**30**	release, remember, regret

Quellenverzeichnis

S. 4/li.ob. Shutterstock.com / Minerva Studio; **S. 4/re.ob.** Shutterstock.com / bsd; **S. 4/re.un.** Shutterstock.com / ASDF_MEDIA; **S. 5** Shutterstock.com / David Hernandez; **S. 8** Shutterstock.com / Africa Studio; **S. 9/un.** Shutterstock.com / ESB Professional; **S. 11/un.** Shutterstock.com / ESB Professional; **S. 16/li.ob.** Shutterstock.com / Raoraby; **S. 17** Shutterstock.com / Designincolor; **S. 18** Shutterstock.com / Intarapong; **S. 22** Shutterstock.com / Stacey Green; **S. 23** Shutterstock.com / PR Image Factory; **S. 24** Shutterstock.com / Asier Romero; **S. 28** Shutterstock.com / Digital Assets; **S. 29** Shutterstock.com / fizkes; **S. 33** Shutterstock.com / El Nariz; **S. 40** Shutterstock.com / Weidong; **S. 42** Shutterstock.com / wavebreakmedia; **S. 45** Shutterstock.com / Rawpixel.com; **S. 50** Shutterstock.com / TaLaNoVa; **S. 52** Shutterstock.com / Polarpx; **S. 53** Shutterstock.com / Chowdhury Sifat; **S. 55** Shutterstock.com / FabrikaSimf; **S. 56** Shutterstock.com / vladwel; **S. 57** Shutterstock.com / Pla2na; **S. 61** Shutterstock.com / LDprod; **S. 62** Shutterstock.com / Alex Kolokythas Photography; **S. 64** Cornelsen / D'Avila Illustration Agency; **S. 71** Shutterstock.com / Patryk Kosmider; **S. 75** Shutterstock.com / Goldenas Marel; **S. 76** Shutterstock.com / ESB Professional; **S. 78** Shutterstock.com / TaLaNoVa; **S. 84** Shutterstock.com / Travel mania; **S. 88** Shutterstock.com / Roman Zaiets; **S. 89** Shutterstock.com / fizkes; **S. 92** Shutterstock.com / Stokkete; **S. 95** Shutterstock.com / fizkes; **S. 102** Shutterstock.com / stickypedro; **S. 104** Shutterstock.com / Rawpixel.com

Business Communication

Workbook

Transcripts and answer key

Cornelsen

Transcripts

01 *Title and copyright*

02 **Unit 1, Part B, Exercise 2**

Helena Hello, you must be Zoe Kline! I'm Helena Sawicki. Welcome to Düsseldorf! It's so nice to meet you at last!
Zoe Hello, Helena. It's nice to meet you, too. I'm so sorry I'm late. I hope I haven't spoiled your plans for this afternoon!
Helena Not at all. Did you have a good flight?
Zoe Apart from the delay it was fine.
Helena Good. Now, can I get you anything before the meeting – tea, coffee, mineral water?
Zoe I'd love a cup of coffee!
Helena Black or white? Sugar?
Zoe Black, no sugar, please.
Helena Here you are.
Zoe Thanks.
Helena Now here's the agenda for the meeting. We've made a few changes but nothing big. And here's the programme for the next two days.
Zoe Thanks.
Helena Now just let me give you my business card, in case you need to phone me on my mobile.
Zoe Thanks. And here's mine.

03 **Unit 1, Part C, Exercise 5**

Chris Good afternoon. Ben Jackson's office. Chris Jones speaking.
Helen Oh, hello, Chris. It's Helen Brown here.
Chris Oh, hello, Helen. What can I do for you?
Helen Well, I'm in Oxford next Tuesday and so I was wondering if I could visit Ben while I'm there. It could save a lot of time.
Chris Sure. Next Tuesday, did you say?
Helen That's right. I'm tied up during the morning,but I'm free all afternoon.
Chris Hang on a moment, Helen. I'll just look in Ben's diary … Helen?
Helen Yes.
Chris Well, Tuesday afternoon is already full, I'm afraid. Ben has a meeting with the bank at 2.30, and then another visitor after that.
Helen Oh, dear. Well, how about a lunch appointment, then? We could meet at that pub in Lion Street, couldn't we?
Chris Well, yes, I suppose so. Look, Helen, … I'll tell you what … why don't we pencil in 12.30 at the Wheatsheaf – that's W-H-E-A-T-S-H-E-A-T – in Lion Street. OK? I'll speak to Ben and confirm by email first thing tomorrow.
Helen OK, I've made a note. Thanks a lot, Chris. Bye now.
Chris Bye, Helen.

04 **Unit 1, Part E, Exercise 1**

Benno Guten Morgen, Berghain GmbH. Koch am Apparat.
Peter Morning, Benno. Peter Michaels here.
Benno Ah, morning, Peter. How are you?
Peter Fine, thanks. And you?
Benno I'm very well, thank you.
Peter Great. Listen, Benno, I'm going to be in Freiburg next week to see a couple of my customers. I'd like to meet you again to discuss the order we talked about at the trade fair last month. Could I possibly make an appointment to come and see you?
Benno Yes, of course, it would be a pleasure.
Peter Great. Well, I'm going to be in town on Monday and Tuesday. Is there a time on either of those days that would suit you?
Benno Well, how about 11 a.m. on Monday? I'm free then.
Peter Oh, I'm afraid I won't be able to make that. I have another meeting then. Could I suggest 1 p.m. on Monday afternoon?
Benno No, unfortunately that won't work. I have to see another supplier.
Peter How would 9 o'clock on Tuesday morning be?
Benno Let me see. No, sorry, that's not possible either. I'm afraid I'm rather busy at the moment. Would you be able to make 3 p.m. on Tuesday?
Peter Oh dear. Sorry, no. I have to catch my plane back at 4 p.m. I have to be at the airport for 3.
Benno Well, then. There's nothing else for it. What are you doing for lunch on Tuesday, Peter?
Peter Nothing as yet.
Benno Well, why don't we meet over lunch? Say about 1 o'clock.
Peter Yes. I think that would work. Splendid. 1 o'clock on Tuesday. Thanks Benno. I look forward to seeing you then.
Benno Great, Peter. See you on Tuesday.

05 **Unit 1, Part F, Exercise 1**

Benno Guten Morgen, Berghain GmbH. Koch am Apparat.
Peter Morning, Benno. Peter Michaels here.
Benno Ah, morning, Peter. How are you?
Peter Fine, thanks. And you?
Benno I'm very well, thank you.
Peter Great. Listen, Benno, I'm going to be in Freiburg next week to see a couple of my customers. I'd like to meet you again to discuss the order we talked about at the trade fair last month. Could I possibly make an appointment to come and see you?
Benno Yes, of course, it would be a pleasure.
Peter Great. Well, I'm going to be in town on Monday and Tuesday. Is there a time on either of those days that would suit you?
Benno Well, how about 11 a.m. on Monday? I'm free then.
Peter Oh, I'm afraid I won't be able to make that. I have another meeting then. Could I suggest 1 p.m. on Monday afternoon?
Benno No, unfortunately that won't work. I have to see another supplier.
Peter How would 9 o'clock on Tuesday morning be?

Benno Let me see. No, sorry, that's not possible either. I'm afraid I'm rather busy at the moment. Would you be able to make 3 p.m. on Tuesday?
Peter Oh dear. Sorry, no. I have to catch my plane back at 4 p.m. I have to be at the airport for 3.
Benno Well, then. There's nothing else for it. What are you doing for lunch on Tuesday, Peter?
Peter Nothing as yet.
Benno Well, why don't we meet over lunch? Say about 1 o'clock.
Peter Yes. I think that would work. Splendid. 1 o'clock on Tuesday. Thanks Benno. I look forward to seeing you then.
Benno Great, Peter. See you on Tuesday.

Unit 2, Part B, Exercise 3

06

1 Your teacher's email address is: catherine.bright@fluent/english.nex. That's C-A-T-H-E-R-I-N-E dot B-R-I-G-H-T at F-L-U-E-N-T slash E-N-G-L-I-S-H dot N-E-X
2 You want to find out more about a new product. You should write to: hotsales@amazing-bikes.nex. H-O-T-S-A-L-E-S at A-M-A-Z-I-N-G hyphen BIKES dot N-E-X.
3 You've got the email address of the job you want to apply for: Damian_HR@InnovatorsLtd.nex. It's capital D-A-M-I-A-N underscore capital H capital R at capital I-N-N-O-V-A-T-O-R-S capital L-T-D dot N-E-X.
4 If you don't like the pullover you bought, you can get your money back. Write to: customer.service@the_apparel_centre.nex. C-U-S-T-O-M-E-R dot S-E-R-V-I-C-E at T-H-E underscore A-P-P-A-R-E-L underscore C-E-N-T-R-E dot N-E-X.
5 This man can help you set up a small business. Mail him at: biljones@freelance-solutions.nex. I'll spell that. B-I-L-J-O-N-E-S at F-R-E-E-L-A-N-C-E hyphen S-O-L-U-T-I-O-N-S dot N-E-X
6 If your computer has a problem, contact: Support@PC-Service.nex. That's capital S-U-P-P-O-R-T at capital P capital C hyphen S-E-R-V-I-C-E dot N-E-X.

Unit 2, Part C, Exercise 5

07

Beatrice Swiss Pharma. Beatrice Kuhn speaking.
John Good morning, Beatrice. This is John Brown from London. How's the weather over there?
Beatrice Good morning, Mr Brown. It's very nice here today. How about London?
John Oh. It's fine here. Sunny.
Beatrice That's nice. How can I help you?
John I'd like to speak to Ms Frey, please.
Beatrice Yes, of course. Just a moment, please. I'll put you through.
Franziska Frey.
Beatrice Franziska. John Brown is on the phone from London.
Franziska Oh, no. I'm just writing a report for him. Could you tell him I'm out?
Beatrice Should I say when you'll be back?
Franziska No, don't do that. Just take a message. Thanks.
Beatrice Mr Brown? It's Beatrice here again.
John Yes. Hello.
Beatrice I'm afraid Ms Frey is out of the office at the moment. Can I take a message?
John Erm. Yes. Could you ask her to call me back?
Beatrice May I ask what it's about?
John It's about the report.
Beatrice The report. Right. I'll ask Ms Frey to call you. Will you be in the office all day?
John Maybe not. Ask her to call me on my mobile please. The number is 0171 49835 double 2 9.
Beatrice 0171 49835 double 2 9. I've made a note of that, Mr Brown, and I'll ask Ms Frey to call you. Thank you for calling.
John Thank you, Beatrice. Have a good day.

Unit 2, Part C, Exercise 6

08

Message 1 This is Liam Watts speaking. I'm not in the office at the moment, but I expect to be back shortly. Please leave your name and number and I'll call you back as soon as possible.
Message 2 Christine Adams. Thank you for your call. I'm sorry I'm not available at present. Please leave your name, number and message and I'll call you back later today.
Message 3 Woods and Company Mechanical Engineers. We regret that all our lines are engaged at the moment. Please call back later. Thank you for your cooperation.

Unit 2, Part D, Exercise 7

09

Zoe Good morning and thank you for calling Rob Heldof's press office. How can I help?
Helena Hello, it's Helena Sawicki in Germany. Is that Zoe?
Zoe Yes, it is. Nice to talk to you again, Helena.
Helena Nice to talk to you too, Zoe. I'm just calling to ask you about holding a press conference with Rob Heldof when he comes here in May. Nina Wittstock wants one either before or after his speech on Thursday evening, and she'd also like him to go on a breakfast TV show the next day.
Zoe Oh right. Just let me look at his diary. I have it here on my phone. OK, go ahead.
Helena When does Rob arrive in Düsseldorf on the first?
Zoe He arrives in the morning, but he'll have jet lag.
Helena Oh, I see. How about a press conference at six o'clock in the evening before his speech?
Zoe He's going shopping with Katie in the afternoon. That'll take about three hours at least. What about eleven o'clock after the conference?
Helena I'm afraid that won't work out because he's having a meal then. How about Friday morning at about 10 am.?
Zoe I'm not sure. He wants to buy some new sunglasses for Rio. And then his flight is at 1.30.
Helena I see. OK. Let's look at Thursday again. What about after his speech at about 9.30 pm.?

Zoe Yes, he's free then, but let's make it ten o'clock to give him a bit more time.
Helena Great!
Zoe I'll check with him and get back to you.
Helena That's marvellous. Oh, and please ask him if he wants to go on the breakfast show on Friday morning.
Zoe What time would that be?
Helena It starts at 6.30 am., but how about eight o'clock?
Zoe Mmm, I'm not sure. I'll ask him and get back to you as soon as possible. Talk to you soon. Bye.
Helena Bye.

Unit 2, Part E, Exercise 1

10

Welcome to this week's 'Your Office Matters' podcast. Today, we're going to talk about the two most common types of business communication – the letter and the email.

I'd like to talk first about three points which some people use to argue against using emails in business.

Point 1: Some people believe that emails are not as business-like as letters. They argue that business letters normally use a formal style and emails tend to be less formal. I don't agree. Whichever medium you choose, you have to write the content in a professional way. Just follow the standards of business letters in your business emails, always use a formal greeting and close with your name, and you can't go wrong.

Point 2: Many people don't want to send sensitive information by email. An email travels to its destination through the internet, so anyone can look at it. You can solve that problem by using email security technology.

Point 3: What about the legal problems? The laws are different from country to country, so you should always find out if an email contract is legally binding in the country you're doing business with. If it isn't, then you must use a letter.

So, now that we have these three points out of the way, I'm going to argue that a business email lets you do exactly the same things as you can do with business letters. In fact, in some cases, the email is more convenient than a letter. For a start, it's faster, and you can contact a lot of people at one time with just one email.

One of the biggest plus points when it comes to choosing between a letter and an email is the cost. Letters are printed on quality paper and use superior-grade envelopes; you have to pay for postage and the cost of using the printer. With email, you only pay for electricity and the internet so email comes out on top when you're trying to save money.

Don't forget, too, that there are more cost advantages if you have to send attachments. When you send extra pages with your business letter, your expenses can be extremely high. Email attachments are almost free.

Last but not least, I'd like to mention the environmental impact. Email communication doesn't need paper. You can easily make your business greener by writing fewer letters and communicating more by email.

Unit 2, Part F, Exercise 2

11

Speaker Guten Morgen, Büro von Herrn Liepe. Was kann ich für Sie tun?
June Guten Morgen, sprechen Sie Englisch? Mein Deutsch ist nicht so gut.
Speaker Sure, English is no problem. How can I help you?
June My name is June Smith and I'm calling on behalf of Rob Heldof. He is due to take part in a TV interview this Sunday morning.
Speaker Yes, Ms Smith, I know about that interview. Please go ahead.
June Well, there are two things we need to sort out. The first is the timing. In Mr Liepe's email he said the interview would take place at half past eight in the morning, but in the email attachment I think it says seven-thirty a.m. Seven-thirty is too early for us.
Speaker Ah, OK. I see. I will clarify that and make sure Mr Liepe knows which time suits you. And the second issue?
June Well, that is connected with the email attachment – the legal form that Mr Heldof is meant to sign. It's in German. I'm afraid Mr Heldof won't sign anything legal if he cannot understand it. Could you send us a copy in English, please?
Speaker I'm sure that will not be a problem, Ms Smith. Is there anything else I can do?
June No, thank you. ... Oh! Yes, one more thing – Mr Heldof doesn't speak German, won't that be strange on German TV?
Speaker No, not at all. We often have English-speaking guests. A translator will translate Mr Heldof's words into German and the viewers will hear that. It's normal here.
June OK, good to know. So we will wait for confirmation of the interview timing and the legal form in English.
Speaker Yes, I will talk to Mr Liepe as soon as possible and you will hear from us shortly.
June Great. Thank you.
Speaker You're welcome, Ms Smith. Goodbye.

Unit 3, Part C, Exercise 5

12

Nadine Hello, Human Resources, Nadine Koch speaking. What can I do for you?
Sarah Good morning. This is Sarah Denby. I'm phoning about your advertisement in yesterday's *Herald* for the position of marketing assistant in Germany.
Nadine Oh yes. Could you just repeat your name, please?
Sarah Yes, no problem. My name is Sarah Denby: I'll spell that for you: D-E-N-B-Y.
Nadine OK. Mmh. You don't mind my taking notes, Sarah, do you?
Sarah No, of course not.
Nadine And could I have your address, please?
Sarah OK. I live at 25 Burns Drive, Aberdeen. And the post code is AB4 6GX. And would you need my phone number as well?
Nadine If you don't mind ...
Sarah The area code is 01224 and the number is: 286437. And my mobile is 0169 8473621.

Nadine I repeat. Your address is 25 Burns Drive, Aberdeen. And your phone number is 01224 for the area and then 286437. And then your mobile phone: 0169 8473621.

Sarah That's correct.

Nadine That's fine then. OK Sarah, now tell me something about yourself, your qualifications and your experience.

Sarah Well, I didn't expect we'd be going as far as that. But … OK. So, I've just finished my honours degree in Marketing at Stirling University and am waiting for the results. I'm expecting a 2.1 actually.

Nadine Sounds good. Hope that all goes well. And your Highers subjects?

Sarah Actually, I didn't go to school in Scotland. I went to school in England so I got A-levels in Economics, History and Social Sciences.

Nadine Any languages, Sarah? How about German?

Sarah Well, I've got GCSE German and French. But I preferred German actually. I've been to Germany regularly because my dad was in the army there.

Nadine And have you got any work experience, done a placement perhaps?

Sarah Well I've been helping out in a coffee bar at weekends during term time. And I've also done two work placements in the PR Department of Aberdeen Development Corporation.

Nadine That sounds absolutely fine. Why don't you send us your CV and then we'll see how it goes from there?

Sarah Yes, no problem. But who do I send it to?

Nadine Well, I'll send you a questionnaire to fill in, and you can send that back with all the usual documents to the address on the questionnaire. OK?

Sarah Yeah. That's fine. I'll do that.

13

Unit 3, Part C, Exercise 7

Interviewer Thanks for coming along to talk to us today, Pat.

Pat Oh, my pleasure. It's nice to be here.

Interviewer Good. Now, today you're going to give us advice about how to prepare for an interview.

Pat Correct. I'm going to go through each of the five stages of a job interview and talk about how candidates can prepare themselves. So, stage one, greetings and introductions. That's perhaps the easiest part of the interview, but it still needs some preparation. First of all, you should find out where the interview location is and how to get there, so that you arrive in good time. Try to give yourself enough time to relax and calm down. You should also make sure that you're wearing appropriate clothes.

Interviewer First impressions count. Would you advise people to buy new clothes specially for the interview?

Pat No, not particularly. Your clothes need to be appropriate for the job, clean and smart, that's all. They don't have to be new.

Interviewer Right. What about body language at the start of the interview?

Pat Body language is important. Walk into the room as confidently as possible, shake hands and make eye contact. Don't be shy. Look directly at the interviewer or interviewers. You'll be asked to take a seat, and there will be a bit of small talk.

Interviewer Talking about the weather, your journey, that kind of thing?

Pat That's right. There might also be a question about where you live or your hobbies.

Interviewer Some people find it difficult to make small talk, even in their own language. What advice can you give us there, Pat?

Pat I think the best thing to do is to simply get into the habit of making small talk in English with a colleague or a friend.

Interviewer That's a good idea. Practise making small talk whenever you can.

Pat That's it. Now, let's move on to the main part of the interview. You'll be asked questions by one or more interviewers.

Interviewer The interview might be conducted by more than one person?

Pat That's correct. Sometimes there's a panel of interviewers. Now, preparation for this part is extremely important. Think about the questions you might be asked and make a list. You'll definitely be asked to talk about yourself. Perhaps the interviewer will ask you about your strengths and weaknesses. Write down the questions – and think about how you're going to answer. And always remember to relate your answers to the job on offer.

Interviewer Yes, that's important. Keep focused on the job. What should a candidate do if he or she doesn't understand a question?

Pat If you don't understand a question, ask the interviewer to clarify. You can say: 'Could you explain what you mean by … ?' – whatever it is. A good interviewer will ask the question again in a slightly different way.

Interviewer Hmm. I hope so. Now, earlier you mentioned questions from the candidate. I remember my very first interview. I had no idea what to ask.

Pat Oh, dear. Some preparation would have helped. It's important to do some background research into the company before you go for the interview. Find out about the company's most recent developments and the future prospects of the company you hope to work for. Go to the firm's homepage on the internet, read the business section of your newspaper, or look through business magazines. As you're doing your research, note down any questions that occur to you concerning the company.

	You should also, of course, prepare some questions about the job itself. Then, when you're asked if you have any questions, this is your chance to show your interest in the company and the job.
Interviewer	Right. Be prepared with questions about the company and the job! And that's the end of the interview and you can say goodbye.
Pat	Well, not quite. Before the interview comes to an end, the interviewer usually says when the candidate can expect to hear from the company, or if there's to be a further interview or a test – hmm – say, in the form of an assessment centre evaluation. So, only after these arrangements have been made, then your last task as a candidate is to say thank you and goodbye. Again, a good, firm handshake and a smile, and that's it.
Interviewer	Well, thank you, Pat, for these very helpful interviewing tips. I'm sure our listeners have learned a lot today and that they'll be able to put your tips to good use in their interviews. Now, next week's podcast is about …

14

Unit 3, Part C, Exercise 9

Ann	Good morning, Mr Krug. Welcome to Fitness Products. My name's Ann Butler. I am the HR manager. I'd also like to introduce Frank Wilson, assistant sales manager.
Frank	Hello.
Andreas	Nice to meet you.
Ann	Please take a seat. I hope you had a good journey here.
Andreas	Yes, thank you. The train connections were all on time.
Ann	Good. Do you mind if I call you Andreas?
Andreas	No problem. Please do.
Ann	Well, Andreas, we're running a bit late, so if you don't mind, we'll start right away. I'm going to ask you a few questions first of all, then I have to leave. But Frank Wilson will stay and tell you more about the job and ask you some more detailed questions.
Andreas	OK.
Ann	Well, as you know, the position we are looking to fill is for an assistant to join the sales team. They are going to be on the road a lot in future and they will need somebody here in the office to support them. It's a completely new position. First, could you tell me something about your present position.
Andreas	Since I left vocational school a year ago, I've worked with VIP Services at the airport. We're a company that looks after first-class passengers and makes sure their arrival or departure is problem free.
Ann	That sounds like an exciting first job. So why do you want to leave?
Andreas	Well, yes, it's fun for a year or so. All the rich and famous people I meet. But it's not my world. I'm looking for something more 'normal', where I feel that I'm part of a team.
Ann	Yes, I can understand that, Andreas. Now in a work situation, what would you say are your biggest strengths?
Andreas	Hm. I thought this question might come! My one big strength is that I can get on well with people. I'm tactful and diplomatic.
Ann	Good. How about your weak points? Things you may need to improve with training and practice.
Andreas	I sometimes find it hard to make decisions. I take a long time and I always try not to upset other people.
Ann	That's not always a weakness. Thanks for those answers. Now you say in your résumé that you also speak Polish. How well do you speak it?
Andreas	My mother is Polish. So I speak it fluently, although I don't write it very well.
Ann	Well, that would be very useful for the team. Now we have a lot of applicants for this job, Andreas, as you can imagine. Is there a special reason why you want to work for us?
Andreas	There are several reasons. I'd like to work with a team, and sales has always interested me. I'd like the opportunity to use my Polish language and deal with people from Eastern Europe. I also like the natural products which you sell very much.
Ann	Good. I'm sorry if I have to rush off in a minute. But before I leave, do you want to ask me any questions?
Andreas	I read that you I have plans to expand your business in Eastern Europe. Is that the reason for this new position?
Ann	I see you've done your research! Yes, that's certainly one of the reasons.

(Knock on the door, it opens.)

Voice	We're ready Ms Butler.
Ann	OK. I'm coming. It was really nice to meet you, Andreas. We can't say anything today, but you'll definitely hear from us before the end of the week. *(fade)*

15

Unit 3, Part D, Exercise 2

Spielberg	Spielberg. Guten Morgen.
Mathers	Good morning, Mr Spielberg. It's Brendan Mathers here from Hermes Freight Forwarding. I'm phoning about the position you applied for as Export Clerk. Do you mind if we speak English?
Spielberg	No, not at all. Good morning, Mr Mathers. It's nice to hear from you.
Mathers	Mr Spielberg, I read through your CV and covering letter and would be very interested to meet you to find out a bit more about you. You wrote in your covering letter that you'd be available for an interview at short notice. Is that still the case?
Spielberg	Yes, certainly. When would suit you?
Mathers	Well, I'm actually in Nuremberg on business from Wednesday, 29 July until Monday, 3 August. What about Thursday, 30 July?
Spielberg	I'm sorry. I'm busy all day on 30 July.
Mathers	What about the next day? Would Friday be convenient for you, at about 5 pm?

Spielberg Friday is fine, but I'm afraid 5 pm is a bit too early for me. I don't finish work until 4 pm, and it will take me an hour and a half to get to Nuremberg. Are you still free at 6 pm?

Mathers 6 pm? Yes, that's OK with me. Now, I was thinking we could meet at Restaurant Backstein. Do you know it?

Spielberg Yes, I think so. It's on Hauptstraße, isn't it?

Mathers That's right. There's just one more thing. Would you mind giving me your mobile number, just in case there are any changes to the plan?

Spielberg No problem. It's 0176 438 05 783.

Mathers Thank you. Right, well, I'll see you on Friday, 31 July at 6 pm, and if that doesn't work out, then I'll be in touch again when I get back to England and we can arrange a phone interview.

Spielberg OK, no problem. Thank you for calling, Mr Mathers. Goodbye.

Mathers Goodbye.

16

Unit 4, Part B, Exercise 3

Zoe Good morning. Wessex Fitness Technology. Zoe van Dijk speaking.

Jo Hi. It's Top Fit Studios in Cologne here. I'm calling about our enquiry for digital …

Zoe Sorry, can we take it one step at at time, please? Who's speaking, please?

Jo Oh, sorry. My name's Jo Clarke. That's Jo without an 'e', and Clarke with one.

Zoe Fine. And you're calling from?

Jo Top Fit Studios, Cologne.

Zoe OK, I've got that. Now, you're ringing about an enquiry, right?

Jo Right. I'm calling about our enquiry for digital pulse counters.

Zoe Can you give me the details, please? I need the date, reference number, if any, and if possible, the catalogue number, OK?

Jo Sure. The date's 21 October. The reference number's J–C slash 2–1–1–0 slash P–C, and the catalogue number is D–P–C hyphen 4–X.

Zoe OK, I've got that. Now, what's the trouble exactly?

Jo Well, we still haven't received your offer, and things are getting a bit urgent this end. We already have several orders ourselves.

Zoe Oh, dear. Something's gone wrong here, I'm afraid. Could you hold on a moment, please? … Hello?

Jo Hello.

Zoe Well, I can't understand it. This offer went out by post on 25 October. You should have got it, well, a week ago.

Jo Oh, the post again. Great. Look, could you do me a favour? Could you email us a copy?

Zoe Of course. I don't understand it. We normally do that automatically. What's the address? It'll save me …

Jo Sure. It's Top.Fit@Training.nex. That's capital T-o-p dot capital F-i-t at capital T-r-a-i-n-i-n-g dot n-e-x.

Zoe Fine. Capital T-o-p dot capital F-i-t at capital T-r-a-i-n-i-n-g dot n-e-x, right?

Jo That's right. Oh, and I don't want to put you under pressure, but could you do that very soon?

Zoe Don't worry. I'll do it immediately.

Jo Great. Bye now.

Zoe Bye.

17

Unit 4, Part D, Exercise 1

Kim Good morning. Star Car Hire. I'm Kim Cameron. Can I help you?

Joe Hi. My name's Joe Davis. Look, I've got a question first. Is it possible to hire a car at Aberdeen Dyce airport but return it at Glasgow Airport?

Kim No problem, sir. There's a Star office at all Scottish airports.

Joe Fine. In that case, what would a car cost for five days, please?

Kim What class of car were you thinking of, sir? We have five groups, from a VW Polo or a Ford Fiesta in Group A through to luxury limosines in Group E.

Joe Well, the car's not for me, actually. It's for my boss. But I know she wants to do a lot of touring, so the car should be comfortable. She doesn't want anything luxurious, though.

Kim In that case, I'd suggest Group C, sir. What about an Audi A4 or a Peugeot 307, for example?

Joe The Peugeot sounds good. She drives a Peugeot herself. How much is the 307, then?

Kim Well, that depends on the day of the week. Weekends are much cheaper.

Joe Well, she wants to pick the car up at 9 am on Monday, 16 March at Dyce and return it at six pm on Friday, 20 at Glasgow Airport.

Kim Thanks. So that's Group C for four days and nine hours during the week. Just a moment, please. Er … that's two hundred and eleven pounds ninety-nine.

Joe Good heavens. That's a lot, isn't it? Does that price include a full tank of petrol?

Kim No, it doesn't, sir. The tank's full when you pick up the car, of course, but you have to give it back with a full tank as well. If you don't, you have to pay a ten pound surcharge in addition to the cost of our filling the tank, I'm afraid.

Joe I see. Are there any other extras?

Kim No. Petrol is the only extra. The price includes full insurance and unlimited mileage.

Joe Ah, so there's no mileage surcharge?

Kim No, sir – and that's important if you're touring.

Joe OK, then. Look, can I get back to you later? I'm sure it'll be OK, but I'd better check with my boss before making a firm reservation.

Kim Sure. No problem, sir. We're open at Dyce until 10 pm, by the way.

Joe Fine. Well, thanks for your help. Bye now.

Kim You're welcome. Goodbye, sir.

18

Unit 4, Part E, Exercise 1

Kim Good morning. Star Car Hire. I'm Kim Cameron. Can I help you?

Joe Hi. My name's Joe Davis. Look, I've got a question first. Is it possible to hire a car at

Aberdeen Dyce airport but return it at Glasgow Airport?

Kim No problem, sir. There's a Star office at all Scottish airports.

Joe Fine. In that case, what would a car cost for five days, please?

Kim What class of car were you thinking of, sir? We have five groups, from a VW Polo or a Ford Fiesta in Group A through to luxury limosines in Group E.

Joe Well, the car's not for me, actually. It's for my boss. But I know she wants to do a lot of touring, so the car should be comfortable. She doesn't want anything luxurious, though.

Kim In that case, I'd suggest Group C, sir. What about an Audi A4 or a Peugeot 307, for example?

Joe The Peugeot sounds good. She drives a Peugeot herself. How much is the 307, then?

Kim Well, that depends on the day of the week. Weekends are much cheaper.

Joe Well, she wants to pick the car up at 9 am on Monday, 16 March at Dyce and return it at six pm on Friday, 20 at Glasgow Airport.

Kim Thanks. So that's Group C for four days and nine hours during the week. Just a moment, please. Er ... that's two hundred and eleven pounds ninety-nine.

Joe Good heavens. That's a lot, isn't it? Does that price include a full tank of petrol?

Kim No, it doesn't, sir. The tank's full when you pick up the car, of course, but you have to give it back with a full tank as well. If you don't, you have to pay a ten pound surcharge in addition to the cost of our filling the tank, I'm afraid.

Joe I see. Are there any other extras?

Kim No. Petrol is the only extra. The price includes full insurance and unlimited mileage.

Joe Ah, so there's no mileage surcharge?

Kim No, sir – and that's important if you're touring.

Joe OK, then. Look, can I get back to you later? I'm sure it'll be OK, but I'd better check with my boss before making a firm reservation.

Kim Sure. No problem, sir. We're open at Dyce until 10 pm, by the way.

Joe Fine. Well, thanks for your help. Bye now.

Kim You're welcome. Goodbye, sir.

19

Unit 5, Part C, Exercise 1

Beate FreiLuft Austria. Beate Quint, Einkauf. Kann ich ...

Anjali Hi, Beate. It's Anjali Sen from Apex Leisure in Nottingham.

Beate Oh, hello, Anjali. How're you?

Anjali Fine, thanks. And you?

Beate Oh, I'm fine, too, thanks. Anyway, what can I do for you?

Anjali Well, it's about your enquiry of ... ah, yes ... 10 February. As it seems quite urgent, I thought I'd call you with an offer, if that's OK.

Beate Of course – the sooner the better, in fact.

Anjali Well, we can supply three hundred Champion 200 solar lamps, colour green and silver, model number CSL200, on the usual terms.

Beate So that'd be a trade discount of 15% below list, plus a 2.5% cash discount for payment within 15 days of delivery.

Anjali That's right.

Beate And delivery?

Anjali Usual terms, too. By road, DDP Linz, dispatch within 12 hours of receipt of order, if that's OK.

Beate That sounds fine, Anjali. Let me just repeat that, though, just to be on the safe side. Here goes. Three hundred Champion 200 solar lamps, colour green and silver, model number CSL200 at 15% below list, plus 2.5% cash discount, DDP our Linz stores, dispatch within 12 hours of receipt of order, right?

Anjali You've got it.

Beate OK, then, Anjali. Well, thanks for your ...

Anjali Hold on a moment, Beate. I'm not through yet, I'm afraid. There's your other enquiry about ...

Beate Oh, of course. The cool boxes.

Anjali Yes. Look, no problem there, either, OK? We're talking 12 volt Arctic Star cool boxes, quantity one hundred and fifty, colour blue and white, capacity 30 litres, model number CB12, OK?

Beate OK. Everything's the same as in our enquiry.

Anjali Right. Anyhow, we'd supply on the same terms as for the lamps, of course. No problem. Any questions, just get in touch, Beate, OK?

Beate Sure, but here it is again, though, just ...

Anjali ... to be on the safe side. I know.

Beate Right. So here goes. One hundred and fifty 12 volt Arctic Star cool boxes, blue and white, 30 litres, model number CB12, OK?

Anjali OK.

Beate Terms 15% below list, 2.5% cash discount, DDP Linz, dispatch within 12 hours of receipt of order.

Anjali Right.

Beate Well, I'll just check with my boss, but I'm pretty sure I'll be able to fax you an order early tomorrow, 16 February.

Anjali That'd be great, Beate. Thanks. Goodbye for now.

Beate Bye now, Anjali.

20

Unit 5, Part D, Exercise 1

Beate FreiLuft Austria. Beate Quint, Einkauf. Kann ich ...

Anjali Hi, Beate. It's Anjali Sen from Apex Leisure in Nottingham.

Beate Oh, hello, Anjali. How're you?

Anjali Fine, thanks. And you?

Beate Oh, I'm fine, too, thanks. Anyway, what can I do for you?

Anjali Well, it's about your enquiry of ... ah, yes ... 10 February. As it seems quite urgent, I thought I'd call you with an offer, if that's OK.

Beate Of course – the sooner the better, in fact.

Anjali Well, we can supply three hundred Champion 200 solar lamps, colour green and silver, model number CSL200, on the usual terms.

Beate So that'd be a trade discount of 15% below list, plus a 2.5% cash discount for payment within 15 days of delivery.

Anjali That's right.

Beate And delivery?

Anjali Usual terms, too. By road, DDP Linz, dispatch within 12 hours of receipt of order, if that's OK.

Beate That sounds fine, Anjali. Well, thanks for your ...

Anjali Hold on a moment, Beate. I'm not through yet, I'm afraid. There's your other enquiry about …
Beate Oh, of course. The cool boxes.
Anjali Yes. Look, no problem there, either, OK? We're talking 12 volt Arctic Star cool boxes, quantity one hundred and fifty, colour blue and white, capacity 30 litres, model number CB12, OK?
Beate OK. Everything's the same as in our enquiry.
Anjali Right. Anyhow, we'd supply on the same terms as for the lamps, of course. No problem. Any questions, just get in touch, Beate, OK?
Beate Well, I'll just check with my boss, but I'm pretty sure I'll be able to fax you an order early tomorrow, 16 February.
Anjali That'd be great, Beate. Thanks. Goodbye for now.
Beate Bye now, Anjali.

21

Unit 6, Part A, Exercise 2

Alan Good Business Equipment. Alan speaking.
Katrin Good morning. This is Katrin Troll from A to Z Logistics in London.
Alan Good morning, Ms Troll. How can I help you?
Katrin I'd like to place an order for a flip chart with stainless steel legs. The item number is 0-
Alan Oh, sorry. Can I just interrupt you here? I'm afraid that the flip chart with the stainless steel legs isn't in stock at the moment.
Katrin When will it be in stock again?
Alan In two to three weeks. Do you need it urgently?
Katrin Yes, I do. It's very urgent.
Alan Well, we have another flip chart in stock. It's a good, basic piece of equipment. It does the job just as well as the other one.
Katrin Is that the cheaper one?
Alan Yes. £62.42. It's very light.
Katrin Is it really light?
Alan Oh, yes. It's not heavy at all. You can move it quite easily.
Katrin How quickly can you deliver that one?
Alan You're in London, so if I send it out today, you'll have it tomorrow.
Katrin All right. If you can guarantee quick delivery, I'll take it.
Alan Good. I'll just call up an order form. So that's item number 01FC, moveable flip chart. Quantity, one. Price, £62.42. What about paper?
Katrin Yes. I'd like to order two packets of paper, please.
Alan Right. Item number 03FC. Flip chart paper. Quantity, two. Price per pack, £18.99. Is that everything?
Katrin Yes. I think so.
Alan Good. That will be a total of one hundred pounds and forty pence. Oh. That's lucky. Over £100, so that means free delivery for you. How would you like to pay?
Katrin Cash on delivery.
Alan COD. Now, the last thing I need from you is your delivery details. May I have your postcode, please?
Katrin Yes, it's London N7 9EJ.
Alan Right. I've got it. A to Z Logistics, North Park Industrial Estate.
Katrin That's right. And my name's Katrin Troll. That's T-R-O-double L, email address is …

22

Unit 7, Part A, Exercise 4

Jenna Good morning, Anton. How're you?
Anton Hi, Jenna. I'm fine, thanks. How about you?
Jenna Oh, I'm OK, Anton. Too much work, of course, but I suppose that's a good thing, isn't it?
Anton Sure. And I'm afraid I'm about to add to it – the work, I mean.
Jenna Oh, dear. Why's that? Has something gone wrong?
Anton Yes, I'm afraid it has. The last consignment hasn't been delivered yet. According to the delivery schedule, it should have arrived here last Thursday, 10 October, but it didn't turn up. That's four days ago.
Jenna I'm sorry to hear that, Anton. Look, let me find out what's happened, and I'll get back to you as soon as I can, OK?
Anton Fine, Jenna, but … Well, look, I don't want to put you under any pressure, but could you treat this as urgent, please? Our stocks are getting very low and we have an awful lot of orders to fill. A few of our own customers are already beginning to get a little restless, in fact.
Jenna Oh, I'm sorry to hear that, Anton. But don't worry. I'll get on with it immediately and call you back within an hour or so, OK?

23

Unit 7, Part B, Exercise 4

Jenna Hi, Anton. It's Jenna again.
Anton Hi, Jenna. That was quick. What have you found out?
Jenna Well, the consignment left our stores last Monday afternoon as planned. I've been in touch with our forwarding agents, and they told me that the truck was on schedule until it was involved in a bad pile-up in fog on the motorway near Nuremberg in Bavaria on Wednesday.
Anton Oh, that's bad. Was our consignment damaged in the accident?
Jenna Well, the forwarding agents say no, it wasn't. It's being transferred to another truck today, and it should arrive in Vienna at about eleven o'clock tomorrow morning, 15 October.
Anton Good heavens. What took so long? Nuremberg's not all that far away. It's only about 500 kilometres or so.
Jenna Sure, but I'm afraid it's the old story, Anton. As far as I can see, on the continent the weekend starts about Friday midday. Anyhow, I'll confirm all this by email, OK?
Anton Fine, Jenna. I'd appreciate that.
Jenna Well, I'm very sorry about this, Anton, but I suppose it could have been worse, couldn't it? Goodbye.
Anton Goodbye, Jenna. And thanks a lot for your help.

24

Unit 7, Part C, Exercise 1

Melissa Guten Morgen. Verkaufsabteilung. Melissa Wolf am Apparat.
Jerzy Oh. Hello. Erm. Do you speak English?
Melissa Yes, of course. How can I help you?
Jerzy Oh. Good. This is Jerzy Adamczyk calling from the Denta Dental Clinic in Warsaw. Is that the Sales Department?

Melissa Yes, this is the Sales Department. My name's Melissa Wolf.

Jerzy Ah. Mrs, erm, Ms Wolf. Hmm. Is, erm, are you the correct person to take a complaint about a delivery?

Melissa It depends on what it's about. Could you give me some details?

Jerzy It's about my order for x-ray machines. Both of the x-ray machines were damaged. One of them – the glass on one of the machines is scratched, and the other machine is dented. I mean, the metal casing is dented. I think that there was a problem during transport.

Melissa Oh, I'm sorry to hear that. Could you give me the order number, please?

Jerzy It's 942761.

Melissa Just a moment, please. Right. 942761. I have it here. Two x-ray machines. And you say that both of them are damaged?

Jerzy That is correct. I am sorry, but I have to say that I am disappointed about this business. This is a trial order but I had to complain last week because the equipment did not arrive on the date we agreed. Now the machines are here and I can't use them.

Melissa Oh, dear. I'm extremely sorry to hear that you've had so much trouble. I'm sure my superior would like to discuss this with you. Can I ask her to phone you when she comes in to work tomorrow?

Jerzy Yes. All right. I'll be at home all day tomorrow so she should call me there. The number is 0048 129 546 993.

Melissa 0048 129 546 993. Yes. You'll get a call from my superior tomorrow, Mr Adamczyk.

Jerzy Could you tell me her name, please?

Melissa It's Mia Richter.

Jerzy Mia Richter. Good. Thank you very much, Ms Wolf.

Melissa You're welcome, Mr Adamczyk. Thank you for calling.

Jerzy Goodbye.

25 Unit 7, Part D, Exercise 1

Melissa Guten Morgen. Verkaufsabteilung. Melissa Wolf am Apparat.

Jerzy Oh. Hello. Erm. Do you speak English?

Melissa Yes, of course. How can I help you?

Jerzy Oh. Good. This is Jerzy Adamczyk calling from the Denta Dental Clinic in Warsaw. Is that the Sales Department?

Melissa Yes, this is the Sales Department. My name's Melissa Wolf.

Jerzy Ah. Mrs, erm, Ms Wolf. Hmm. Is, erm, are you the correct person to take a complaint about a delivery?

Melissa It depends on what it's about. Could you give me some details?

Jerzy It's about my order for x-ray machines. Both of the x-ray machines were damaged. One of them – the glass on one of the machines is scratched, and the other machine is dented. I mean, the metal casing is dented. I think that there was a problem during transport.

Melissa Oh, I'm sorry to hear that. Could you give me the order number, please?

Jerzy It's 942761.

Melissa Just a moment, please. Right. I have it here.

Jerzy I am sorry, but I have to say that I am disappointed about this business. This is a trial order but I had to complain last week because the equipment did not arrive on the date we agreed. Now the machines are here and I can't use them.

Melissa Oh, dear. I'm extremely sorry to hear that you've had so much trouble. I'm sure my superior would like to discuss this with you. Can I ask her to phone you when she comes in to work tomorrow?

Jerzy Yes. All right. I'll be at home all day tomorrow so she should call me there. The number is 0048 129 546 993.

Melissa Yes. You'll get a call from my superior tomorrow, Mr Adamczyk.

Jerzy Could you tell me her name, please?

Melissa It's Mia Richter.

Jerzy Mia Richter. Good. Thank you very much, Ms Wolf.

Melissa You're welcome, Mr Adamczyk. Thank you for calling.

Jerzy Goodbye.

26 KMK mock exam, Aufgabe 1, Hörverstehen, Teil 1

Natalie Hello and welcome back to 'Business Instinct' here on Radio Nova. I'm Natalie Richardson, and today I'm speaking to well-known motivational speaker Lewis Schelling. Welcome, Lewis!

Lewis Thanks, Nat. It's great to be here.

Natalie Work is an essential part of life, so if you aren't happy at work, you can't be happy in life! But it isn't easy to find a job you love, especially when many employers prioritize profit over employee happiness. Lewis, you spent ten years working in an office for a large company. What was your experience?

Lewis That's right: my first job after graduating from university was in PR for a large media company in Leeds. To be honest, it confirmed all my worst fears about corporate culture. The offices were grey and lifeless, and the work was dull. There was so much red tape: every new idea had to pass three stages of approval! All my colleagues were bored too. It created a bad atmosphere in the office.

Natalie Having been in that position, how would you advise someone who is currently struggling with boredom at work?

Lewis I'd push them to make a positive choice: either they stay in the job and try to make it fun, or it's time to leave. Personally, I'd always choose to leave. As long as you're in a job you dislike, you can never realize your full professional potential – nor can you feel as happy or fulfilled as you would in a job that inspired you.

Natalie Yes, that's an important point. But what if the boss is making your life difficult – how can you deal with that?

Lewis Well, again, you have two options. You can try to train your boss – and yes, I know that *they* are supposed to train *you*! But most bosses are willing to change their ways if it will make their employees happier and more productive. Sometimes that just won't work, though. Studies have shown that around five to ten per cent of managers have psychopathic traits, compared to two per cent of the general population. You can't reason with these people. Their lack of empathy means they don't – they *can't* – care about you. If you suspect your boss has such traits, get away as fast as you can! Find a job in a different team or even at a new company.

Natalie It isn't usually as simple as that, though. People have responsibilities; they have to earn money – and the job market is tough! So how can our listeners break the monotony of the working day without taking such drastic steps?

Lewis Oh, there are a million ways to bring some variety into your routine. Why not do something nice for a co-worker tomorrow? Perhaps bring them a coffee out of the blue. Or even treat your whole team: bring doughnuts to a meeting, compliment people on their achievements, or ask about their plans for the weekend. Anything that helps bring some fun to the office and creates a personal connection between colleagues.

Natalie Thank you for your fascinating insights, Lewis. Those are some great tips to end on.

27 KMK mock exam, Aufgabe 1, Hörverstehen, Teil 2

Good morning, this is Arturo Mendez Reverte from Buenos Aires, Argentina speaking. I will spell my name for you. It's: A-R-T-U-R-O M-E-N-D-E-Z R-E-V-E-R-T-E.

I am calling about my business trip to Munich from 12 to 14 March. I will be arriving at the airport at 9:00 in the morning. Since I have never been to Germany before I would really appreciate it if you arranged for somebody to pick me up. Also, can you please confirm the hotel reservation you have made for me and confirm you have booked a quiet room? I desperately need a room that is facing the garden. I need the room to be very quiet as I am a light sleeper and if I don't get enough sleep, I will not make it through the entire meeting.

Also, it would be fantastic if you could get tickets for me to see the Munich versus Chelsea football match.

My email address is: am_reverte@buenos-aires.com.

Thank you. Goodbye.

28 IHK mock exam, Aufgabe C, Vermerk in Deutsch über ein Gespräch in Englisch

Martin Spielberg. Guten Morgen.

Brendan Good morning, Mr Spielberg. It's Brendan Mathers here from Hermes Freight Forwarding. I'm phoning about the position you applied for as Export Clerk. Do you mind if we speak English?

Martin No, not at all. Good morning, Mr Mathers. It's nice to hear from you.

Brendan Mr Spielberg, I read through your CV and covering letter and would be very interested to meet you to find out a bit more about you. You wrote in your covering letter that you'd be available for an interview at short notice. Is that still the case?

Martin Yes, certainly. When would suit you?

Brendan Well, I'm actually in Nuremberg on business from Wednesday, 29 July until Monday, 3 August. What about Thursday, 30 July?

Martin I'm sorry. I'm busy all day on 30 July.

Brendan What about the next day? Would Friday be convenient for you, at about 5 pm?

Martin Friday is fine, but I'm afraid 5 pm is a bit too early for me. I don't finish work until 4 pm, and it will take me an hour and a half to get to Nuremberg. Are you still free at 6 pm?

Brendan Yes, that's OK with me. Now, I was thinking we could meet at Restaurant Backstein. Do you know it?

Martin Yes, I think so. It's on Hauptstraße, isn't it?

Brendan That's right. There's just one more thing. Would you mind giving me your mobile number, just in case there are any changes to the plan?

Martin No problem. It's 0176 438 05 783.

Brendan Thank you. Right, well, I'll see you on Friday.

Martin OK, no problem. Thank you for calling, Mr Mathers. Goodbye.

Brendan Goodbye.

Unit 1 Getting started

A INTRODUCING YOURSELF AND OTHER PEOPLE

1
freie Lösung

2
1g; **2**e; **3**c; **4**j; **5**i; **6**f; **7**b; **8**h; **9**d; **10**a

B WELCOMING A VISITOR

1
1 meeting, Dusseldorf;
2 her flight was delayed;
3 haven't;
4 an hour

2
1 Welcome to;
2 nice to meet you;
3 sorry I'm late;
4 have a good flight;
5 can I get you anything;
6 I'd love;
7 Here you are;
8 here's the agenda;
9 give you my business card;
10 here's mine

C WRITING A THANK-YOU EMAIL

1
Lösungsvorschlag
Dear Helena

Thank you very much for your kind welcome and the useful meeting we had in Dusseldorf. It was very nice to meet you personally. My flight back to Oslo was fine – no delay this time! I was most impressed with your company and its products, and I hope we can work together in the future.

I am looking forward to seeing you again soon.

Best wishes
Zoe Kline

2
1g; **2**d; **3**i; **4**h; **5**b; **6**a; **7**c; **8**f

3
1 to; **2** to; **3** at; **4** to; **5** back; **6** at; **7** by; **8** on, for; **9** for; **10** of

4
1 make;
2 improve;
3 change;
4 work;
5 have;
6 ask;
7 do;
8 listen

5
1 Oxford;
2 Tuesday;
3 morning;
4 afternoon;
5 lunch;
6 12.30;
7 pub;
8 Lion Street;
9 Wheatsheaf;
10 tomorrow morning

D MAKING AN ONLINE TRAVEL BOOKING

1
1 logged in;
2 clicked on;
3 enter;
4 select;
5 return;
6 available;
7 filter your search;
8 breakfast included;
9 facilities;
10 payment method;
11 booked;
12 confirmation

2
1c; **2**a; **3**d; **4**b; **5**f; **6**e

E KMK EXAM PRACTICE

1
1 er fährt nach Deutschland (Freiburg) und will sich mit Benno treffen
2 Montag/Dienstag
3 er hat schon eine andere Besprechung
4 er fliegt um 4 Uhr nach England zurück und muss schon um 3 Uhr am Flughafen sein
5 sie treffen sich zum Mittagessen (1 Uhr am Dienstag)

2
Lösungsvorschlag
To: HelenBrown@bobblemail.nex
From: ChrisJones@Jackson.nex
Subject: Meeting with Ben Jackson
Dear Helen

Ben has confirmed your meeting in Lion Street on Tuesday. However, he will not be able to be there before 1 p.m. because he has another meeting before yours. He will wear a red scarf so that you can recognize him. He will have a maximum of two hours for your discussion. He has to leave at 3 p.m. because he is flying to London.

I hope that is OK with you.

Kind regards
Chris

3
1 stets freundlich sein, auch wenn sie beschäftigt sind; Augenkontakt herstellen, mit Handgesten zeigen, dass sie gleich verfügbar sind; Hilfe anbieten, wenn sie mit dem Telefonieren fertig sind
2 ein Plakat im Empfang aushängen, was der Gast begrüßt
3 Augenkontakt schaffen; lächeln; den Besuch begrüßen; Hilfe anbieten
4 sauber, einladend und aufgeräumt, nicht nur Empfang; Wände sollen sauber sein; Teppich soll nicht alt aussehen; sollte keine alte Zeitschriften im Wartebereich geben
5 eine Dankeskarte oder kleines Geschenk verschicken

F IHK EXAM PRACTICE

1
Lösungsvorschlag

Für: Marie Hufnagel		
Verfasst von: Benno Koch	am:	15. März
Gesprächspartner/in: Peter Michaels		
Betrifft: Termin in Freiburg		
Herr Michaels wird nächste Woche auf Kundenbesuch in Freiburg sein und möchte sich mit mir treffen; es geht um die Bestellung, die wir letzten Monat auf der Messe besprochen haben. Das Treffen wird am Dienstag um 13 Uhr bei einem Mittagessen stattfinden (ein anderer Zeitpunkt war nicht möglich, da wir beide viele Termine haben).		

2
Lösungsvorschlag
To: HelenBrown@bobblemail.nex
From: ChrisJones@Jackson.nex
Subject: Meeting with Ben Jackson
Dear Helen

Ben has confirmed your meeting in Lion Street on Tuesday. However, he will not be able to be there before 1 p.m. because he has another meeting before yours. He will wear a red scarf so that you can recognize him. He will have a maximum of two hours for your discussion.

He has to leave at 3 p.m. because he is flying to London.

I hope that is OK with you.

Kind regards
Chris

3
1 impression; **2** premises; **3** for; **4** staff; **5** answering; **6** greeting; **7** takes; **8** their; **9** much; **10** to; **11** who; **12** entrance; **13** desks; **14** around; **15** attending; **16** on; **17** where; **18** healthy; **19** appreciated; **20** competition

Unit 2 Basic communication

A WRITING BUSINESS LETTERS

1
1 Letterhead (A); **2** Reference 1 (B); **3** Reference 2 (B); **4** Date (C); **5** Inside address (D); **6** Attention line (E); **7** Salutation (F); **8** Subject line (G); **9** Body of the letter (H); **10** Complimentary close (F); **11** Signature (I); **12** Enclosure(s) (J)

2
Your ref.: UA/be
Our ref.: MN/sk
19 June 20..

Julia Roch
Gamma Photo Agency
33 Avenue Napoléon
75019 Paris
France

Dear Ms Andrews

Photo selection

I enjoyed our discussion in Cologne last week and was very pleased with the photos you took of our stand at the trade fair. Please find enclosed my choice for our new brochure.

Could you let us have price details asap?

Kind regards
Marianne Neumann
Marketing Director

Encs

3
Dear Sir or Madam, Yours sincerely, Best wishes, Kind regards

4
1 Tel. 33 (0)1 40 00 00 11,
2 Our ref: UA/be;
3 23 June 20..;
4 Ms Neumann,
5 Photo selection;
6 hearing from you soon;
7 Yours sincerely;
8 Encs

B WRITING EMAILS

1
1f; **2**a; **3**b; **4**e; **5**d; **6**c

2
1d; **2**g; **3**a; **4**c; **5**b; **6**e; **7**f; **8**h

3
1 catherine.bright@fluent/english.nex
2 hotsales@amazing-bikes.nex.
3 Damian_HR@InnovatorsLtd.nex.
4 customer.service@the_apparel_centre.nex
5 biljones@freelance-solutions.nex
6 Support@PC-Service.nex.

4
1d; **2**f; **3**a; **4**e; **5**b; **6**c

5
Lösungsvorschlag
1 New date for meeting;
2 Presentation: information, please;
3 Out-of-office;
4 Details for stand at Bionord Fair;
5 Link to website;
6 Lunch appointment

6
1 wishes; **2** sincerely; **3** Good; **4** Hello/Hi Paul; **5** wishes/regards; **6** All the; **7** writing; **8** note/line/mail/letter; **9** to your; **10** hearing; **11** from you soon

7
Lösungsvorschlag
To: gdoyle@irishnation.nex
From: halltown@globalmail.orx
Subject: Meeting with Inge Pedersen at Industrial Fair

Dear Mr Doyle

Ms Pedersen would like to arrange a meeting with you to finalize the contract. She would like to meet you at the Industrial Fair in Frankfurt next week. She suggests either Thursday 26 any time in the morning until 1 p.m. or Friday 27 between 12.30 and 6.30 p.m. The meeting will take about three hours. Please let me know if either of these dates is suitable. I hope to hear from you by tomorrow as I need time to organize a conference room.

Best regards
(name)

8
Lösungsvorschlag
To: paulholliday@irishnation.nex
From: gdoyle@irishnation.nex
Subject: Cancel Thursday breakfast

Hi Paul

Just a quick note to let you know I have to cancel our breakfast meeting on Thursday. Sorry, I have a meeting to finalize a contract. Could we perhaps meet on Thursday evening for dinner? How about that nice French restaurant near the entrance to the fair?

If you let me know soon, I can reserve a table for 7.30.

All the best
Gary

C TELEPHONING

1
1 Guten Morgen, ich heiße …
2 Guten Tag. Hier spricht … von …
3 Wie kann ich Ihnen behilflich sein?
4 Am Apparat.
5 Wie geht es Ihnen?
6 Wie ist das Wetter bei Ihnen?
7 Ich würde gern mit Herrn/Frau … sprechen.
8 Könnten Sie mich bitte mit der … abteilung verbinden?
9 Ich möchte mich nach … erkundigen.
10 Ich hätte gerne Näheres zu/über … gewusst.
11 Können Sie mir etwas zu/über … sagen?
12 Kann ich eine Nachricht hinterlassen?
13 Ich rufe später noch einmal an.
14 Danke für Ihre Hilfe.

2
1d; **2**b; **3**i; **4**a; **5**k; **6**f; **7**h; **8**g; **9**c; **10**e

3
1 who's calling, please;
2 spell your name;
3 repeat that;
4 hold the line;
5 trying to connect you;
6 unavailable;
7 someone else;
8 put you through;
9 is engaged;
10 leave a message

4
Lösungsvorschlag
A Hello? Steve Brown speaking.
B Hello, Steve. This is …. speaking. How are you?
A Fine, thanks. Everything's going well here. How can I help you?
B Steve, could you put me through to Diana Wilson, please?
A I'm afraid Diana is not in the office today. She's on holiday. Would you like to leave a message?
B Yes. Would you tell her that I can't keep our appointment on Friday, and I'll ring her to arrange a new one?
A OK. I have made a note of that, and I'll pass it on.
B Thanks, Steve. Bye for now.
A Bye.

5
1b; **2**c; **3**b; **4**c

6
1 to be back shortly;
2 leave a name and number;
3 call back as soon as possible;
4 is not available at present;
5 leave a name, number and message;
6 call back later;
7 all their lines are engaged at the moment;
8 call back later;
9 his/her cooperation

D COMMUNICATING BY EMAIL AND PHONE

1
1c; **2**a; **3**b

2
1 confirm;
2 arrive;
3 suitable;
4 book;
5 change;
6 arrange

3
1j; **2**f; **3**a; **4**i; **5**b; **6**h; **7**g; **8**k; **9**c; **10**e

4
1c; **2**f; **3**e; **4**b; **5**d; **6**a; **7**g

5
1b; **2**a; **3**b; **4**b

6

noun	**verb**	**noun**	**verb**
confirmation	confirm	booking	book
Bestätigung	bestätigen	Reservierung, Buchung	reservieren, buchen
arrangement	arrange	invitation	invite
Vereinbarung	vereinbaren, organisieren	Einladung	einladen
meeting	meet	enquiry	enquire
Besprechung	treffen	Anfrage	sich erkundigen
presentation	present	information	inform
Präsentation	präsentieren	Information(en)	informieren
arrival	arrive	apology	apologize
Ankunft	ankommen	Entschuldigung	entschuldigen

7
1 ~~June~~ May;
2 ~~Tuesday~~ Thursday;
3 ~~computer~~ phone;
4 ~~evening~~ morning;
5 ~~after~~ before;
6 ~~sightseeing~~ shopping;

7 ~~TV show~~ conference;
8 ~~clothes~~ sunglasses;
9 ~~10.30~~ 1.30;
10 ~~show~~ speech;
11 ~~one~~ ten;
12 ~~Sunday~~ Friday;
13 ~~p.m.~~ a.m.

E KMK EXAM PRACTICE

1
Vorteile: schneller; man kann mit einer E-Mail mehrere Leute gleichzeitig erreichen; geringere Kosten; umweltfreundlich
Nachteile: manche Leute halten E-Mails für zu informell für Geschäftskorrespondenz; mögliche Sicherheitslücken im Internet; mögliche Probleme mit der rechtlichen Verbindlichkeit von Vertragsabschlüssen per E-Mail

2
Lösungsvorschlag
To: halltown@globalmail.orx
From: gdoyle@irishnation.nex
Subject: Meeting at Industrial Fair

Dear Ms Hall

Thank you for your email. An appointment at the Industrial Fair on Thursday 26 at 9.30 would suit me best. Your assistant needn't book a conference room as my company has a stand with a small meeting room attached (Hall 3, stand number 75). I look forward to seeing you then.

Best wishes
Gary Doyle

3
Lösungsvorschlag
Dear Sir or Madam

I wish to reserve a stand for my company in Hall 2 at the WORKPLACE trade fair from 18 to 20 November in Earls Court, London.

The stand should be as near to the main entrance as possible and have a minimum area of 280 m^2.

We assume that all stands are equipped with telephone and internet connections. Ideally, we would also like to have a separate meeting room.

Please confirm our reservation as soon as possible.

Yours sincerely
(Name)

4
Lösungsvorschlag
Dear Ms Giles

I am writing to you about an interesting report on business travel which I found on the internet. It may answer some of your questions.

50% of all companies have changed from business trips to virtual conferences. The advantage of this is,for example,that people who take part in a meeting don't feel stressed about being late because of traffic. On the other hand not all business trips can be digital because many businesses believe that personal contact is very important.

When they go on a business trip, 59% of people said that they try to plan several appointments to save costs and emissions. Half the people asked said, they travel by train rather than by plane or renting a car. In addition, managers in every second company said they don't carry paper printouts with them, but they take digital copies instead. However, one thing they were not interested in doing was car sharing.

I hope you will find these results interesting.

Best regards

F IHK EXAM PRACTICE

1
Lösungsvorschlag
Dear Sir or Madam

I wish to reserve a stand for my company in Hall 2 at the WORKPLACE trade fair from 18 to 20 November in Earls Court, London.

The stand should be as near to the main entrance as possible and have a minimum area of 280 m^2.

We assume that all stands are equipped with telephone and internet connections. Ideally, we would also like to have a separate meeting room.

Please confirm our reservation as soon as possible.

Yours sincerely
(Name)

2
Lösungsvorschlag

Für: Thomas Liepe		
Verfasst von: *Name*	am:	*Datum*
Gesprächspartner/in: June Smith		
Betrifft: Rob Heldofs Interview am Sonntagvormittag		
Frau Smith hat angerufen, um die genaue Uhrzeit des Interviews zu bestätigen: In Ihrer E-Mail steht 8.30 Uhr, in der angehängten Datei jedoch 7.30 Uhr, was Herrn Heldof zu früh ist. Außerdem ist das Formular, das Herr Heldof unterschreiben soll, auf Deutsch. Er versteht kein Deutsch und wird es daher nicht unterzeichnen. Wir möchten ihm bitte eine englische Version schicken. Außerdem wollte Frau Smith wissen, wie im Interview das Sprachproblem gelöst wird. Ich habe ihr erklärt, dass beim Interview gedolmetscht wird, und ihr zugesagt, dass wir uns mit dem englischsprachigen Formular und der Bestätigung des Interviewtermins wieder bei ihr melden.		

3
1 has shown;
2 more;
3 if;
4 be used to;
5 written;
6 to;
7 negative;
8 globalized;
9 may be;
10 mean;
11 for;
12 we are writing to;
13 formal;
14 Because of;
15 is expressed;
16 surnames;
17 such;
18 using;
19 it;
20 of;
21 write;
22 then;
23 This;
24 recipient;
25 permission;
26 person's;
27 their;
28 become;
29 don't forget;
30 should always begin

Unit 3 Applying for a job

A JOB ADVERTISEMENTS

1

1 Bürokauffrau
2 Terminverwaltung, Arbeit am Empfang, Praxisleiter/in assistieren, Begrüßen von Kundschaft
3 gut organisieren können, fähig unter Druck zu arbeiten, fähig in typischen Büro-Software, gute Maschinenschreibkenntnisse, gutes Telefonverhalten, Kenntnisse von Englisch und eventuell eine weitere Fremdsprache
4 optionale Sprachunterricht
5 Bewerbungsbogen ausfüllen und Lebenslauf und Begleitschrieben anhängen

2

1 candidate;	**5** CV;
2 responsibility;	**6** covering letter;
3 administration;	**7** permanent;
4 application;	**8** salary

3

A2; **B**1; **C**3; **D**5

4

1 The company is looking for trainees for its training programme.
2 The trainees can participate in the in-house training scheme.
3 A customer adviser talks to different people.
4 The animator will give classes in dancing and aerobics.
5 A bank trainee should be good at handling cash.
6 The company has a vacancy for an events clerk.
7 The clerk will deal with the public.
8 The team gives out brochures to the public.
9 The company says there is the possibility of a better job later.
10 The assistant needs to come with good language skills.

B JOB APPLICATIONS

1

1e; **2**f; **3**h; **4**c; **5**a; **6**g; **7**b; **8**d

2

1 Personal details;	**5** Skills and achievements;
2 Personal statement;	**6** Hobbies and interests;
3 Work experience;	**7** References
4 Education and training;	

3

A German CV includes more personal information, e.g: date of birth, place of birth, marital status. Details about education and work experience are given in chronological order.

4

1 team-oriented;	**5** skills;
2 certified	**6** flexible;
3 health insurance;	**7** fluent;
4 participation;	**8** referee

5

freie Lösung

6

1B; **2**D; **3**A; **4**E; **5**C

7

Lösungsvorschlag
(your address)

Ms Rebecca Potter
NYNY Events
76 Broadway
New York
NY 11580
USA

(date)

Dear Ms Potter

Experienced events clerk

The position of events clerk with your company in New York as advertised on the 'Jobs in the USA' website has caught my interest.

I am interested in the job you are offering as I feel sure it will give me the opportunity to develop in my career as well as personally. I am particularly keen to work in an English-speaking country where I can use my knowledge of English on a daily basis. Although I am successful in my present position, I feel that it is time for me to look for a new challenge at work, and I believe a year or two abroad would provide this.

As you can see from the enclosed CV, I am currently employed in a German events company in Munich. My duties include dealing with the general public, giving out information about events and distributing tickets by post and email. Because of my experience and the fact that I speak fluent German (mother tongue) and English, I believe I would be particularly suitable for the post advertised.

Enclosed is my CV. If you wish, I am happy to provide the names of two referees.

I would appreciate it if you would consider my application.

I look forward to hearing from you soon.

Yours sincerely

...

C JOB INTERVIEWS

1

Lösungsvorschlag
Ein telefonisches Bewerbungsgespräch kann ebenso entscheidend sein wie ein persönliches Vorstellungsgespräch. Man sollte dabei gleich den bestmöglichen Eindruck machen und sich deshalb gut vorbereiten. Es ist wichtig über das Telefon nicht zu entspannt zu werden, formell zu bleiben, und besonders aufmerksam zuhören, da man den anderen nicht sehen kann. Am besten geht man das zu erwartende Gespräch gründlich in Gedanken durch. Als praktische Vorbereitung sollte man das Stellenangebot, das eigene Bewerbungsschreiben, den Lebenslauf und die Zeugnisse greifbar und übersichtlich bereit halten. Eine zuvor erstellte Liste mit Notizen zu besonderen

Fähigkeiten und Stärken ist nützlich. Papier und Schreibzeug nicht vergessen!

2
1d; **2**c; **3**a; **4**b; **5**e

3
1 How would you describe yourself?
2 What are your strengths and weaknesses?
3 Why did you choose to train at a vocational college?
4 Why do you want to work for this company?
5 What would you like to achieve in the next five years?
6 What languages do you speak?

4
freie Lösung

5
1 25 Burns Drive, Aberdeen;
2 AB4 6GX;
3 01224 286437;
4 0169 8473621;
5 Honours degree in Marketing;
6 A-levels in Economics, History, Social Sciences;
7 German, French;
8 two work placements in the PR Department of Aberdeen Development Corporation

6
1d; **2**g; **3**e; **4**f; **5**h; **6**b; **7**a; **8**i; **9**c

7
1 in good time;
2 to relax and calm down;
3 clothes;
4 impressions count;
5 language;
6 confidently as possible;
7 make eye contact;
8 shy;
9 the weather, your journey, where you live, hobbies;
10 small talk in English with a colleague or a friend;
11 by one or more interviewers. Sometimes there's a panel;
12 make a list;
13 strengths and weaknesses;
14 ask the interviewer to clarify;
15 background research into the company before the interview;
16 most recent developments and the future prospects;
17 homepage on the internet;
18 the business section of newspapers;
19 business magazines;
20 questions about the company;
21 questions about the job itself;
22 the candidate can expect to hear from the company;
23 thank you and goodbye;
24 firm handshake and a smile

8
a7; **b**8; **c**4; **d**2; **e**1; **f**5

9
1 HR manager, assistant sales manager;
2 assistant in the sales team to support them when they are on the road in future; a completely new position;
3 looks after first-class passengers at the airport; but not his world –wants something more normal, to be part of a team;
4 Strength: gets on well with people, tactful and diplomatic, Weakness: finds it hard to make decisions, always tries not to upset other people;
5 wants to work in a team, interested in a sales job, opportunity to use Polish, likes the natural products the company sells

D KMK EXAM PRACTICE

1

1 völlig andere Kultur, eine der am schnellsten wachsenden Volkwirtschaften der Welt
2 Ingenieurwesen, IT, Finanzen, Vertrieb und Marketing.
3 Durch persönliche Kontakte findet man am besten einen Job. Hat man diese nicht, bietet das Internet viele Möglichkeiten.
4 Chinesischkenntnisse sind ein Türöffner, ein Universitätsabschluss ist von großem Vorteil, außerdem Fremdsprachenkenntnisse, Teamfähigkeit, gute Organisation.
5 Beim Lebenslauf und im Vorstellungsgespräch bescheiden auftreten und bei den Fakten bleiben; kurzes Begleitschreiben, Zeugnisse und Zertifikate mit der Bewerbung schicken

2
1 Interessiert sich für Martins Lebenslauf und möchte wissen, ob Martin für ein Vorstellungsgespräch zur Verfügung steht;
2 geschäftlich;
3 Er arbeitet bis 16.00 Uhr;
4 anderthalb Stunden;
5 Freitag, 31. Juli, um 18.00 Uhr;
6 0176 438 05 783

E IHK EXAM PRACTICE

1
Lösungsvorschlag
From: (Ihr Name)@kpmj.de
An: patobrien@outlook.eix
Subject: Your enquiry about our job advertisement (ref. no. 2021915IE)

Dear Mr O'Brien,

Thank you very much for your email requesting further information regarding our job advertisement. We are happy to help you with your queries:

· The relocation package that we offer depends on the personal circumstances of the candidate, for example whether they have children or whether they have a mortgage or rental payments to pay, etc. Unfortunately, we cannot confirm details of this package until the second round of interviews at the earliest but I can assure you that previous candidates from Ireland and the UK were satisfied with the packages they received.

· There is a probationary period of six months.

· I'm afraid we cannot give details about which qualifications are recognized here in Germany but can recommend you look this up on the information portal for foreign qualifications online and select the federal state of Hessen.

I hope this information provides some assistance and would further suggest you look at the candidate submission checklist on our company website.

We wish you the best of luck with your application.

Yours sincerely,

2

Lösungsvorschlag

Herr Traynor teilt uns die Ergebnisse des ersten Abschnitts unserer Rekrutierungskampagne in Irland mit. Er hat eine detaillierte Aufstellung mitgeschickt, fasst aber seine ersten Erkenntnisse in seinem Brief zusammen. Die Erfolgsquote lag mit 60% oder 30 Kandidat/innen unter unserem Ziel von 50 geeigneten Kandidat/innen. Die Rücklaufquote zu unserer Werbung und direkten Ansprache über soziale Medien wie LinkedIn und Profis.eix war ebenfalls niedrig. Auf die Frage, weshalb sie kein Interesse an einer Bewerbung bei Sellbycom hätten, haben angesprochene Fachkräfte folgende Gründe genannt: unattraktives Gehalt, unzureichende finanzielle Beihilfe beim Umzug und fehlendes Wissen über das Leben in Deutschland insbesondere für Leute, die kein Deutsch sprechen. Herr Traynor meint allerdings, dass wir mit einigen kleinen Änderungen unsere Erfolgsquote deutlich steigern können. Fachkräfte in Irland orientieren ihre Gehaltsvorstellungen an den hohen Lebenshaltungskosten in Irland. Diese sind in Deutschland jedoch erheblich niedriger, und für uns kommt es daher darauf an, potentiellen Bewerbern dieses Gefälle deutlich zu machen. Vorschläge dazu hat Herr Traynor mitgeschickt und freut sich auf unser Feedback. Für die zweite Planungsbesprechung in ca. zwei Wochen bittet er darum, einen Termin zu vereinbaren. Unser Assistent soll sich bei ihm melden.

Unit 4 Making and dealing with enquiries

A A FIRST ENQUIRY

1

1 False. He works for a company in Germany.
2 False. He found information in a trade magazine.
3 False. Gartenmöbel Limbach imports garden furniture.
4 True.
5 False. He asks The Greenhouse BV to send him a catalogue.
6 True.
7 False. He may be prepared to place regular orders.
8 True.

2

1 advertisement; 2 delivery; 3 payment; 4 trade magazine; 5 range of products; 6 importer; 7 place an order; 8 grateful

3

1 We saw your advertisement …
2 Our company is a leading German importer …
3 We are planning to …
4 … a wide range of …
5 Please let us have details …
6 If we are satisfied with your company's products …
7 We would be happy to supply references …
8 We look forward to hearing from you soon.

4

1 director; 2 imports; 3 range; 4 advertisement; 5 greenhouse; 6 manufacturer; 7 magazine; 8 enquiry; 9 request; 10 information; 11 company's; 12 in; 13 payment; 14 a business; 15 closed; 16 Yours faithfully

B AT A TRADE FAIR

1

1l; **2**k; **3**e; **4**g; **5**j; **6**c; **7**d; **8**a; **9**b; **10**h

2

1 I represent;
2 Are you familiar with;
3 If you have a spare moment;
4 I'll explain the advantages of;
5 is available in;
6 It includes;
7 Would you like me to send you a quotation;
8 give a detailed presentation of all our products;
9 I'll contact you after the fair;
10 supply you with further information

3

Caller: Jo Clarke
Company: Top Fit Studios
Date of enquiry: 21 October
Reference number: JC/2110/PC
Catalogue number: DPC-4X
Date of offer sent: 25 October
Email address for resend: Top.Fit@Training.nex

C ENQUIRY ABOUT OFFICE EQUIPMENT

1

Lösungsvorschlag

(date)

Glasgow Office Furniture plc
Tayside Industrial Estate
Glasgow G1 3GH
United Kingdom

Dear Mr McTavish

Enquiry about office furniture

We have seen your advertisement in a trade magazine. We note that your company makes office furniture. Our company is a well-known importer of office furniture in Germany, and we are looking for a new supplier.

Please send a brochure and price list and details of your terms of delivery and payment. We look forward to hearing from you soon.

Yours sincerely …

2
Lösungsvorschlag

Office Props
Am Winterhafen 7
D-80930 Munich
Tel. +49 89 22344

(date)

Office Inc
149 Moulton Way
Cork City T12 T997
Ireland

Dear Sir or Madam

Enquiry about WLan OfficeInc 3.0

I saw your advert for the WLan OfficeInc 3.0 printer in Fortune magazine and I am very interested in this product. Office Props is a retail company which sells office machines, and we specialize in high-quality products. As our customers are always interested in the latest developments in the computer branch, we would like to include the WLan OfficeInc 3.0 in our range of products.

Our purchasing department is planning a meeting next week. Therefore we urgently require detailed information. Would you be so kind and send us the following information as soon as possible:
- detailed description of the product
- full details of your terms of delivery and payment
- your current price list including discounts
- information concerning minimum orders

If your company's product meets our requirements, we will be happy to place a large order with you.

Looking forward to hearing from you soon.

Yours faithfully

D KMK EXAM PRACTICE

1
1 Aberdeen (Dyce) Flughafen;
2 Glasgow Flughafen;
3 für die Chefin von Joe Davis/des Anrufers;
4 an Wochenenden;
5 Montag, den 16. März, um 09.00 Uhr;
6 £ 211.99;
7 Man muss für das Auftanken plus zehn Pfund extra bezahlen.;
8 Versicherung und unbegrenzte Kilometerzahl

2
Lösungsvorschlag
(date)

Finland Paper
Bulevardi 49
FI-55000
Finland

Dear Sir or Madam

Enquiry about printing paper

We have been given your address by our business partner in London, Ian McKenzie, Office Stationery Suppliers. Our company is one of the leading printers of trade magazines for the German-speaking market.

We hope you might be able to supply us with printing paper and would like you to send us samples of different types of paper which we could use. Please also let us have details of your terms of delivery and payment.

Mr McKenzie will be happy to supply references.

We look forward to hearing from you soon.

Yours faithfully

3
Lösungsvorschlag
Teilnahme an Messen bringt mehrere Vorteile:
1 Eine Firma wird dadurch besser bekannt. Mit einer auffallenden Gestaltung des eigenen Standes oder Logos ist ein Weg dieses zu erreichen.
2 Eine Messe ist eine gute Gelegenheit neue Geschäftsbeziehungen zu knüpfen. Man sollte im Messeprogramm nach Events schauen.
3 Für die Verkaufsabteilung ist eine Messe einen perfekten Ort, da die Käufer wissen was sie suchen und gut vorbereitet sind. Der Messestand sollte die neusten Produkte attraktiv darstellen, um die Kunden zu interessieren.
4 Es ist eine perfekte Gelegenheit zu schauen, was die Konkurrenz macht. Man sollte herumlaufen, die Stände anschauen und Notizen machen.
5 Letztlich sollte man nicht vergessen sich weiterzubilden und sich über neue Entwicklungen zu informieren. Man sollte im Messe Programm die Veranstaltungen notieren, die mit den eigenen Geschäftsbereichen zusammenhängen.

E IHK EXAM PRACTICE

1

Für: Linda Paschke		
Verfasst von: Joe Davis	am:	8. April
Gesprächspartner/in: Kim Cameron		
Betrifft: Autovermietung bei Star Car Hire		
Star Car gibt es an jedem schottischen Flughafen, daher ist es auf jeden Fall möglich, ein Auto am Flughafen Aberdeen zu mieten und am Flughafen Glasgow abzugeben. Es stehen fünf Mietwagenklassen zur Verfügung mit VW Polo und Ford Fiesta in Klasse A bis zu Luxuslimousinen in Klasse E. Die Mitarbeiterin empfiehlt wegen des Fahrkomforts Klasse C, z. B. einen Audi A4 oder Peugeot 307. Der Mietpreis hängt vom Wochentag ab und ist am Wochenende viel günstiger. Ein Auto der Klasse C von Montag, 16. März, 9.00 Uhr ab Aberdeen Dyce bis Freitag, 20. März, 18.00 Uhr nach Glasgow würde 211,99 £ kosten. Benzin kommt noch dazu (das Auto wird vollgetankt übernommen und muss vollgetankt zurückgegeben werden, sonst werden die Kosten dafür zzgl. einer Gebühr von 10 £ aufgeschlagen). Versicherung und unbegrenzte Kilometer sind im Preis inbegriffen. Das Büro ist bis zum 22 Uhr geöffnet und kann Reservierungen entgegennehmen.		

2
Lösungsvorschlag
(date)
Finland Paper
Bulevardi 49
FI-55000
Finland

Dear Sir or Madam

Enquiry about printing paper

We have been given your address by our business partner in London, Ian McKenzie, Office Stationery Suppliers. Our company is one of the leading printers of trade magazines for the German-speaking market.

We hope you might be able to supply us with printing paper and would like you to send us samples of different types of paper which we could use. Please also let us have details of your terms of delivery and payment.

Mr McKenzie will be happy to supply references.

We look forward to hearing from you soon.

Yours faithfully

3

1 for	**11** them;	**22** check;
2 There;	**12** make;	**23** competition;
3 hardly;	**13** increase;	**24** some;
4 occasions;	**14** These;	**25** around;
5 investment;	**15** little;	**26** take notes;
6 value;	**16** at;	**27** up to date with;
7 Whether you are;	**17** department;	**28** technologies;
8 better;	**18** well;	**29** on;
9 are;	**19** staff;	**30** with
10 impression;	**20** selling points;	
	21 latest;	

Unit 5 Making offers

A REPLYING TO ENQUIRIES

1

1. Yes. Everything in the catalogue is in stock.
2. If he pays within 10 days, he will get a discount.
3. They deal with orders immediately.
4. He can contact Lara Smit /The Greenhouse BV.

2

1. Our prices are quoted EXW.
2. For payment within 10 days we offer a 2.5% cash discount.
3. We are pleased to hear that you are interested in our products.
4. Please contact us if you require further details.
5. Our products are carefully packed.
6. We deal with orders immediately and guarantee an efficient and reliable service.
7. We feel sure that a trial order will convince you of the quality of our products.

3

1 insurance;	**5** freight;
2 unloaded;	**6** place;
3 on;	**7** paid;
4 Free;	**8** insurance;

4

2 FOB;	**5** EXW;
3 CIF;	**6** CPT
4 DAP;	

5

1 F; **2** T; **3** F; **4** T; **5** F; **6** T

6

1 cash discount;	**4** date of invoice;
2 cash with order;	**5** credit transfer;
3 credit;	**6** cash in advance

B OFFERS

1

Herr Nordstern aus der Abteilung Export-Verkauf bedankt sich für die Anfrage. Er stellt seine Firma vor und hat einen Prospekt beigefügt, dem der Kunde weitere Informationen über die Firma und den Schalter entnehmen kann. Das Angebot lautet: Bei einer Mindestbestellung von 1000 Schaltern 6.00 pro Schalter. Die Liefer- und Zahlungsbedingungen sind: frei an Bord Hamburg, für eine Erstbestellung Kasse bei Auftragserteilung. Die Lieferung erfolgt ca. 1 Monat nach Eingang der Bestellung. Das Angebot gilt bis 30.06.20..

2

Lösungsvorschlag

Glasgow Office Furniture plc
Tayside Industrial Estate
Glasgow G1 3GH
United Kingdom

(date)

Bürowelt
Landstraße 250
80469 Munich
Germany

Dear Mr/Ms …

Your enquiry about office furniture

Thank you for your enquiry of (date). We are pleased to note that you are interested in our products.

As requested, we enclose a brochure and price list. All goods mentioned in the price list are in stock, so we can guarantee immediate delivery.

We would like to point out that our prices are quoted DDP. We offer a cash discount for payment within 14 days.

We look forward to receiving your order soon. Please contact us if you need further details.

Yours sincerely …

3

1g; **2**i; **3**a; **4**h; **5**b; **6**c; **7**e; **8**f

4

Lösungsvorschlag

Office Inc
149 Moulton Way
Cork City T12 T997
Ireland
Tel. +35 3214 / 27947

(date)

Office Props
Am Winterhafen 7
80930 Munich
Germany

Dear Mr/Ms …

Your enquiry about the Wlan OfficeInc 3.0 printer

Thank you for your enquiry of March 14th. We are pleased to note that you are interested in our product. Please find enclosed detailed information about the Wlan OfficeInc 3.0 printer as requested.

We would like to point out that the price of €298.90 is really most favourable. The printer is not available anywhere else at such a low price. In addition, we can offer you a quantity discount of 15% on orders for 50 or more printers.

Our offer is valid as long as stocks last. We recommend you to place your order as soon as possible as demand for this special offer is high.

We look forward to receiving your order. If you need any further information, please do not hesitate to contact us.

Yours sincerely …

5

	Chen Bike Co. Ltd.	Konrad Dynamos GmbH
Price	€137 per unit	€140 each for 100+ units
Discounts	7% for 50+ units	3% cash discount payment within 10 days
Terms of delivery	FCA: seller pays only to airport	DAP: seller pays all costs
Terms of payment	Cash with order; later 60 days' credit	within two weeks of invoice
Delivery time	dispatch (to airport) within two weeks	immediate delivery
Valid for …	10 days	long as stocks last

1 Chen: €127.41; Konrad: €135.80
2 No extra costs for order from Konrad; with Chen have to pay transport, insurance, duty from Taiwan
3 Konrad for first order; Chen if there is a later order

C KMK EXAM PRACTICE

1

Notiz 1
Menge: 300; Farbe: grun/silber; Modellnummer: CSL200; Nachlässe: 15% unter Listpreis, 2,5% Rabatt für Zahlung innerhalb 15 Tagen; Transport- und Lieferbedingungen: per LKW, DDP Linz; Abfertigung: innerhalb 12 Stunden

Notiz 2
Menge: 150; Farbe: blau-weiß; Fassungsvermögen: 30 Liter; Modellnummer: CB 12; Nachlässe: 15% unter Listenpreis, 2,5% Rabatt für Zahlung innerhalb 15 Tagen; Transport- und Lieferbedingungen: DDP Linz; Abfertigung: innerhalb 12 Stunden

2

Lösungsvorschlag

Liebe Frau Thiel

Die ‚Basic Sales Course' ist für mich gerade richtig. Die Schulung dauert nur ein Tag und ist an Mitarbeitern gerichtet, die neu im Verkauf sind.

Unter den Trainingszielen sind eine Einführung in den Grundprinzipien des Verkaufs sowie das Selbstvertrauen der Teilnehmer im Verkaufsgespräch am Telefon oder in Person zu entwickeln. Besonders wichtig im Kursprogramm finde ich das Thema wie man ein Verkaufsgespräch richtig öffnet. Erste Eindrücke und nonverbales verhalten werden thematisiert. Ebenso wichtig ist wie man ein Gespräch zu Ende bringt, prüft, ob Kauf Interesse besteht und nach den nächsten Schritten fragt.

Manche Teilnehmer/innen waren begeistert. Eine/r hat geschrieben, dass der Kurs ihm/ihr die Kenntnisse und das Selbstvertrauen gegeben hat, um in der Lage zu sein raus zu gehen und zu verkaufen.

Ich würde mich sehr freuen, wenn ich am Kurs teilnehmen dürfte.

Mit freundlichen Grüßen

3

Lösungsvorschlag

Firma World Navigator GmbH
Querstraße 20
90762 Fürth
Germany

(date)

Ms Aileen O'Reilly
Purchasing Director
Whitefriar Trekking Ltd
31 Wicklow Street
Dublin 8
Irland

Dear Ms O'Reilly

Your enquiry about GPS devices

Thank you very much for your enquiry of 25 September 20.. To download our catalogue and export price list please visit our website, where you will also find more information about our company.

As regards the goods required, we are pleased to submit the following quotation:

- GPS device type "eTreck" with touch screen, article no. eT49 at 250 per item
- GPS hand device type "Xpedition", article no. XP1 at 100 per item

A quantity discount of 10% is granted on orders for 10 or more devices. Our prices are quoted DDP your premises in Ireland. Delivery is made within 14 days after receipt of order.

We hope our offer is to your liking and look forward to doing business with you.

Yours sincerely

D IHK EXAM PRACTICE

1

Notiz 1
Menge: 300; Farbe: grun/silber; Modellnummer: CSL200; Nachlässe: 15% unter Listpreis, 2,5% Rabatt für Zahlung innerhalb 15 Tagen; Transport- und Lieferbedingungen: per LKW, DDP Linz; Abfertigung: innerhalb 12 Stunden

Notiz 2
Menge: 150; Farbe: blau-weiß; Fassungsvermögen: 30 Liter; Modellnummer: CB 12; Nachlässe: 15% unter Listenpreis, 2,5% Rabatt für Zahlung innerhalb 15 Tagen; Transport- und Lieferbedingungen: DDP Linz; Abfertigung: innerhalb 12 Stunden

2
Lösungsvorschlag

Firma World Navigator GmbH
Querstraße 20
90762 Fürth
Germany

(date)

Ms Aileen O'Reilly
Purchasing Director
Whitefriar Trekking Ltd
31 Wicklow Street
Dublin 8
Irland
Dear Ms O'Reilly

Your enquiry about GPS devices

Thank you very much for your enquiry of 25 September 20.. To download our catalogue and export price list please visit our website, where you will also find more information about our company.

As regards the goods required, we are pleased to submit the following quotation:

- GPS device type "eTreck" with touch screen, article no. eT49 at 250 per item
- GPS hand device type "Xpedition", article no. XP1 at 100 per item

A quantity discount of 10% is granted on orders for 10 or more devices. Our prices are quoted DDP your premises in Ireland. Delivery is made within 14 days after receipt of order.

We hope our offer is to your liking and look forward to doing business with you.

Yours sincerely

3
Lösungsvorschlag
From: (Ihr Name)@schmidtsport.nex
To: m_alkubaidi@sunsand.dux
Subject: Enquiry about football clothing
Dear Ms Al Kubaidi

Thank you for your email enquiring about our products.

We are sorry that you haven't received the promised catalogue and details of our terms and payment but Mr Dietrich became ill shortly after the trade fair and has not been in the office.

I have now attached our current catalogue and price list to this email and once Mr Dietrich is back in the office, he will get in touch with you directly.

Please do not hesitate to contact us again if you require further details.

Yours sincerely

Unit 6 Placing and acknowledging orders

A PLACING ORDERS

1
1N; **2**F; **3**T; **4**N; **5**F; **6**T; **7**T; **8**F

2
Address: N7 9EJ; item number: 01FC; description: moveable flip chart; quantity: 1; price: £62.42; item number: 03FC; description: flip chart paper; quantity: 2; price: £18.99 (per pack); total: £100.40; method of payment: COD

3
1i; **2**c; **3**f; **4**j; **5**b; **6**a; **7**k; **8**g; **9**e; **10**l

4
Correct: 1, 4, 7, 8
Incorrect: 2, 3, 5, 6
Corrections: The discount is 30%. VAT is 19%.
The final price is 25,823.00.
The seller pays the transport costs to the port of destination, i.e. Rotterdam.
The buyer wants the goods by (i.e. before or on) 30 June 20..

5
1 for your quotation of;
2 agree to your;
3 place an order;
4 note that your prices;
5 Payment will be made;
6 receipt of goods;
7 acknowledge;
8 receiving the goods as soon as possible

6
Box C:
1 bank transfer;
2 business letter;
3 credit card;
4 clothing company;
5 market research;
6 order form;
7 photo agency;
8 sales representative;
9 trade fair;
10 transport costs;
11 trial order;
12 unit price

Box D:
1 Banküberweisung;
2 Geschäftsbrief;
3 Kreditkarte;
4 Bekleidungsfirma;
5 Marktforschung;
6 Bestellformular;
7 Fotoagentur;
8 Handelsvertreter/in;
9 Messe;
10 Transportkosten;
11 Probebestellung, Probeauftrag;
12 Stückpreis

7
1 pleased;
2 discount;
3 list prices;
4 following;
5 of;
6 item no.;
7 enclosed;
8 delivery;
9 Payment;
10 invoice;
11 within;
12 order;
13 satisfaction;
14 sincerely

8
1e; **2**f; **3**b; **4**g; **5**d; **6**c

9
1 for; **2** on; **3** by; **4** of; **5** at; **6** to; **7** by; **8** on

B ACKNOWLEDING ORDERS

1
1c,h; **2**h,b; **3**f; **4**d; **5**g; **6**e; **7**a

2
1 4 July 20.. for banner material
2 the above-mentioned order.
3 We are pleased to confirm the details as listed below.
4 Payment of 30% of the total amount is now due. Payment of the remaining 70% will then be due.
5 We expect to complete your order in approx. 20 days' time. ... the goods will be transported to the Port of Shanghai for shipment, and we will send you our advice of dispatch.
6 Thank you for placing your order with the China Canvas Company.

3
Lösungsvorschlag
Dear Mr Schwarz

Your order number AB 54321
Thank you for the above-mentioned trial order for greenhouses of 1 July 20..
We are pleased to confirm the order and can assure you that it will be dealt with immediately.
We are sure that the goods will arrive in good condition and look forward to further orders in the future.

Yours sincerely
Lara Smit
Sales Manager

C KMK EXAM PRACTICE

1
1 Firmen ohne Marketing-Budget und ohne Büro in den entsprechenden Ländern
2 Sie bewerben ihre Produkte auf Webseiten und hoffen, dass jemand sie entdeckt und sie kontaktiert.
3 alle Dienstleistungen (davon 3): detaillierte Marktanalyse; Analyse zu bestimmten Produkten und Dienstleistungen in der Region (Wettbewerbersituation, Käufersituation, Importstatistiken); Information zu Einfuhrzöllen und -vorschriften; Unterstützung bei Werbemaßnahmen
4 Unterstützung bei der Auswahl der passenden Werbemedien und der Art der Werbung
5 welche Art Unternehmen als potentielle Kunden gesehen werden
6 Zahlungs- und Lieferbedingungen, Mindestbestellmenge, Mengenrabatte, Verpackung, Versicherung
7 Übersetzung (großer Pool von Übersetzern)
8 Provision bei erfolgreichen Geschäftsabschlüssen

2
Lösungsvorschlag
Firma TT Autobeschriftung GmbH
Tempelstr. 99
47918 Tönisvorst
Germany

(date)
Guangzhou Materials Ltd
Unit 2099

Panyu District
511450 Guangzhou
China
Attn. Ms Susan Wang

Dear Ms Wang

Order number VF247

With reference to our telephone call of (date), we now wish to place an order for the following goods:

Quantity	Description	Catalogue No.	Unit price ($)	Total ($)
100 rolls	Go faster tape, 0.08 mm × 1.07 m	VF8107	$7.50	$750
100 rolls	Self-adhesive film, 0.10 mm × 1.27 m	SAF10127.	$9.00	$900
			Total price	$1,650

Delivery: CIF Rotterdam within 30 days after receipt of order

Payment: 30% in advance, 70% after completion by transfer to your a/c at the Bank of China

We look forward to receiving your confirmation of order and advice of dispatch in the near future.

We trust the goods will arrive punctually and in good condition.

Yours sincerely

3
Lösungsvorschlag
The article is about the things you need to check before you start a company which imports or exports goods. There are many rules and laws that you need to follow. One of the first things to do is to write a business plan. This will help you to work out the details of your business idea and it's necessary for a meeting with a bank adviser about finance.

Before you start an import company, you must know where in the foreign country you can find the goods you need with the right quality and the price. And find out how high the transport costs are. Check also if export from the country is allowed or if there are certain rules you must follow. Do you have the necessary knowledge of the market or how can you find the right business partner in the country?

New markets in other countries for your products offer sales opportunities. But for a small export company it's a big challenge. It's often difficult to understand the market because of language and cultural differences. You must be sure that your product is suitable for transport. Find out also about import standards and the duty you have to pay. How will you organize sales and marketing in the foreign country? Finally, there is the cost of launching the product to consider.

D IHK EXAM PRACTICE

1

Lösungsvorschlag

Frau Smit freut sich, dass wir mit der Qualität der *Solargro*-Gewächshäuser zufrieden sind und regelmäßige Bestellungen erwägen. Sie schickt uns ihren aktuellen Katalog mit der neuen Produktlinie *Solargro Next*. Für die neue Linie bietet sie uns einen Einführungsrabatt von 5% für Bestellungen von 5 bis 10 Stück bzw. 7,5% für Bestellungen von mehr als 10 Stück. Außerdem bietet sie uns ein offenes Zahlungsziel mit vierteljährlicher Abrechnung mit Zahlung innerhalb von 30 Tagen nach Abrechnungsdatum.

2

Lösungsvorschlag

To: j_ryan@skyhigh.ei
From: sales@trixiemode.nex
Subject: Your order no. 42BK

Thank you for your email about the above-mentioned order.

The acknowledgement of order should have arrived with you as we sent it a week ago. We hope this hasn't caused any inconvenience and thank you again for your payment that we received on time.

I have attached a copy of our acknowledgement of order and advice of dispatch to this email for your convenience.

Thank you once again for your order and please don't hesitate to contact us should you have further questions.

Yours sincerely

3

1 due;	**8** within;	**15** requirements;
2 unable;	**9** receipt;	**16** accept;
3 ship;	**10** advance;	**17** discount;
4 agreed;	**11** after;	**18** that;
5 provide;	**12** account;	**19** understanding;
6 confirmation;	**13** making;	**20** trust
7 follows;	**14** fulfil;	

Unit 7 Making and adjusting complaints

A MAKING COMPLAINTS

1

1. Two x-ray machines were not delivered on the agreed date of delivery.
2. The writer (Mr Adamczyk) would like the addressee (Melissa Wolf) to look into the matter and let him know when he can expect the machines.
3. He needs the machines urgently.
4. He mentions that this is a trial order. If it is not handled well, there will be no further orders.

2

1. on 18 April;
2. by 3 May;
3. needs the containers as soon as possible;
4. has been waiting for delivery since;
5. have been doing business with each other for over five years;
6. never sent a complaint before;
7. as soon as possible

3

1. Regarding our order …;
2. the agreed date of delivery was …;
3. to date …;
4. Please look into the matter …;
5. We need the equipment urgently;
6. We feel sure that you will understand …

4

1. she has a lot of work;
2. Thursday, 10 October;
3. 14 October;
4. their stocks are getting low (and they have orders to fulfill);
5. are beginning to get restless;
6. call Anton back within an hour or so

5

1. delay / Wir hatten verstärkt darauf hingewiesen, dass uns pünktliche Lieferung sehr wichtig ist.
2. poor quality / Die Hosen haben nicht die erwartete Qualität.
3. goods / Wir hoffen, Sie können uns die korrekte Ware ohne Verzögerung schicken.
4. part of delivery is missing / Da wir die gesamte Bestellmenge dringend benötigen, sorgen Sie bitte dafür, dass uns die fehlenden 100 Teile unverzüglich zugeschickt werden.
5. damaged goods / Wir sind bereit, die zerkratzten Geräte zu behalten, wenn Sie uns einen Preisnachlass von 20% gewähren.

6

1 complaint;	**7** replacement;
2 arrived;	**8** suppliers;
3 waiting;	**9** damaged;
4 reduction;	**10** delivery;
5 prepared;	**11** testing;
6 receipt;	**12** solution

7

4, 1, 6, 3, 2, 7, 11, 8, 5, 10, 9, 13, 16, 12, 14, 15, 17

B ADJUSTING COMPLAINTS

1

1. The delay was caused by a late delivery of materials from one of Swedish Metals' business partners.
2. The order was dispatched two days ago.
3. It has / They have sent the equipment by rail so that it is not interrupted by the weekend.

2

1. We are sorry for the delay;
2. this was caused by …;
3. Your order was dispatched two days ago;
4. consignment;

5 We hope the goods arrive safely;
6 We apologize once again for ...

3

1 complaint;
2 delay in delivery;
3 business partners;
4 dispatched;
5 advice of dispatch;
6 consignment;
7 consignment/goods;
8 apologize

4

1 ~~Tuesday morning~~ Monday afternoon;
2 ~~snow~~ fog;
3 ~~main road~~ motorway;
4 ~~yes, it was~~ no, it wasn't;
5 ~~train~~ truck;
6 ~~nine~~ eleven;
7 ~~13~~ 15;
8 ~~300~~ 500;
9 ~~in Bavaria~~ on the continent;
10 ~~at four o'clock~~ midday;
11 ~~letter~~ email

5

1c; **2**a; **3**b

6

1c; **2**e; **3**a; **4**f

7

1	regret;	8	expense;
2	connection;	9	address;
3	packing;	10	inconvenience;
4	well;	11	placing;
5	staff;	12	executed;
6	consignment;	13	care
7	return;		

C KMK EXAM PRACTICE

1

1 Verkauf
2 Gerät 1: zerkratztes Glas, Gerät 2: Gehäuse verbeult
3 942761;
4 Probeauftrag
5 letzte Woche
6 Ausrüstung nicht pünktlich geliefert
7 0048 22 546 99;
8 Mia Richter

2

1 Zeit, Ressourcen
2 gelungene Problemlösung fördert Kundenbindung und -vertrauen
3 falsche/beschädigte Waren; dem Kunden zu viel berechnen; Versicherungsprobleme
4 ruhig, angemessen, einfühlsam mit sanfter Stimme
5 den Kunden unterbrechen
6 hilft dem Kunden, sich zu beruhigen; zeigt dem Kunden, dass man ihm helfen will
7 das Problem wiederholen; darlegen, welche Maßnahmen man ergreifen wird, um das Problem zu lösen; ggf. Problem an jemand anderen weiterleiten
8 sich mit dem Kunden in Verbindung setzen und nachfragen, ob alles in Ordnung ist; dies zeigt dem Kunden, dass Ihrem Unternehmen seine Meinung am Herzen liegt

D IHK EXAM PRACTICE

1

Lösungsvorschlag

Für: Mia Richter		
Verfasst von: *Name*	am:	15. September
Gesprächspartner/in: Jerzy Adamczyk		
Betrifft: Beschwerde zu Bestellnummer 942761		
Herr Adamcyzk von der Firma Denta Dental Clinic in Warschau hat angerufen, um sich wegen der Bestellung Nr. 942761 zu beschweren. Beide gelieferten Geräte sind beschädigt: Bei einem ist das Glas zerkratzt, beim zweiten ist das Metallgehäuse verbeult. Herr Adamcyzk vermutet, dass dies beim Transport passiert ist. Er ist besonders verärgert, da es sich um einen Probeauftrag handelt und er sich schon letzte Woche beschweren musste, weil die Geräte verspätet eingetroffen waren. Bitte rufen Sie ihn unter 0048 129 546 993 an – er wird den ganzen Tag zu Hause sein.		

2

Lösungsvorschlag

Cécile Nixer von Événements Merveilleux beschwert sich über die Bestellung Nr. CG25005 vom 17. Dezember 20.. über 300 Champagnegläser. Die Lieferung ist noch später als erwartet eingetroffen. Wir hatten in unserer E-Mail vom 21. Dezember erklärt, dass wir Probleme mit unseren Lieferanten haben und dass die Lieferung 1 bis 2 Wochen verspätet ankommen würde. Tatsächlich kam sie dann 4 Wochen später an, was Frau Nixer inakzeptabel findet. Außerdem sei in einer Kiste mit 50 Gläsern fast jedes Glas zerbrochen und die restliche gesprungen. Fotos hat sie mitgeschickt, die auch den Lieferwagen zeigen, sodass deutlich wird, dass die Lieferung bereits beschädigt ankam. Frau Nixer erwartet, dass wir die beschädigten Artikel schnellstmöglich und ohne zusätzliche Kosten ersetzen.

1	Re;	11	instead;	21	make;
2	regarding;	12	which;	22	delivery;
3	consignment;	13	out of stock;	23	priority;
4	this;	14	who;	24	an;
5	than;	15	into;	25	at;
6	However;	16	immediately;	26	let me know;
7	when;	17	urgently;	27	to receive;
8	opened;	18	losing;	28	do;
9	found;	19	reasons;	29	wrong;
10	they;	20	ask;	30	sincerely

Unit 8 Dealing with payments and reminders

A CHECKING A COMMERCIAL INVOICE

1
Quantity should be 50, not 55
Total price should be 2,500 USD, not 2,750 USD
Delivery should be FOB Shanghai, not FAS Shanghai
Terms of payment should be 30% in advance, 70% after completion, not 50% in advance, 50% after completion

2
D: 1, 4, 6, 7, 9
I: 2, 3, 5, 8, 10

3
1 I am afraid some mistakes have been made
2 It seems the quantity is not correct
3 An error also appears to have been made with the payment and delivery terms
4 We would appreciate it if you could send us a corrected invoice without delay
5 it would be unfortunate if such mistakes were to happen again

B DEALING WITH LATE PAYMENTS

1

German	English	German	English
Mahnung	reminder	fällig sein	(to) be due
überweisen	(to) remit	überfällig	overdue
unbemerkt bleiben	(to) escape notice	offenstehend	outstanding
Saldo	balance	obengenannt	above-mentioned

2
1 escaped;
2 notice;
3 outstanding;
4 balance;
5 above-mentioned
6 was;
7 due;
8 overdue;
9 remitted;
10 reminder

3
1 set a final deadline;
2 regret to note;
3 would welcome;
4 refer to;
5 will result in;
6 will be remitting;
7 to charge

4
2nd: 2,3,6
3rd: 1,4,5,7

5
Lösungsvorschlag

Wir Fahren Gut GmbH
Elbchaussee 498
22588 Hamburg

4.10.20..
Foyle Foods
Donore Road Industrial Estate
Donore Road
Drigheda
Irland

Dear Sir or Madam

Invoice number 21-1549

We write to you concerning the above-mentioned invoice for €10,454 which should have been paid on 21st September. We sent a reminder email on 25th September, but unfortunately received no reply. Therefore, we would appreciate an explanation as to why the invoice has not yet been paid and furthermore remind you again that the payment should be settled without further delay.

We trust we will receive payment in the next few days.

Yours faithfully
Ines Steven
Head of Accounts

C KMK EXAM PRACTICE

1
This article discusses how you can encourage customers to pay their invoices on time and deal with late payments. It offers these five recommendations:
1 Keep short payment timeframes. A deposit in advance along with payment at different milestones such as 25% at time of order, 25% at dispatch and 50% upon delivery help keep your cashflow flowing smoothly and helps with longer term projects or sales.
2 Automated reminders. It is easy to let an invoice slip to the bottom of your to-do list. Using a CRM system or automatic reminders helps to make sure you don't forget anything and that late-payers are always gently reminded when an invoice isn't paid.
3 Keep up your relationships. If you have a good relationship with your customers built on trust, you reduce the chance of customers disappointing you by paying late because they won't want to damage the relationship.
4 Offer incentives. It pays to offer discounts for early or on-time payments. This helps you keep your accounts accurate and encourages people to pay on time. Amounts like 10% or 15% are generous but still make business sense. Print the discount in bold on the invoice and you will see how quickly customers pay when it means saving a little money.
5 Accept newer payment methods to encourage customers to pay you more quickly. Nobody uses cheques anymore and credit cards are a must for all businesses. Also think about accepting PayPal payments, direct bank transfers, and maybe even cryptocurrencies, such as Bitcoin, but make sure to do some research first, especially on cryptocurrencies.

2

MegaKauf Großhandel GmbH
Oberkasseler Str. 200
40545 Düsseldorf
GERMANY

5 April 20..
Ms Sheena Murray
Accounts Director
Winter Gear Ltd

222 Grampian Road
Aviemore PH22 1RH
UNITED KINGDOM

Dear Ms Murray

Statement no. GBST/375 dated 2 April 20.. for €31,550.00

Thank you for the above-mentioned statement.

Having checked it against our records, we must point out that it is incorrect in the following points:

- The discount granted on items 1 and 2 for skiing boots is only 15% instead of 50%, as promised.
- You have not included our credit note no. RBM/6 dated 15 March 20.. for €185.00.

We are therefore returning your statement and would request you to send us an amended statement for €25,065.00, which we will pay by transfer to your account after receipt.

Please do not hesitate to contact us should you have any queries.

Yours sincerely

3

From: accounts@wfg.dex
To: seanduignan@foyle.ei
Subject: Your invoice no. 21-1549

Dear Mr Duggan

Thank you for your email with your explanation for the late payment. However, I'm afraid that the outstanding sum of €10,454 is now almost three weeks late and we can accept no further delays. We must set a final deadline asking you to settle the payment within the next seven days and furthermore charge you an extra late payment fee of €200.

If we have not received your payment within the next seven days, we will have to instruct our solicitors to take legal action.

We trust we will receive payment in the next days.

Yours sincerely
Ines Steven

D IHK EXAM PRACTICE

1

Frau O'Connor von Green Isle Gardens Limited hat uns am 27.02 mitgeteilt, dass wir eine offene Rechnung haben (Rechnungsnummer GIG-45129 vom 15.10.20.. über 9.995,00€). Diese sollte bereits vor vier Wochen bezahlt werden; eine Erinnerungs-E-Mail wurde am 2. Februar, eine zweite Erinnerung am 10. Februar geschickt. Da Frau O'Connor nichts von uns gehört hat, setzt sie uns eine endgültige Frist von 10 Werktagen. Hinzu kommt eine Säumungsgebühr in Höhe von 526€, was dem ursprünglich angebotenen 5% Rabatt für die Bezahlung innerhalb von 7 Tage entspricht. Wenn wir den Betrag von 10.521,00€ nicht bis zum 9. März begleichen, wird unser Konto bei Green Isle Gardens gesperrt und Frau O'Connor wird eventuell rechtliche Schritte einleiten.

2

MegaKauf Großhandel GmbH
Oberkasseler Str. 200
40545 Düsseldorf
GERMANY

5 April 20..
Ms Sheena Murray
Accounts Director
Winter Gear Ltd
222 Grampian Road
Aviemore PH22 1RH
UNITED KINGDOM

Dear Ms Murray

Statement no. GBST/375 dated 2 April 20.. for €31,550.00

Thank you for the above-mentioned statement.

Having checked it against our records, we must point out that it is incorrect in the following points:

- The discount granted on items 1 and 2 for skiing boots is only 15% instead of 50%, as promised.
- You have not included our credit note no. RBM/6 dated 15 March 20.. for €185.00.

We are therefore returning your statement and would request you to send us an amended statement for €25,065.00, which we will pay by transfer to your account after receipt.

Please do not hesitate to contact us should you have any queries.

Yours sincerely

3

From: accounts@wfg.dex
To: seanduignan@foyle.ei
Subject: Your invoice no. 21-1549

Dear Mr Duggan

Thank you for your email with your explanation for the late payment. However, I'm afraid that the outstanding sum of €10,454 is now almost three weeks late and we can accept no further delays. We must set a final deadline asking you to settle the payment within the next seven days and furthermore charge you an extra late payment fee of €200.

If we have not received your payment within the next seven days, we will have to instruct our solicitors to take legal action.

We trust we will receive payment in the next days.

Yours sincerely
Ines Steven

KMK mock exam

1

1. hässliche/graue Büros; langweiliger Job; zynische/unzufriedene Atmosphäre
2. bleiben und versuchen, etwas draus zu machen, oder die Firma verlassen
3. psychopathische Tendenzen, kein Mitgefühl, interessiert sich nicht für andere
4. sich schnellstmöglich aus dem Staub machen
5. Kollegen/Team/Abteilung etwas Gutes tun (ungefragt Kaffee mitbringen/Süßigkeiten im Meeting verteilen); anderen Komplimente machen; Interesse zeigen (nach dem Wochenende fragen)

Anrufer	Arturo Mendez Reverte
Grund des Anrufs	Geschäftsreise nach München vom 12. bis 14. März
Inhalt des Anrufs	Herr Reverte kommt um 9 Uhr am Flughafen an und bittet darum, abgeholt zu werden. Er bittet um Bestätigung der Hotelreservierung. Bitte bestätigen lassen, dass das Zimmer auf der Gartenseite liegt und absolut ruhig ist. Er schläft schlecht und hält sonst die Verhandlungen nicht durch. Bitte Karten für das Fußballspiel München gegen Chelsea besorgen.
E-Mail-Adresse	am_reverte@buenos-aires.com

2

1 in Regierungs- und finanziellen Angelegenheiten
2 die Wahrung der Interessen bzw. des Wohls aller Bürger
3 wenn ein Firmenbankrott das Gemeinwohl bedroht; Regierung muss die Firma unterstützen
4 Angestellte, Kunden, Investoren
5 Investitionen direkt vor Ort
6 Strom- und Wasserversorgung, Gesundheitsfürsorge
7 jeder, aber am meisten die, die am wenigsten Macht haben
8 Das Unternehmen muss Maßnahmen ergriffen haben, die eigene finanzielle Situation zu verbessern; und diese Maßnahmen haben nicht gewirkt.

3

Lösungsvorschlag

Dear Sir or Madam,

We just received your latest delivery. Unfortunately, there are several discrepancies between our order and what we received. Listed below are the problems we came across:

- We ordered 10,000 pages of photocopying paper but only received 1,000 pages.
- We ordered 50 glue sticks, but you sent us 100.
- We didn't get the 20 rolls of tape at all.
- We wanted 20 packets of whiteboard pens, but instead you sent 20 packets of pens to use on transparencies.
- Last but not least, we wanted 10 bigger-sized files in DIN A4 but you sent us the thinner ones.

This is all quite dissatisfying, especially since we are a loyal customer of yours. I would like to ask you to send us the missing items as soon as possible and to offer us a discount to make up for the inconvenience. Also, in order to send back the items we didn't order, we would like to get a returns voucher so we don't have to pay the postage.

I really hope this was a one-off incident. We have been doing business with you for such a long time, and it would be a shame if we had to look for another company to order our goods from.

Yours faithfully,

4

Lösungsvorschlag

Sieben Tipps für die Organisation einer perfekten Konferenz

1 Wie weit ist die Anreise der Teilnehmer? Die Anreisezeit sollte in einem angemessenen Verhältnis zur Dauer der Konferenz stehen.
2 Bei der Wahl des Tagungsorts spielt auch das Thema oder die Form der Konferenz eine Rolle.
3 Der Zeitpunkt des Verschickens der Einladungen ist sehr wichtig. Seine Kollegen kann man mit großzügigem Vorlauf informell Bescheid geben, damit sie sich den Termin vormerken können. Offizielle Einladungen sollten folgen. Teilnehmer aus anderen Unternehmen sollten ihre Einladungen nicht allzu weit im Voraus erhalten, weil Zusagen meist zeitnah gegeben werden oder die Konferenz sonst vergessen wird.
4 Ein effizientes Anmeldeverfahren ist sehr wichtig. Es gibt webbasierte Systeme, bei denen sich Teilnehmer über einen Link in der Einladungs-E-Mail anmelden können, und sogar ihre Unterkunft reservieren und die Reisebuchung vornehmen können.
5 Es muss klar kommuniziert werden, wer wofür bezahlt und was in der Konferenzgebühr enthalten ist.
6 Es sollte einen straffen Zeitplan mit genügend Spielraum für Unvorhergesehenes geben. Angemessene Kleidung ist ebenfalls wichtig, um einen guten Eindruck zu hinterlassen.
7 Nach der Konferenz sollten Konferenzprotokolle elektronisch oder in Druckform verschickt werden.

IHK mock exam

A

Lösungsvorschlag

Speedy GmbH
Karolingerstraße 56
85059 Ingolstadt

(date)

Pete's PCs
Ballycoolin Industrial Estate
Dublin 15
Irland

Dear Sir or Madam

Enquiry about laptops

We have visited your home page on the internet. We note that your company sells computer hardware and your prices are competitive.

Our company is a medium-sized freight forwarder. Our business is growing and we are planning to buy ten laptops for our staff to use in their home offices. The laptops should come with 13-inch screens and not weigh more than 1.5 kilos.

We need the laptops urgently and we would expect delivery two weeks after we place an order. I hope this is not a problem.

Please send us details of suitable laptops together with your current price list and information about possible special offers and quantity discounts. Please also let us have full details of your terms of delivery and payment.

If the laptops meet our requirements, we will be happy to place a second order.

We look forward to hearing from you.

Yours faithfully

B

Lösungsvorschlag

From: int_sales@gesundum.dex
To: helenom@dubhs.ei
Subject: Enquiry about battery-powered wheelchairs (item no. BP075)

Dear Ms O'Meara

Thank you for your enquiry of … *(date)*.

We are pleased to note that you are interested in our battery-powered wheelchairs (Product no. BP075).

The price for each chair is €2,320. Our discount for your order of ten wheelchairs is 2%.

Our tems of delivery are DAP Dublin, delivery within two weeks of order.

The terms of payment are 1/3 with order, 2/3 on delivery.

We enclose our catalogue and a price list as requested.

We look forward to hearing from you soon.

Yours sincerely

C

Lösungsvorschlag

Für: XX		
Verfasst von: *Name*	am:	*Datum*
Gesprächspartner/in: Martin Spielberg		
Betrifft: Termin für Vorstellungsgespräch		
Herr Spielberg hat sich für eine Stelle als Außenhandelskaufmann beworben und Herr Mathers möchte sich mit ihm treffen, während er vom Mittwoch, 29. Juli bis zum Montag, 3. August in Nürnberg ist. Als Termin haben sie Freitag, den 31. Juli um 18 Uhr vereinbart und treffen sich im Restaurant Backstein in der Hauptstraße. Sollte der Termin verschoben werden, meldet sich Herr Mathers bei Herrn Spielberg unter 0176 438 05 783.		

D

Lösungsvorschlag

Frau Fiona Murphy von Safety First in Dublin hat sich am 21. Juni über die Lieferung von 5000 Rauchmeldern beschwert, die am 12. Juni geliefert wurde (Bestellung Nr. VBF900 vom 12.05.20..). Die Firma hatte die Rauchmelder an verschiedenen Kunden in Großbritannien verschickt. Dort stellte sich heraus, dass einige Rauchmelder keine Batterien und Befestigungsschrauben enthielten und einige weitere nicht funktionierten. Außerdem waren 200 Geräte nicht weiß, sondern gelblich verfärbt. Fotos wurden mitgeschickt. Frau Murphy möchte eine Erklärung, wie das passieren könnte, und erwartet, dass alle Artikel schnellstmöglichst kostenlos ersetzt werden.

E

Text 1

1 about;
2 Many;
3 major;
4 reputation;
5 brochure;
6 enclosed;
7 range;
8 visit;
9 agreed;
10 supply;
11 with;
12 FCA;
13 initial;
14 CWO;
15 references;
16 approximately;
17 receipt;
18 hesitate;
19 require;
20 receiving

Text 2

1 use;
2 candidates;
3 sensitive;
4 their;
5 them;
6 help;
7 already;
8 professional;
9 an;
10 keep;
11 Personnel;
12 supposed;
13 many;
14 presence;
15 won't;
16 didn't get;
17 so;
18 retail;
19 about;
20 good look;
21 might;
22 This;
23 previous;
24 employer;
25 have been;
26 interview;
27 direct;
28 policy;
29 work contract;
30 regret